WHERE
ANGELS WALK

JOAN WESTER ANDERSON

WHERE ANGELS WALK

TRUE STORIES OF HEAVENLY VISITORS

Guideposts

New York

This Guideposts edition is published by special arrangement with Loyola Press, A Jesuit Ministry, 3441 N. Ashland Avenue, Chicago, Illinois 60657, (800) 621-1008, www.loyolapress.com

Originally published in the United States by Ballantine Books, an imprint of The Random House Publishing Group, a division of Random House, Inc., New York, and simultaneously in Canada by Random House of Canada Limited, Toronto.

Grateful acknowledgment is made to the following for permission to reprint previously published material:

Chosen Books (Old Tappan, NJ, 1986): Excerpt from *Angels Watching Over Me* by Betty Malz, Copyright © 1986 by Fleming H. Revell Co. Reprinted by permission.

"The Day We Saw the Angels" by Dr. S. Ralph Harlow originally appeared in *Guideposts* magazine and is used by permission of Guideposts. Copyright © 1970 by Guideposts All rights reserved.

"Angel of Vietnam" by Joan Wester Anderson originally appeared in *Angels on Earth* magazine and is used by permission of Guideposts. Copyright © 2007 by Guideposts. All rights reserved.

All Scripture quotations are taken from the *Holy Bible, New International Version*, Copyright © 1973, 1978, 1984 by International Bible Society. Used by permission of Zondervan Publishing House.

Sr. Miriam Pollard, OCSO. *Neither Be Afraid* (San Francisco: Ignatius Press), pp. 189–190. www.Ignatius.com

"Bonus Stories about Angels" originally appeared on Guideposts.org or in *Angels on Earth* magazine and are reprinted with permission from Guideposts. Copyright © 2016 by Guideposts. All rights reserved.

Original cover art credit: Medioimages/Photodisc/Thinkstock.
Cover design of Guideposts edition: Müllerhaus
Cover photograph of Guideposts edition: Shutterstock

ISBN-13: 978-0-8294-4470-4
ISBN-10: 0-8294-4470-X
Library of Congress Control Number: 2016949346

Printed in the United States of America.

20 19 18 17 16 15 14 13 12 11 10 9 8 7 6 5 4 3 2 1

To those who took a step in faith, sharing information, opinions, and wonderful stories. Without you, my angels, these pages would not exist.

Farewell! I did not know thy worth,
But thou art gone, and now 'tis prized,
So angels walked unknown on earth,
But when they flew were recognized.
—THOMAS HOOD, "TO AN ABSENTEE"

CONTENTS

Foreword by Colleen Hughes   **xi**

Introduction by Gary Jansen   **xiii**

Where Angels Walk: The Original Stories

The Beginning . . .   **3**

Searching for Answers   **8**

Angels All around Us   **14**

Angel in the Cockpit   **22**

Night Guide   **26**

Invisible Intervention   **30**

Neither Wind nor Rain   **34**

The Safety Inspector   **38**

Angels on the Highway   **41**

A Pat on the Back from God   **45**

Angels on Guard   **50**

Special Delivery   **53**

Message from Beyond   **56**

The Man in White   **59**

Scaling the Heights   **64**

The Flutter of Wings   **68**

Brian's Angel   **72**

Unseen Protectors   **76**

Tender Touches   **79**

A Tiny Piece of Heaven   **83**

Contents

The Light of Love   **87**

Angel in the Andes   **90**

The Hands of a Comforter   **94**

Bedside Companion   **97**

Twice Blessed   **100**

He Will Send Angels   **105**

Callers in the Night   **108**

A Voice from Beyond   **111**

Master Builders   **113**

Julia's Visitor   **118**

The Gray Lady   **120**

Rescue on the Tracks   **125**

Winged Warriors   **128**

Companion through the Storm   **132**

The Angels and the *Padre*   **136**

Heavenly Directions   **139**

"Like Touching God"   **142**

The Boy Who Drowned   **145**

Watcher in the Woods   **148**

The Quiet Protectors   **151**

Silent Circle   **156**

A Smiling Child   **159**

The Boy in the Blue Suit   **162**

Strangers in Distress   **166**

Angels with Nightsticks   **171**

Heavenly Housekeeper   **174**

Leonor's Choice   **177**

The Day We Saw the Angels   **181**

Another Beginning   **185**

CONTENTS

New Stories about Angels

"Where the Pictures Came From"   **189**

Angel of Vietnam   **191**

Susan's Story   **195**

O Holy Night   **199**

Where Are the Children?   **201**

Angels Unaware   **205**

Willow's Mystery   **208**

10 Percent Solution   **210**

Miracle in Missouri   **214**

My Twenty-Five Years with the Angels   **219**

Bonus Stories about Angels

Special Note from the Author   **233**

To Sir, with Love   **236**

Guardian in Their Midst   **243**

Old Dog, New Trick   **250**

More Than Man's Best Friend   **253**

Views from the Bridge   **260**

Snow Angel   **264**

Doggone Darling   **270**

A Rose for Margaret   **273**

An Angel to Catch Her   **278**

A Motorcycle Miracle   **279**

A Small Gift Becomes an Angelic Sign   **282**

Comfort, When She Was Sick   **284**

Her Spirit Was in the Pink   **287**

The Mysterious Diver That Saved Her   **289**

A Vehicle of God's Love   **292**

Help for Nuns in Angel White   **294**

Contents

An Earth Angel on the Trail **296**

The Angel on the Beat-up Bike **298**

No Batteries Required **300**

The Nest Egg **302**

When Angels Have No Names **304**

Angel in the X-ray Room **310**

An Angelic Rescue **312**

Did an Angel Help Her Get to Her Dying Mom's Side? **314**

An Angel's Message in Stone **316**

What Do the Little Ones See? **318**

Stranded on a Dark Mountain Pass **322**

Vision of God's Love **324**

Acknowledgments **327**

Endnotes **329**

About the Author **331**

FOREWORD

~⊗~

It's hard to believe the first time I picked up *Where Angels Walk* by Joan Wester Anderson was nearly twenty-five years ago. I've since gone back to it many times. I should have known right away the impact this book would have. As it turned out, *Where Angels Walk* was at the forefront of America's angel renaissance.

As editor of *Angels on Earth* magazine, I and countless other readers have come to know Joan and her stories, and I'm always stunned by the same thing: encounters with angels happen to regular people just like you and me. People who've known troubled times and in a moment of despair saw glorious wonders. People who've prayed for a miracle and as a result met just the right person who could make it happen. People who've been lost, only to discover a new path laid out for them.

Where Angels Walk features heartfelt and dramatic stories, including the one that started Joan on her own angel journey. Her son and his friend were stranded on the side of the road during an eighty-below windchill on Christmas Eve. After praying for help, they were rescued by a stranger who towed their car to safety and then vanished without a trace—tow truck and all. You'll also read the incident of a woman whose grief over the loss of her young nephew threatened to undo her, until the perfect angel came to comfort her. And the account of a pilot and his passenger guided through the fog by an air traffic controller whose very existence could never be explained. Every page of this book offers thrilling evidence that angel encounters do happen to people. They happen every day.

This Guideposts exclusive edition of *Where Angels Walk* will no doubt lead you to rediscover your own appreciation for God's heavenly helpers. You'll find that each angel is unique and special in God's eyes, as is the person in need of protection, comfort, and love. As unique, in other words, as you.

Colleen Hughes
Angels on Earth Editor-in-Chief

INTRODUCTION

"Who, if I cried out, would hear me among the angels' hierarchies?" wrote the poet Rainer Maria Rilke in the early years of the twentieth century, as dark forces were laying the groundwork for what would culminate in World War I.

This is a despairing question and arguably one of the most angst-ridden lines of poetry in all of Western literature. But at the same time, for someone like Joan Wester Anderson, Rilke's words might sound a bit, well, comical, akin to the old joke that asks, "Who's buried in Grant's tomb?" The answer, of course, is Grant.

So who, if we cried out, would hear us among the angelic orders? For Anderson the answer is simple: the angels, that's who.

Back in the 1990s, as we inched closer to a new millennium and an unknowable future, angels were all around us, offering guidance and protection. Joan Wester Anderson's *Where Angels Walk*, published in 1992, appealed to the zeitgeist of the moment. Her book, which fits very nicely in the Judeo-Christian tradition—angels as God's messengers, helpers, and warriors—offered inspiring stories of modern-day encounters with holy, supernatural beings, with each story reassuring us that indeed our prayers were being heard on high.

Where Angels Walk sold well over a million copies and sat on the *New York Times* best seller list for more than a year. A phenomenal feat. Around the same time, Sophy Burnham's *A Book of Angels*, positioned for more of a New Age audience, was also a celebrated best seller. Yet, millions and millions of people weren't just reading about angels; they were also watching them on the big screen in movies such as *City of*

Angels starring Nicholas Cage; listening to songs such as "Angel" by Sarah McLachlan; and tuning in every week for the popular TV show *Touched by an Angel* starring Roma Downey and Della Reese. Even *Newsweek* and *Time* featured angels as their cover stories. The underlying message from all these forays into popular consciousness was simple: Do not be afraid. You're not alone. Someone has your back.

The mark of the new millennium came and went. The world did not end. Y2K—that computer bug that was going to shut down all technology and plunge us into darkness—is looked upon now as a bit of silliness that never amounted to much of anything. In those early days, the twenty-first century was looking pretty good. Here in the West, things *seemed*, in general, safe and secure. Then the terrorist attacks happened on September 11, 2001, and for a few moments we thought that maybe fate had been running a little late. Thousands of people lost their lives in a series of acts, wars ensued, the economy later busted, and everything seemed to come crashing down around us. The ominous lines of William Butler Yeats's poem "The Second Coming" seemed terribly prescient: "Things fall apart; the centre cannot hold. / Mere anarchy is loosed upon the world."

Where were the angels during all of this? Where were our protectors? If angels were all around us in the 1990s, they seemed to have cut their losses, packed their bags, and headed for warmer climates. Certainly, though, there were stories of rescues and angelic intervention in the 2000s. Anderson recounts a number of them in her most recent book, *In the Arms of the Angels*. Yet angels generally had faded from our collective consciousness. We weren't paying attention to them anymore. Instead, our focus turned to heaven.

In recent years, books such as the best sellers *Proof of Heaven* by Eben Alexander and *Heaven Is for Real* by Todd Burpo and Lynn Vincent have sold in excess of seven million copies combined (and that is a conservative figure). Angels were out, and near-death experiences (NDEs)—firsthand accounts of people dying, encountering God, and coming back to life—were in.

Maybe this wasn't such a bad thing. Angels, as I'm sure Anderson would agree, are not ends in themselves, but a way of leading us to God, of reminding us that God is present. In an old Bruce Lee movie, there is a line where the teacher tells a student that the secret to life is like a finger pointing to the moon. As the student stares at the finger, the teacher slaps the boy on the head and says, "Don't focus on the finger or you will miss all the heavenly glory." Maybe the angels had become like that finger and needed to stand aside to shift the focus back to what was most important.

Or maybe the rise of technology has caused our consciousness to shift. As more and more of us stop paying attention to the world around us and instead shift our focus to the screens of our smartphones, the more we may be missing the angels around us. Fewer and fewer of us are looking to the sky these days. Instead, we're checking Facebook or e-mail and in turn blocking out the realities that surround us every day. Myopia isn't conducive to angelic encounters.

Still, the winds are beginning to shift again, and angels seem to be coming in for a landing. As an author, editor, and publisher, I've come across at least a dozen book proposals in the past year that center on angels. Recent best-selling books such as Anthony DeStefano's *Angels All Around Us* and Ptolemy Tompkins and Tyler Beddoes's *Proof of Angels* are helping pave a whole new runway for our heavenly friends. Question: What does this all mean? Answer: That there is an angelic renaissance on the way. And what better way to help usher in that new awareness than to celebrate *Where Angels Walk*, this classic inspirational work that reaffirms God's ultimate message of love and abiding presence in our lives.

In this book, you'll find stories of angelic intervention: a seven-foot, white-clad mystery man who scares away a gang of thugs; an angelic helper who whisks a boy to his mother after a potentially fatal snakebite; and a heavenly voice that helps a lost pilot and his passenger land a plane in dense fog, to name just a few.

Because I have been a fan of Anderson's book for years, and because I'm lucky enough to talk about spiritual matters for a living, many people have asked me over the years why they've never had an encounter with an angel. I don't really have a perfect answer for that, but as the stories here attest, we can't *will* an angel to appear. We can certainly pray. We can ask for assistance. We can have faith. We can petition. But in the end, angels are wild and mysterious and can't be tamed by our desires. God made them that way for good reason. Think of all the trouble we'd get into if we could control the angels!

So we can't make an angel appear before us. Still, this doesn't mean that we can't prepare a place at the table in hopes of an angelic visit. How do we do that? First, through stillness. If angels have a playground, it's a very quiet playground. Certainly, the angels intercede during times of crisis (one of my favorite stories in *Where Angels Walk* is Anderson's story about her son being saved by angels on a terribly cold Christmas Eve), but in the Bible many encounters with our angelic friends happen during times of stillness. Angels appear to Jacob in the stillness of a dream, to Mary in the stillness of an ordinary day, to the shepherds in the stillness of a desert night, to Peter in the stillness of a cold prison cell.

When there is too much chatter in your head, you can't hear the voice of God or the beautiful songs of the angels. If you don't believe me, start a conversation with a friend and then ask that friend to talk at the same time as you. How well do you understand each other? You don't. All you have is confusion. Or try listening to a friend tell you about her day while you're writing an e-mail on your phone. How many of us have been on either end of that encounter? It's not pleasant, and it undermines true communication. If we want angels in our lives, I think we need to be respectful and we need to practice stillness throughout the day. You need to be quiet to hear and see all that is visible and invisible.

Try this experiment. If you're looking to have a better relationship with God's angels, ask God to help you be aware of their presence. The next time you go to work, to the grocery store, or to the doctor, ask God to send your guardian angel ahead to prepare the way for you. Ask God to have your angel help you with a crisis. Worrying about the job? Ask God to have the angels guide you in discerning what to do. Ask God in prayer for angelic assistance. Many of us, in our day-to-day lives, fail to ask God for anything. But ask. And see what happens. Don't focus on angels during the day. Make your petition, put God first in all that you do, and go about your day. See what happens. I'm sure Joan Wester Anderson would love to hear about the results.

And read. Read more about the angels. You won't find a better book than the one you are reading now. We know from grammar school that when a sentence begins with a word such as *when* or *who* or *where*, someone is asking a question. But, unlike Rilke, Anderson isn't asking a question in the title of her book *Where Angels Walk*. She's making a declaration. She's declaring that they walk among us, especially during such tumultuous times as these. We have a companion with us always. That companion is God, and God sends His messengers, these mirrors of grace, to illuminate the way for us.

Embrace this book. Embrace the angels. Your life will never be the same.

Gary Jansen

Author of *The 15 Minute Prayer Solution* and *Station to Station*

WHERE ANGELS WALK:
THE ORIGINAL STORIES

THE BEGINNING . . .

❧

A guardian angel o'er his life presiding,
Doubling his pleasures, and his cares dividing.
—SAMUEL ROGERS, "HUMAN LIFE"

It was just past midnight on December 24, 1983. The Midwest was shivering through a record-breaking cold spell, complete with gale-force winds and frozen water pipes. And although our suburban Chicago household was filled with the snug sounds of a family at rest, I couldn't be a part of them, not until our twenty-one-year-old son pulled into the driveway. At the moment, Tim and his two roommates were driving home for Christmas, their first trip back since they had moved east last May. "Don't worry, Mom," Tim had reassured me over the phone the night before. "We're going to leave before dawn tomorrow and drive straight through. We'll be fine!"

Kids. They do insane things. Under normal circumstances, I figured, a Connecticut-to-Illinois trek ought to take about eighteen hours. But the weather had turned so dangerously cold that radio reports warned against venturing outdoors, even for a few moments. And we had heard nothing from the travelers. Distressed, I pictured them on a desolate road. What if they ran into car problems or lost their way? And if they *had* been delayed, why hadn't Tim phoned? (This was long before we had cell phones.) Restlessly I paced and prayed in the familiar shorthand all mothers know: *God, send someone to help them.*

As I later learned, the trio had stopped briefly in Fort Wayne, Indiana, to deposit Don at his family home. Common sense suggested that Tim and Jim stay the rest of the night and resume their trek in the morning. But when does common sense prevail with invincible young adults? There were only four driving hours left to reach home. And although it was the coldest night in Midwestern history and the highways were snowy and deserted, the two had started out again.

They had been traveling for only a few miles on a rural access road to the Indiana tollway when they noticed that the car's engine seemed sluggish, lurching erratically and dying down to ten or fifteen miles per hour. Tim glanced uneasily at Jim. "Do not"—the radio announcer intoned—"repeat, *do not* venture outside tonight, friends. There's a record windchill of eighty below zero, which means that exposed skin will freeze in less than a minute." The car surged suddenly, then coughed and slowed again.

"Tim," Jim spoke into the darkness, "we're not going to stall here, are we?"

"We can't," Tim answered grimly as he pumped the accelerator. "We'd die for sure."

But instead of picking up speed, the engine sputtered, chugged, and slowed again. About a mile later, at the top of a small incline, the car crawled to a frozen stop.

Horrified, Tim and Jim looked at each other in the darkened interior. They could see across the fields in every direction, but, incredibly, theirs was the only vehicle in view. For the first time, they faced the fact that they were in enormous danger. There was no traffic, no refuge ahead, not even a farmhouse light blinking in the distance. It was as if they had landed on an alien, snow-covered planet.

And the appalling, unbelievable cold! Never in Tim's life had he experienced anything so intense. They couldn't run for help; he knew that now for sure. He and

Jim were young and strong, but even if shelter was only a short distance away, they couldn't survive. The temperature would kill them in a matter of minutes. "Someone will come along soon," Jim muttered, looking in every direction. "They're bound to."

"I don't think so," Tim said. "You heard the radio. Everyone in the world is inside tonight—except us."

"Then what are we going to do?"

"I don't know." Tim tried starting the engine again, but the ignition key clicked hopelessly in the silence. Bone-chilling cold had penetrated the car's interior, and his feet were already growing numb. *Well, God,* he prayed, echoing my own distant plea. *You're the only one who can help us now.*

It seemed impossible to stay awake much longer. Then, as if they had already slipped into a dream, they saw headlights flashing at the car's left rear. But that was impossible. For they had seen no twin pinpricks of light in the distance, no hopeful approach. Where had the vehicle come from? Had they already died? But no. For, miraculously, someone was knocking on the driver's-side window. "Need to be pulled?" In disbelief they heard the muffled shout. But it was true. Their rescuer was driving a tow truck.

"Yes! Oh, yes, thanks!" Quickly, the two conferred as the driver, saying nothing more, drove around to the front of the car and attached chains. If there were no garages open at this hour, they would ask him to take them back to Don's house, where they could spend the rest of the night.

Swathed almost completely in a furry parka, hood, and a scarf up to his eyes, the driver nodded at their request but said nothing more. They noted that he was calm as he climbed into his truck, seemingly unconcerned about the life-threatening circumstances in which he had found them. *Strange that he's not curious about us,* Tim mused, *and isn't even explaining where he came from or how he managed to approach without our seeing him.* And had there been lettering on the side of the truck? Tim hadn't noticed any. *He's going to give us a big bill, on a night like this. I'll have to borrow some money from Don or his dad.* But Tim was exhausted from the ordeal, and gradually, as he leaned against the seat, his thoughts slipped away.

They passed two locked service stations, stopped to alert Don from a pay phone, and were soon being towed back through the familiar Fort Wayne neighborhood. The streets were hushed, Christmas lights long since extinguished and families asleep. Still, Don's street seemed the most welcoming they'd ever been on. The driver maneuvered carefully around the cul-de-sac and pulled up in front of Don's house. Numb with cold, Tim and Jim raced to the side door where Don was waiting, then tumbled into the blessedly warm kitchen, safe at last.

Don slammed the door against the icy blast. "Hey, what happened?" he began, but Tim interrupted.

"The tow-truck driver, Don—I have to pay him. I need to borrow—"

"Wait a minute." Don frowned, looking past his friends through the window. "I don't see any tow truck out there."

Tim and Jim turned around. There, parked alone at the curb, was Tim's car. There had been no sound in the crystal-clear night of its release from the chains, no door slam, no chug of an engine pulling away. There had been no bill for Tim to pay, no receipt to sign, no farewell or "thank you" or "Merry Christmas." Stunned, Tim raced back down the driveway to the curb, but there were no taillights disappearing in the distance, no engine noise echoing through the silent streets, nothing at all to mark the tow truck's presence.

Then Tim saw the tire tracks traced in the windblown snowdrifts. There was only one set of marks ringing the cul-de-sac curve. And they belonged to Tim's car.

When Christmas carols fill the air and our worries regress in a temporary whirl of holiday nostalgia, everyone believes in angels. But it's harder to accept the likelihood that the "multitude of heavenly host" on that long-ago Bethlehem hillside has relevance in our lives, too, that God's promise to send his angels to protect and rescue each of his children is a faithful pact, continuing for all eternity, throughout every season of the year.

Angels don't get much attention today. If the spirit world is acknowledged at all, it's usually the dark side, tales of demons or alien invaders or other apocalyptic threats. Yet there is evidence that good spirits are also at work here on Earth—combating evil, bringing news, warning us of danger, consoling us in our suffering, then vanishing, just as the angels did on that first Christmas night.

Angels don't submit to litmus tests, testify in court, or slide under a microscope for examination. Thus, their existence cannot be "proved" by the guidelines we humans usually use. To know one, perhaps, requires a willingness to suspend judgment, to open ourselves to possibilities we've only dreamed about. "The best and most beautiful things in the world cannot be seen or even touched," Helen Keller said. "They must be felt with the heart."

Was it an angel? Our family will never know for sure.

But on Christmas Eve in 1983, I heard the whisper of wings as a tow-truck driver answered a heavenly summons and brought our son safely home.

SEARCHING FOR ANSWERS

We not only live among men, but there are airy hosts, blessed spectators,
sympathetic lookers-on, that see and know and appreciate our thoughts
and feelings and acts.
—HENRY WARD BEECHER, *ROYAL TRUTHS*

Angels. What did I really know about these celestial beings? As a Catholic, I was certainly aware of their existence. During childhood, I had learned a prayer to my guardian angel, and in college I had studied the hierarchy of angels, the nine choirs, each with its own function and assignment. But after Tim's curious rescue, I began to research angels with deeper interest.

One of the first facts I uncovered was a Gallup poll suggesting that more than 60 percent of Americans believe wholeheartedly in angels. Although scholars differ about specifics, their existence is accepted by all three of the great Western religions—Judaism, Christianity, and Islam. Angels are mentioned more than three hundred times in sacred Scripture, acting alone or in great gatherings, carrying out God's commands, forming a heavenly court, and—significantly—protecting and bringing messages to people. They played crucial roles in the Old Testament, including the books of the Jewish Torah, and are cited frequently in the Islamic Koran. Socrates often asked his guardian angel for advice. Many famous saints, as well as Salvation Army founder General William Booth, claimed to have seen angels, and Abraham

Lincoln said he felt their presence frequently. Celestial beings appear in the works of Dante, Milton, and Shakespeare, as well as in the works of contemporary authors.

As civilization evolved, so did humanity's understanding of angels. To early pagans, gods seemed either to be stars and planets or to dwell in the sky, so it was a simple transition to consider angels as winged spirits who could travel easily between heaven and earth.

Interpretations varied as time passed. Early Hebrews contended that the universe was a hierarchy, with God at the top and other entities radiating downward from him. They believed that angels constitute the "court of heaven." In writings they referred to "the angels of God" and *bene Elohim*, "God's sons."

Christians believe that God made angels at or about the time he made the world (Saint Augustine thought the two acts of creation were simultaneous), but before he created human beings. They were given minds and wills, like us, but had no bodies. At some point, according to the book of Revelation, some of the angels wished to be gods and there was a terrible battle in heaven. The defeated angels then became evil spirits, headed by Satan, who roam the world to this day.

The Council of Nicaea in the year 325 declared *belief* in angels a dogma, but a later synod condemned the *worship* of angels.

Muslims also believe that angels were created before man. According to the Koran, when humans were fashioned as God's supreme handiwork, angels were required to bow down before them, an order that prompted Lucifer's rebellion. Before Muhammad united them under one religious banner of Islam, the Arabs had recognized many gods and goddesses and seemed to include angels among them. Muhammad acknowledged biblical writings and thus included angels in his new religion. In fact, after being chosen as Prophet, Muhammad claimed to see a beautiful vision of Gabriel, who promised to guide him in his new role. Muslims believe that angels witness for or against people on the Day of Judgment, and that recording angels are present at prayer in the mosque and elsewhere.

My investigations revealed that, whatever their beginnings, angels have three basic purposes: to worship God, to serve as heralds between God and his people on the earth, and to act as our caretakers while never interfering with our free will. Saint Dionysius, Saint Paul, Pope Gregory, and others further divide angels into nine choirs, listed here in descending order, along with their main duties: Seraphim and Cherubim, who love and worship God; Thrones and Dominions, who regulate angelic duties; Virtues, who work miracles on the earth; Powers, who protect us from demons; Principalities, Archangels, and Angels, who are ministers to and guardians of people.

The four archangels best known to us are Raphael, Michael, Gabriel, and Uriel. Their numbers seem to be infinite, though, and throughout history, others have also been named. One of the oldest shrines in Turkey is dedicated to Michael, who is considered a great healer of the sick in that nation. Although angels are extremely powerful, they are, of course, subject to God in all things.

Religions differ on specifics about angels. For example, most Catholics believe that everyone receives a guardian angel at birth, a life companion especially suited to one's unique personality. Catholic children learn a comforting little prayer to initiate "conversation" with their angel, and the feast day of guardian angels is celebrated on October 2. Ancient Jewish angelology also taught the personal-angel theory. In fact, the Talmud speaks of every Jew being assigned eleven thousand guardian angels at birth! The various Protestant faiths hold divergent views, most believing that we shouldn't pray to angels but that we may ask them to intervene for us.

As angels began to appear in art, around the fourth century, artists gave them wings in order to distinguish them from the apostles or other holy men and women.

We also think of them as dimpled cherubs, or perhaps a white-garbed chorus, as on that first Christmas night. Survivors of near-death experiences, however, cite "bright beings of light" that they met along the way—a reminder that light, symbolized in artists' renditions by halos or luminous bodies, represents heaven and, perhaps, those occupying it.

In Scripture, many angels appear as powerful, fearless soldiers. But there are also Bible stories about men and women meeting angels in human form, angels who look just like ordinary mortals . . . actually, just like Tim's angel. The companion in the book of Tobit and the strangers who visit Lot in Genesis are good examples. And did not Saint Paul admonish the Hebrews—and all who would come after them—to "show hospitality . . . for by doing so some people have shown hospitality to angels without knowing it"?

Even Hollywood gets into the angel act on occasion. Who can forget Clarence in the movie *It's a Wonderful Life*, a lovable, bumbling angel who shows a suicidal man (James Stewart) the value of his life and what would have happened if he had not been true to his principles? Stewart always maintained that the role was his favorite.

And consider the popular television series *Highway to Heaven*, produced by the late Michael Landon. Landon played the role of an angel, Jonathan Smith, sent from heaven to persuade hurting people to help one another. The idea had come to Landon one day while, stuck in traffic on a Los Angeles freeway, he watched drivers angrily honk and yell at one another. If they used even a fraction of that energy on being kind, Landon mused, how the world could be changed! Soon he developed a series based on the idea that kindness, not anger, solves problems, with the central character an angel who could make mistakes but could also be a spiritual catalyst in people's lives.

But Hollywood is fiction. Were *real* angels still around today, still ministering to us by caress, whisper—or in human form? If this dramatic, unexpected, and marvelously loving rescue had happened to my son, would I find that others had similar stories? It seemed logical; since I believe God loves all his children with equal intensity, he would certainly extend to everyone the same protection he had provided for Tim. But maybe few of us recognized this help when it came. Or perhaps we passed such moments off as "lucky breaks" or "coincidence." I would have to dig deeper to find the answers.

But it was one thing to read privately about angels, quite another to ask someone, even a close friend, "Have you ever met an angel?" People vary in their willingness to trust the supernatural, I think. Many consider the idea of heavenly beings walking around helping humans as incomprehensible. We are, after all, creatures of the twentieth century's "theology" of scientific proof. Others agree that such an encounter might occur, that we live in a world where not everything is explainable in logical terms, but they maintain that real miracles wouldn't—*couldn't*—happen to *them*. After all, didn't one have to be exceptionally pious in order to qualify? And if I found people who had had an encounter similar to Tim's, would they be willing to share it?

Taking a deep breath, I went to the post office and rented a box. Then I wrote to magazines where readers were familiar with my byline and asked that my letter be published: "I am looking for people who believe they may have met an angel," I wrote. "I am not talking about human beings who, because of kindly deeds, might rightfully be called 'angels.' I am talking about spirits who appeared in human form to give some kind of help. Please write to me at this box number . . ."

A few of the magazine editors wrote back stating that they didn't publish letters of this kind. They either objected to having their pages used as a means of research or, I suspect, considered my request a bit too weird. From others, I received no acknowledgment. This could mean a decision to discard my letter—or publish it. But even if my request was honored, what if no one responded? What if readers laughed or, worse, said to one another, "That Joan Anderson used to be a nice, normal writer. But I think she's gone round the bend, don't you?"

I waited, kept looking for angel material, and, one day, saw one of my requests in print. A few weeks later I went to the post office, inserted my key into my rented box, and gathered my courage. This was probably what people call "the moment of truth." Today I would discover whether Tim's event was an isolated occurrence—or whether we were members of a great and glorious community of people whose lives had been touched by a heavenly being.

I swung open the mailbox door—and stepped back in amazement. It was filled with envelopes.

ANGELS ALL AROUND US

Yet many will not believe there is any such thing as a sympathy of souls.
—IZAAK WALTON, *LIFE OF DR. DONNE*

I haven't told this to many people. I guess I'm afraid my family or friends would laugh, or think I was having hallucinations."

"If I try to explain what I saw, he gives me That Look, as if he thinks I need counseling."

"It all happened so fast that I didn't consider angelic intervention, not until days later. Then I started putting the pieces together."

The letters were a joy to read. In subsequent months, as other magazines printed my invitations and I developed enough courage to request stories from audiences at my humor speeches and writers' conferences, many strangers shared their "special event" with me. I also corresponded with some authors of angel books already in print, to ask for their insights or to request addresses of people they had interviewed. My files began to grow.

I found it fascinating that, although angel incidents varied, the reaction of those involved was almost always the same, and twofold: first, a hesitancy about sharing; then, once that was overcome, an awe that, even years later, was still powerfully aroused by the memory of the incident.

The reluctance to go public was understandable. Like those who had experienced clinical death, had been revived, and had attempted to tell others what they'd seen, my interviewees had often felt rejected. Gradually, they had learned to ponder such happenings silently, lest their wonder be diminished by the disbelief of others. None wanted to lose that precious conviction that they had been especially blessed, permitted—just for a moment—to look into a world they must usually accept on faith.

The emotional response seemed universal too. One middle-aged woman, talking to me on a stairway during a break in a writers' conference, described a scene from her childhood. Piqued at some trivial matter, she had run off into the woods and had promptly gotten lost. She kept walking as the sky darkened and was horrified to come across her own footprints; she'd been walking in a circle. Suddenly, she felt a gentle hand on her brow, and a tender inner voice told her to "go straight ahead." Immediately she obeyed, and in less than a mile, she saw her house on the horizon.

"It's been forty-five years, but I can still feel that hand and hear that wonderful voice," she said, eyes misting as she swallowed hard and stared over my head into a place I could not follow. Others choked up on the telephone when attempting to describe what they had seen or heard. Though none could fully explain what had happened, all seemed transformed in light of their encounter.

As I separated and categorized the responses, I noticed that they fell into one of several groups. Like the lady in the woods, there were those who hadn't met an angel in human form but had seen lights, heard a voice, or felt a touch. Others mentioned their awareness of a "presence" during significant moments, as if special friends had come to share the occasion.

"I was visiting my neighbor in the hospital," one told me, "and suddenly I felt the company of angels all around us. 'Oh! There are angels here!' I said, before I could help myself. The patient and her sister seemed surprised, but willing to accept my notion."

"The next morning, my neighbor died, and later her sister told me what a comfort it was to know that angels had been in the room with us. It's been forty years, and I've never had a similar experience, but I still remember that indescribable feeling."

Many letters involved deathbeds, where those keeping vigil saw a radiance on the face of the dying one or heard him speak to someone unknown and unseen just before closing his eyes for the last time. "Look, Mother, there are angels all around us, and one is more beautiful than the rest," one eleven-year-old said as he was dying from peritonitis.

"I can't see them, Joey," his mother answered. Thinking her son was delirious, she tried to soothe him, but Joseph was insistent.

"See, they're right here, so close I could touch them," he told her again. Joseph's grieving mother was struck by her son's attitude of profound joy and peace. It became a consolation to the entire family.

F. S. Smythe, who attempted to climb Mount Everest in 1933, wrote of the same "friendly presence" in his account of the expedition. "A strange feeling possessed me that I was accompanied by another. In its company I could not feel lonely, nor could I come to any harm. It was always there to sustain me on my solitary climb up the snow-covered slabs. [When] I halted and extracted some mint cake from my pocket, it was so near and so strong that instinctively I divided the mint into two halves and turned round with one half in my hand to offer it to my companion."[1]

Another respondent told me of a time when she was seventeen and, for several nights in a row, felt a presence at the foot of her bed. "I didn't actually see any-thing," she explained. "It was more the kind of feeling you get when you're aware of someone looking at you when you're in traffic, or reading, or sitting with your back to a doorway."

She sensed that there were two angels standing side by side, facing her. Their mission seemed to be one of simple reassurance, and the young girl felt warm, sheltered, and at peace. The following years were turbulent. "But knowing that two angels had guarded me for those nights—and were probably still nearby—kept me from doubting a loving God."

Theologians maintain that although angels can and do appear as humans, their image is not necessary for their presence to be there; God and his messengers are just as close to those who do not see them as to those who do. Certainly there must be times when we never realize that an angel ministered to us. We feel a nudge, a mysterious urge to do something a bit out of character. Or something is, oddly, taken care of for us. Perhaps a sudden flash of insight is actually a spirit interceding to keep us safe and healthy. "An angel reaches down and gives us a heavenly hug, and we say, 'What a glorious day!'" wrote one believer.

Another group of correspondents did not see anyone protecting them—but others around them did. One reader sent me the well-documented story of Alice Z., a young Seventh-day Adventist selling literature door-to-door in a hostile neighborhood in the Philippines. Alice was welcomed into a house where, curiously, the guard dogs seemed friendly rather than fierce. *Two* chairs were set for her rather than one, and the lady of the house addressed the second chair as if someone were there, and she remarked to Alice that her "companion" certainly looked becoming in white. I found similar episodes where the protected one, like Alice, had no awareness that anyone was there, but the witnesses—all credible and normal—insisted they were seeing people.

The majority of my correspondents told of meeting angels in human form. Some offered messages; others rescued the person from a tricky or dangerous situation. Most often these visitors were of few words—they did their jobs, then left.

⚮

Occasionally, there was something otherworldly about the experience as it was happening, and the person recognized the being as an angel.

For example, preacher John Weaver and some friends had gone hunting for elk in Montana. John was about two-thirds of the way up a ridge when he saw a man coming out of the trees on the next hill. The stranger wasn't wearing hunter orange or carrying a rifle, and though he seemed to be walking at a normal pace, he covered the distance so quickly that it seemed like a matter of seconds.

And he left no footprints in the snow.

"The man walked up to me and shook my hand. 'John, do you know who I am?' he asked me."

And Weaver did, through the enlightened eyes of faith. The man was the same being who had helped John some twenty years before when his car broke down.

The two sat on some rocks, discussed John's current ministry and his needs—just like two friends—and the angel-visitor left, after reassuring Weaver of God's love and faithfulness.[2]

In this case, because of the footprint phenomenon and the immediate spiritual recognition, Weaver knew his visitor was an angel. For most of my correspondents, however, the encounters were so conventional that it was only later that they began to wonder. "It seemed just too coincidental . . ." or "It took awhile before I realized how odd it all was . . ." were classic comments. Because such "visitors" came in human form, initially it was easy to explain them away.

This was not new, I discovered. Throughout time, angels have typically appeared in whatever form the visited person was most willing to accept—perhaps a winged version for children or a benign grandfatherly type for a woman in distress. I found reports of angels speaking in familiar dialects or assuming the same race as the visited one. "Angels, and angels alone, are minds without bodies," observes philosopher Mortimer J. Adler in *The Angels and Us.* "Therein lies their fascination [in that] when they assume bodies, they do so only for the sake of engaging in their earthly ministry."

Nor did it seem to matter—at least to my correspondents—whether they *knew* their helper was an angel; one's recognition or faith wasn't a prerequisite for aid. But there does seem to be one common denominator. Author and angel scholar Betty Malz notes that angelic protection never seems to occur when people are *deliberately* breaking the laws of society or even the natural law—for example, taking risks by speeding down a highway or stealing from or abusing others. Following one's own headstrong will or charging into danger and waiting for God to rescue us, says Malz, apparently moves us out of the "safety zone" in which angels operate. She and others believe, however, that people can intercede for us and perhaps summon spiritual help.

Many of these stories confirm Malz's observation. Contributors were asking for assistance or were somehow tuned in to the heavenly realm when help occurred. Some suggested a similar theory: unless we *deliberately* invoke their aid, angels can help only in a limited way.

Finally, a small group of my letter writers reported seeing a real angel—that is, a being that *looked* the way we all assume angels look. "How can you be sure they aren't . . . you know . . . kooks?" my hairstylist once asked while, over a trim, I told her about my project. I couldn't, actually. And it would probably take faith on any-one's part to accept their stories.

But, once again, these people didn't care whether anyone believed them. Their conviction was powerful in its simplicity. "I know what I saw—and it changed my life," one woman said quietly. That seemed to be enough.

I had started collecting stories because of Tim's experience. Now I found myself with bulging folders that I took along to read while waiting in a dentist's office or riding on the train. The letters deserved a wider audience. I selected several of the most intriguing and began to write a book.

What has this quest taught me? I used to think that angels were minor adjuncts in the spiritual world and that dwelling on them could only distract us from God. But today I believe that angels help us lift our souls heavenward, to God. Through-out time they have been part of the divine plan, so it seems God wants us to know about them and to feel free to ask them for protection for ourselves or loved ones. The subject of angels requires a great deal of discernment and respect. Angels must be treated not as a curiosity but as an entity from which we can learn, and receive, much. In short, they can become our dear and loving companions, if we are willing to allow them into our lives.

"There is a diversity of angel forms to be celebrated, and there is an element of surprise to be realized," wrote G. Don Gilmore in *Angels, Angels Everywhere*, "but unless people revive their childlike wonder and imagination, they may never experi-ence such things."

Jesus put it another way: "Unless you become as little children, you cannot enter heaven." He was speaking of the trust, the wonder, the innocent acceptance of things not provable. In short, he was speaking of faith. "Blessed are they who have seen, and have believed."

The people who have shared their experiences in this book all suspect they have been touched by the same spiritual messengers who graced the world at its beginning; the only thing that has changed is the setting. And they are left with a sense of indescribable wonder and the warm assurance that, whatever their failings, God is holding them gently in the palm of his hand.

As the saying goes, to those who are willing to believe, no explanation of the events on the following pages is necessary. To those who are not willing to believe, no explanation is possible.

Was it an angel? It's up to you.

ANGEL IN THE COCKPIT

~⁓❦⁓~

How sweetly did they float upon the wings
Of silence, through the empty-vaulted night.
—MILTON, *COMUS*

David Moore and his wife, Florence, discovered in July 1971 that Florence's mother was dying of cancer. The Moores lived in the small town of Yoakum, Texas, but they began driving back and forth to Hendersonville, North Carolina, to visit the sick woman. After one trip, David decided to leave the car in North Carolina for Florence to use and take the bus back to Texas.

"It was the worst idea I ever had," he says, laughing. "Forty-six hours of riding and listening to babies cry! On our budget I couldn't afford to fly, but I made a vow to walk if I had to—anything to avoid getting on another bus!"

The following week, as David packed and planned a hitchhiking route to Hendersonville, Henry Gardner phoned. Henry had heard about David's transportation problems, and he volunteered to fly David to North Carolina in his small Cessna 180 and get in some sightseeing at the same time. David accepted gratefully.

David had never flown in a small plane, and he was nervous as the two men taxied down the runway early the next morning. But the little aircraft lifted gracefully, and David sat back to handle his unfamiliar duties as navigator. Within half an hour, however, as they neared Houston, they ran into fog.

"This is no problem," Henry reassured an increasingly nervous David. "We have aviation maps on board, and look—you can see the Houston radio towers rising above the fog. All we have to do is watch the towers, and we can tell where we are."

He was right, and their journey continued. But the fog worsened, and just outside Jackson, Mississippi, the plane's radio and instruments died. Now the pair couldn't see anything on the ground, nor could they talk to people in the control tower.

Just as David was becoming desperate, the fog lifted for a moment to reveal the airport directly beneath them. Henry took the plane down smoothly, and within minutes they had found an airport mechanic. Relieved, the two men grabbed a quick lunch and were soon airborne, with instruments and radio restored and fuel tanks filled.

Everything went smoothly for a while. The sun had come out, and David's tension diminished. He began to enjoy the flight and his bird's-eye view of the ground. As they traveled northeast, he could see Atlanta off to his right. "I was getting excited," David says, "knowing that soon I would be with my wife and daughter again."

But as the plane passed Greenville, South Carolina, the fog, which had been patchy and broken, turned once again into a continuous gray mass. There was enough visibility for Henry to clear the first mountain range, but as the two looked into the distance, they saw a solid wall of fog, and their hearts sank. Henry radioed Asheville's airport for instructions.

"Our field is closed because of fog," the air-traffic controller responded, "and we have no capability for instrument landing. Return to Greenville and land there."

"But I can't," Henry protested. "We're almost out of fuel—we won't have enough to fly back to Greenville."

There was a silence. Then, "Okay," the radio voice snapped. "We'll get the ground crew ready. Come in on an emergency landing."

David gripped the sides of his seat. They seemed to be flying in a dense gray blanket, and the Asheville control tower couldn't possibly see them. How were he and Henry going to land? "We can use the aviation maps, just like we did before," Henry reassured David, and after a brief scan of the blueprint, he began his blind descent. The airport runway *should* be beneath them—but what if it wasn't?

Suddenly a voice came over the radio: "Pull it up! Pull it up!"

Henry immediately pulled up on the stick. As he did so, the men saw a split in the fog, and the view beneath sent tremors of fear through each of them. Instead of being over the runway, they were above an interstate highway! Had they descended a few feet farther, they would have hit a bridge and certainly crashed.

The two looked at each other. They were almost out of fuel, and inside the grayness it was impossible to know where they were. Henry tried to descend again but almost hit the tips of some trees poking above the fog. Again, he pulled up sharply. There seemed to be no way out of their dilemma. Without enough fuel—or guidance from the control tower—how could they possibly land?

Then, with enormous relief, they heard the controller's composed voice breaking into the tense silence in the cockpit. "If you will listen to me," he said, "I'll help you get down."

"Go ahead," Henry radioed back in relief.

The controller began his instructions. "Come down just a little," he said. "Now over to the right. Down a little more . . ."

David gripped the seat, praying intently. Thank God the controller had been able to pick them up on radar, despite the airport's apparent lack of the necessary instruments. But would they make it in time? It seemed impossible. The fuel needle hovered on E, but the voice went on with calm authority: "Not so fast. Easy, easy now . . ." Was this nightmare flight ever going to end? And would he see his wife and daughter again?

"Raise it up a little now. No, you're too far left." The journey seemed to be taking forever. But all of a sudden the controller said, "You're right over the end of the runway. Set it down . . . now!"

Obediently, Henry dropped the plane through the fog, and the two men recognized the beginning of a runway just ahead, with lights along both sides. It was the most welcome sight they had ever seen. Within minutes, they had touched down. Tears of gratitude and relief filled David's eyes when he saw Florence standing at the end of the runway.

The plane taxied to a stop, and the two men offered a quick prayer of thanksgiving. Then Henry turned the radio on again. "Thanks so much," he told the air-traffic controller, his voice shaky with relief. "You probably saved our lives."

But the controller's response stopped both men in their tracks. "What are you talking about? We lost all radio contact with you when we told you to return to Greenville."

"You *what?*" Henry asked, incredulous.

"We never heard from you again, and we never heard you talking to us or to anyone else," the controller told them. "We were stunned when we saw you break through the clouds."

David and Henry looked at each other. Who had guided them through the grayness and onto safe ground? They would never know for sure. But even today David never hears a small airplane without thinking of that flight. "I know now that, insignificant as I may be in this big world, God always has his eye on me," he said. "He sustains me through the storm and the fog."

Night Guide

We are like children, who stand in need of masters to enlighten us and direct us; and God has provided for this, by appointing his angels to be our teachers and guides.
—Saint Thomas Aquinas

William and Virginia Jackson, native New Englanders, had lived in Florida for several years. Virginia often asked for her angel's help. Once, the couple drove from Las Vegas to El Paso through long, hot and desolate stretches—and only later discovered that their car's fan belt hadn't been functioning at all. How had they managed to cross a treacherous desert without a vital piece of engine equipment? Virginia believed they were protected by spiritual beings.

But it was during another journey that angelic guardianship seemed especially vivid. The Jacksons had visited their daughter in nearby Hudson and were driving home on a Sunday evening. "We try never to travel then, because in the area where we live, everything is closed and deserted," Virginia said. "If you get in trouble on the road, there's no place to go for help."

They had covered only a small distance when their car headlights went out. What to do? William pulled over, raised the hood, and looked hopefully down the road. Virginia started to pray.

Almost immediately a policeman drove up. "Do you know of a garage open on Sunday nights around here?" William asked.

The trooper thought a minute. "There may be one. Why don't you put your hazard lights on and follow me."

The Jacksons did so, but the garage was closed. Since they lived in a neighboring county, the policeman wasn't able to leave his route and escort them farther. Instead, he led them to Route 41. "Park here along the road," he suggested. "Someone's bound to come along who can guide you closer to where you live."

As the policeman was speaking, a car pulled up ahead, and William and the policeman went over to talk to the driver.

"Aren't we fortunate?" William said to Virginia as he got back into the car and the policeman drove off. "That fellow ahead is driving right past our town. He'll go slowly, and I told him that when we get to Route 44, we'll turn off. What luck, out here, to find someone going in our direction!"

Virginia was not so sure it was luck. She kept praying.

The couple honked as they reached their exit, and the Good Samaritan ahead waved and drove on. Now the Jacksons crawled to the Mid-State Bank, right in the center of their deserted town. They were only a few miles from home, but the dark drive would be extremely dangerous without lights.

"Why don't we sit here for a while, in case someone we know drives by?" Virginia suggested.

A few minutes passed. Then a red car approached. Instead of parking or leaning out the window to inquire about them, the driver, an indistinguishable figure in the darkened interior, slowed down and pulled in front of the Jacksons. In the bank's parking-lot lights, Virginia could see the first few digits on the car's license plate, and they seemed familiar.

"I think that's someone we know," she told William.

"Well, he seems to be waiting for us to follow him." William started the car and eased behind the stranger, who pulled away very slowly.

The last leg of the Jacksons' journey was almost over. What a relief. It could have been so dangerous, and yet they had been protected every inch of the way. Virginia continued to look at the car in front of them as they drove. Although she couldn't see the driver, she was able to read, a little at a time, the remaining digits on the license plate. "Oh, I know who that is!" she finally told William. "I recognize the number. That car sits in a driveway a block from our house. I pass it all the time—no wonder it seemed familiar."

Sure enough, when the driver approached that house, he tooted and turned into the driveway. William and Virginia waved their thanks, then went on to their own house, glad to relax after their ordeal.

The next day they decided to thank the driver personally, and they walked down to the house. The same red car, with the same license plate, stood in the driveway where they had watched it turn in last night.

A woman answered their knock, and as the Jacksons offered their thanks, she grew more and more mystified. "I wasn't out at all last night," she protested. "I never drive at night."

"Then it was your husband," Virginia concluded.

"That's impossible," the woman said. "My husband couldn't have led you home."

"Oh, but he did," Virginia said. "Without his help, we'd probably still be parked at the bank. I saw your license-plate number. And that red car definitely turned into this driveway."

The woman shook her head. "You don't understand," she told Virginia. "I'm the only driver, and I haven't moved the car in several days. It couldn't have been my husband. He doesn't drive anymore. You see, he's blind."

The Jacksons later discovered that the man in the house was indeed blind. And for some time, whenever Virginia met her, the woman would give Virginia a look as if to say, "What kind of hallucination have you had today?"

The couple has puzzled over their rescue since then. But however it happened, one thing is certain. "I was praying for help during the whole journey," Virginia summed it up. "Why should I be surprised that we received it?"

INVISIBLE INTERVENTION

The angel of the LORD encamps around those who fear him,
and he delivers them.
—PSALM 34:7

Corrie ten Boom was a middle-aged spinster who led an uneventful life as a watchmaker in Haarlem, Holland. When Hitler's armies conquered much of Europe in the early 1940s, Corrie's brother, a minister in the Dutch Reformed Church, began to shelter Jewish refugees. Eventually, as German troops occupied Holland, Corrie decided to help too, by hiding Jewish friends in a secret passage within her home until they could be smuggled out of the country.

Gradually, the ten Boom household became the center of the city's resistance movement, with hundreds of Jews passing through, and some being hidden permanently. "My room resembled a beehive, a sort of clearinghouse for supply and demand," she wrote in *A Prisoner, and Yet.*[3]

On February 28, 1944, Corrie, her sister Betsie, and their father were betrayed and arrested. Although the Gestapo searched their house, the secret room had been so cleverly designed that they could find no evidence of smuggling. Since the ten Booms refused to reveal the house's hiding place, they were convicted of stealing food-ration cards and sent to prison. (All but one of their guests ultimately reached safety.)

Corrie's father lived for only ten days after being sentenced, but for Corrie and Betsie, the next year was hell itself. And yet through their indomitable spirit and firm faith in God, the sisters brought hope and kindness to many suffering prisoners. To Corrie's knowledge, she never saw an angel "in the flesh," but she found evidence of angelic intervention.

At one point, as she and other inmates arrived at the dreaded Ravensbrück, a women's extermination camp, Corrie realized in horror that all their possessions, including warm clothes, were being taken from them. They would freeze in this desolate wasteland. And what of her little Bible? She wore it on a string around her neck, and it had been her consolation through the hard days thus far. But surely it would be confiscated.

Before it was Corrie's turn to be stripped and searched, she asked permission to use the bathroom. There she wrapped the Bible in Betsie's and her woolen underwear, laid the bundle in a corner, and returned to the row of waiting prisoners. Later, after Corrie and Betsie had been dressed in the prison's regulation undershirt and dress, Corrie hid the roll of warm underwear and her Bible under her clothes. It bulged considerably, but she prayed, *Lord, send your angels to surround me.*

Then, realizing that angels were spirits, she amended the prayer: *Lord, don't let them be transparent today, for the guards must not see me!*

Calmly, she then passed the guards. Everyone else in line was searched from side to side and top to bottom, every bulge and crease investigated. The woman in front of Corrie had hidden a woolen vest under her dress, and it was immediately spotted and confiscated. Behind her, Betsie was searched.

But Corrie passed without being touched—or even looked at—by anyone. It was as if no one saw her in line. At the outer door, as a second row of guards felt the body of each prisoner, she was again unnoticed.

Bibles were forbidden property. To be found with one meant a doubling of the prison sentence as well as a cutback on rations, which were already just above starvation level. Corrie lived for several months at this cruelest of institutions and was subjected to many searches. She and Betsie also conducted clandestine worship services and Bible study for inmates of all faiths and nationalities. But there seemed to be an invisible wall of protection around her Bible, for the guards never found it.

In Ravensbrück, prisoners had to surrender most medicines, but they were allowed to keep a few toilet articles. Corrie kept a bottle of Davitamon, a liquid vitamin compound, that, at the time she entered Ravensbrück, was about half full.

Vitamin deficiency was one of the worst hazards to prisoners, and Corrie's instinct was to hoard the precious vial for Betsie, who by now was emaciated and ill. But the others were sick too, "and it was hard to say 'no' to eyes that burned with fever, hands that shook with chill," she wrote in *The Hiding Place*.[4] Soon the number receiving a daily dose was more than thirty, and still, "every time I tilted the little bottle, a drop appeared at the top of the stopper. Many times I lay awake trying to fathom the marvel of supply lavished upon us." Although she could not understand how it was happening, the drops kept coming.

One day someone who worked in the prison hospital smuggled to Corrie a yeast bag containing vitamins, asking that she dispense them to as many prisoners as possible. Corrie gave each woman enough to last her for a week. But when she opened her own little bottle of Davitamon, the bottle was dry. However, the yeast bag took its place, continuing to yield vitamins for many weeks. Corrie always believed that angels had a hand in these unaccountable events.

Betsie died in prison from starvation and illness. A short time later, Corrie was called into the warden's office and released. Her suffering had ended. But life would never again be the same.

Corrie began a new career, opening homes for people who had been damaged by brutal treatment during the war, places where they could heal their bodies and minds. To support her homes, she went around the world giving lectures. It was not until 1959, however, that Corrie discovered the most significant "invisible intervention" she had received. She was revisiting Ravensbrück as part of a pilgrimage honoring the ninety-six thousand women who died there, when she learned that her own release had been the result of a clerical error. A week after she'd been granted freedom, all the women prisoners her age had been taken to the gas chambers.

NEITHER WIND NOR RAIN

❧❧

Millions of spiritual creatures walk the earth
Unseen, both when we wake and when we sleep.
—MILTON, *PARADISE LOST*

If Corrie ten Boom's angels encamped around her to make her invisible, what else can a ring of determined protective spirits do for us? I found the story of a couple who were staying at a hotel when a fire broke out. It was two-thirty in the morning, and the hall was full of flames. At first, the couple believed they were doomed. But the husband called upon God for help, picked up his wife, and ran down the hall. The flames and smoke seemed to roll back, he said, until they reached the safety of the lobby.[5]

Another woman wrote of a time when, just divorced, heartsick, and praying for help, she drove her truck through a severe rainstorm. Her son was the first to notice that the rain wasn't hitting their truck. In the side and rearview mirrors, they could see the deluge beating down, flattening foliage, pelting houses and barns. But their windshield, without wipers, was perfectly clear! This tender gesture lifted the woman's spirits and gave her courage for the difficult road that lay ahead.[6]

Lucille Johnson, a teacher, believed she experienced an "encampment" too. In 1949, a polio epidemic swept through the area of Iowa where Lucille taught, and she contracted the disease, probably from her students.

"I was hospitalized for over six months and finally 'graduated' with two sawed-off crutches with arm supports called 'Kenny sticks,'" Lucille told me. "I went back to college to finish my degree, then taught again." Through her career, her marriage, and the birth of her daughter, Lucille managed to get around first with two crutches, then with one, and finally, "due to vanity," she says, without any props.

But polio left her with a weak right side. In order to support her body, she still had to lock her knee when she walked and usually used a cane. "I fall very easily, and I once broke a kneecap," she explained. "High and gusty winds are especially dangerous, as they thrust me off balance. Even when I was much younger, I avoided going shopping in downtown Davenport because when that famous Iowa wind blew, I could hardly manage to cross the street without being pushed over!"

In 1977, Lucille and her family built a house near New Salisbury, Indiana, and Lucille got involved in Saint Michael's congregation. As their first Christmas in the new house approached, Lucille decided to thank God for her blessings by attending Mass every day during December.

Each day of the first week, Lucille drove the seven miles to Saint Michael's. But on Monday morning of the second week, she awakened to the sound of her nemesis, the wind. Weather reports warned of extreme gusts, a condition that could topple Lucille and severely injure her. Should she take the risk? *God*, she prayed, *I know I promised you . . . and I'll do my part.*

Cautiously, Lucille drove to Saint Michael's. The wind pushed and bounced her car the whole way, but it was especially nervewracking whenever she came to a clearing or unprotected area and the vehicle shuddered like a toy that easily could be tossed. Exhausted from gripping the steering wheel and riding the brake, Lucille finally parked about half a block away from the church entrance and looked around hopefully. Was anyone approaching, someone with a strong arm who wouldn't mind letting her hang on?

No. She seemed alone, and she almost decided to turn back. The wind sounded as though it was rising, and, even parked, her little car bucked and quivered. But she had come this far in safety. Reluctantly she opened the door and stepped out into the turmoil.

Strangely, the wind seemed to have died suddenly, for Lucille felt nothing at all. "I was expecting to be blown nearly off my feet, but to my surprise, I didn't feel the slightest puff, not even a breeze. There didn't seem to be any air moving at all." God had apparently heard her prayer and calmed the wind for her.

What a loving Father! she thought.

Then Lucille looked up at the trees in the churchyard. Far from being motionless, they were swaying wildly, and she could actually hear the branches creak with the strain. But Lucille *felt* nothing, not even a slight current of breeze to ruffle her hair. How could this be?

She didn't know, but she began the walk to the church doors with growing confidence. The wind was probably blowing high and not low, she decided. If that was possible, it would explain the phenomenon. But then she saw, rushing past her in a whirlpool of motion, several dead brown leaves, obviously propelled by a force that was at ground level yet not touching her at all.

Lucille climbed the cracked church steps one at a time, holding on tightly to the iron railing and forcing her body up with her left arm. But again, no wind fought her. Reaching the top, she pulled open the heavy door with ease and stepped inside, the door closing slowly behind her but not quite.

Caught by a powerful draft, the door began to fly back open. Lucille caught it and felt the terrible force as the gust fought her. As she struggled to pull the door shut, a friend grabbed the other side and half plunged inside. "This is the worst gale I've ever felt!" she exclaimed to Lucille, then looked at her more closely. "Why, you're not even rumpled!" she said. "Didn't you just come in?"

"She was right. My hair was not tossed or tumbled, nor were my clothes in any kind of disorder," Lucille reported. "I was completely calm and unruffled, even though a storm continued to rage outside."

Lucille would never know for sure if an encampment of angels had thrown rings of protection around her, rings that even gale-force winds could not penetrate. But although the presence of angels is perhaps more difficult to grasp than the wind itself, many believe it is entirely possible.

THE SAFETY INSPECTOR

An angel! or, if not,
an earthly paragon!
—WILLIAM SHAKESPEARE, *CYMBELINE*

Jean Hannan Ondracek of Omaha was one of the first to answer my request for angel stories. Hers is a memory she treasured ever since it happened in 1958.

Jean had gone to a spa in the Ozarks with her sister Pat and two girlfriends, young adults enjoying a weekend of sunning and fun. Because Jean was the only one who knew how to swim, she decided on Saturday morning to venture into the lake. Her companions planned to stay on shore and work on their tans. "There were other people in the area," Jean remembered, "but no one very close to our spot on the shore. There were no lifeguards patrolling this section of beach. As far as I knew, I was the only swimmer in the lake."

The sun was warm, the water refreshing, and time—and distance—passed more quickly than Jean had anticipated. At a point much farther from shore than she had thought—and where the lake was quite deep—Jean suddenly ran out of breath. Shocked, she realized that she did not have enough energy to get herself back to shore.

She called and waved frantically, but she could hardly make out the tiny figures on the sand. And no one was looking her way. As her fear increased, Jean realized that she could drown. "God, help me! Help me!" she prayed aloud.

Suddenly she saw something bobbing in the water to her left. A boat! It looked like an old abandoned canoe. If she could get to it, perhaps she could row it back. With the last of her energy, Jean paddled over to the boat, but her heart sank when she saw it. It was old, all right, without oars, and apparently chained or anchored in some way to something at the bottom of the lake. She could hold on for a moment, steady herself and catch her breath, and that was surely a blessing. But the respite was at best temporary.

How long could she hang on before Pat and the others noticed her absence? Or would they simply assume she had come ashore on another stretch of beach, and not put out any alarm for her? What would happen when the sun's rays began to burn her, or she became thirsty, or her arms, clutching the slippery sides, became tired? What if the old boat splintered under her weight? Jean started to cry. "Help!" she called again. "Somebody, help!"

To her right, Jean suddenly heard splashing. She turned to see a man a few years older than she gliding easily through the waves, then treading water in front of her. "Hi," he greeted her calmly, as if it were the most natural thing in the world to be passing by. "Having trouble?"

"I—I'm out of breath and can't get back," she answered, relief flooding her. "Where did you come from? I didn't see anyone swimming—and I was certainly looking for help!"

The young man shrugged casually. "Oh, I'm a safety inspector, and one of my jobs is saving lives in water, if I have to. Do you think you can swim back?"

"Oh, no." Jean shook her head. "I'm exhausted."

"Come on, you can do it!" The young inspector smiled confidently. "I'll swim beside you the whole way, until you reach shore. If you get in any trouble, I'll hold you up."

"Well . . ." He seemed so confident. Maybe she *could* do it, especially if he was there to catch her if she faltered.

Jean somehow summoned the energy to swim the entire distance. The safety inspector didn't say much, but true to his word, he matched his strokes to hers and watched her carefully. In a final burst of power, Jean stumbled triumphantly onto the beach's sandy shore. Pat and the others, still lounging on their blankets, looked at her as she splashed through the shallows. "What happened to you?" Pat called. "You've been gone such a long time."

"I almost drowned," Jean panted, dragging herself toward them. "If it wasn't for the lifeguard . . ."

"What lifeguard?" Pat was looking past Jean.

"The guard, the safety inspector who swam back with me." Jean turned around to point to him.

But there was no young man on the shore, no one swimming away in the lake, no one walking on the shoreline in either direction. Nor had Jean's friends seen any-one accompanying her.

Jean never saw her rescuer again, but she did discover that the resort didn't have any lifeguards or "safety inspectors" on the payroll. Perhaps he was a guard of a dif-ferent kind.

ANGELS ON THE HIGHWAY

*"See, I am sending an angel ahead of you to guard you
along the way . . ."*
—EXODUS 23:20

One of the first things I noticed as I opened my mail was that my son Tim had plenty of company—many people seemed to meet angels when driving! When you consider how much trouble we can get into in traffic, it's reasonable that our angels would be kept busy. For example, a minister's wife told me of a trip she took across central Kentucky. On one two-lane stretch she found herself stuck behind a coal truck, and after carefully peeking around, she swung out to pass. Horrified, she saw a huge semi coming toward her.

"The coal-truck driver saw my dilemma and inched over to the right as far as he could go, but there was not going to be enough space for three vehicles to pass, nor was there enough time for me to get back in my lane," she recounted. Frozen, she waited for the inevitable crash.

But as the truck approached her, it melted from view.

Shocked, she moved back behind the coal truck, checking her rearview mirror. The semi wasn't there. "There were five of us in the car," she told me. "All of us saw the truck coming. None of us saw what happened to it."

Sharon W. (not her real name) doesn't drive often, so when she set out one rainy evening for a coworker's house, her roommate gave her explicit directions. But the rain turned to snow, and Sharon became nervous. She knew she didn't have enough experience driving in rough Michigan weather.

Traveling too fast through an intersection, Sharon tapped the brake, but her car skidded dangerously toward a light pole instead. "Oh, angels, help me!" she cried. Immediately the car righted itself.

"It was as if it had actually been picked up and turned around," she said. "I found myself on the right side of the street, heading in the right direction." None the worse for wear, Sharon drove on to her destination.

When she arrived home, Sharon told her roommate about the near miss. "I'm not surprised," her friend replied. "After you left, I began worrying about you driving in this weather. So I sent my guardian angel to accompany you."

⚜

Bernadine Jones was driving north on a two-way street in Denver and approached an intersection where she could either continue on a straight path or go left into a curve. She was planning to turn left, but she was unfamiliar with the avenue, so when she heard a voice command her, "Slow down now!" she responded without thinking.

Coming almost to a stop, Bernadine was astonished to see an oncoming car speed across the left-hand curve, just where she would have been had she not stepped on the brake.

It was only later that Bernadine realized the voice had come from within her car. But she was alone.

Mae Warrick left the optometrist and walked toward her car. As she opened the front door, she heard a man's voice say, "Fasten that seat belt!" Mae turned and looked back, expecting to see someone, but the street was deserted.

Was someone playing a trick on her? Puzzled, she fastened the belt. She drove to her favorite highway cafe and started to turn left into the driveway. Too late, Mae realized that a truck was in the driveway and she couldn't complete her turn. An oncoming car, unable to stop in time, plowed into Mae's automobile.

"Even with my seat belt on, I sustained a cracked rib and bruises," said this eighty-year-old. "I wonder what shape I would have been in had I not obeyed my angel's orders!"

Janet Notte-Corrao obeyed orders, too, one night. She was sitting in the passenger seat next to her husband, their two children in the back. Janet was not really alarmed to hear a voice as the car went around a curve—she had heard her angel before. Although the message was not audible to the others, Janet heard: "Pray, Janet! There is a car coming that will hit you as you turn into your driveway. Pray!"

As she heard the words, Janet also received a vision of the vehicle hitting her family's car. *Oh, God*, she prayed, *please surround our car with your heavenly host of angels!*

Janet's husband was driving carefully. Without warning, there was the sound of screeching tires, and then a jolt as he slammed on the brakes.

"I was still so deep in prayer that the motion was almost a surprise," Janet said. "It thrust me forward—thanks to my seat belt, *not* through the windshield—but the cars hadn't crashed. We were so close that their headlights were shining into our eyes."

Before Janet's astonished husband could react, the other car sped off, as quickly as it had appeared. But her prayer had been answered. "There was just a tiny space between the two cars," she noted with a smile. "A space the width of an angel."

⌒⟨⟩⌒

Driving home on a Saint Louis freeway one rush hour, Andrew (not his real name) had almost reached his exit. Checking his mirrors, he began to move into the right-hand lane. But the steering wheel didn't budge. What was happening? Andrew attempted to swerve again, but the wheel seemed stuck.

He would have to force it in order to get off the freeway and find a service station right away. Trying not to panic, Andrew looked back to see what was behind him.

Directly at his rear, in the blind spot, was a compact car. "It was too far back to be picked up by peripheral vision, too far forward to be seen in my rearview mirror. Had the steering not locked, I would have turned directly into the other vehicle, at fifty-five miles per hour."

Andrew braked a little, to let the other vehicle pass, before forcing his steering wheel to the right. But as soon as the little car went by, Andrew's wheel responded normally. There was no reason to find a service station after all.

Andrew drove the car another eighteen months, and later, his son and daughter-in-law drove it. No one found any abnormalities in the steering, or anything else.

A PAT ON THE BACK FROM GOD

❧

The guardian angels of life sometimes fly so high as to be beyond our
sight, but they are always looking down upon us.
—JEAN PAUL RICHTER

Here's one more story about driving. It was January 1948 when young Father Anthony Zimmerman arrived as a freshly minted Catholic missionary priest at Yokohama port in Japan. He was the first of his order, the Society of the Divine Word, to journey from America after World War II had ended, but he would eventually be joined by many more, along with priests being sent out of China before the communists could catch up with them.

Father Anthony still remembered how he felt when his feet touched the pier after riding the waves for twelve days. "I felt myself swaying," he said, "and I watched as my 117 trunks of luggage were lined up for inspection." Inside were many articles for the war-deprived missionaries: army-surplus shoes, winter underwear, jackets, canned goods, even a bicycle and tiny motorcycle. General Douglas MacArthur had given the word that missionaries were welcome in Japan, and his command apparently cut the red tape—Japanese tax officials gave only a cursory inspection to the luggage, and Father Anthony was waved on to start his new life in Japan.

"The missionaries in our Tokyo house gave me a warm welcome that night," Father Anthony recalled. "We went to chapel right away to thank God for the safe journey. I don't remember whether I thanked my guardian angel specifically, but I usually kept in touch with him at morning and evening prayers, so I probably nodded to him then, too, asking that he accompany me during my future in Japan."

He went first to a mission in Tajimi, where he would study Japanese and teach English. Those were the days of food and fuel rationing, when Japanese families sold precious heirlooms at bargain prices to buy the necessities of life. As they saw Americans helping them, giving them food and fuel and kind treatment, the environment slowly changed to mutual acceptance and tolerance. Yet living conditions were not comfortable.

"Traveling took a long time, there was no flush plumbing, and we didn't always like the food. When I once asked my superior what that terrible smell was, he answered, 'Either it's supper or the toilet.'" Father Anthony added that he commuted on rocky and deserted roads on a little putt-putt motorcycle.

"Looking back, I think my guardian angel did not approve of all the risks I took, but I prayed to him daily and tried to keep him on my good side just in case."

By 1950, Father Anthony had relocated to Ehocho parish in Nagoya, but he still commuted to various sites to teach English, visit the hospitalized, and, if the Japanese people were willing, discuss the Christian message of healing and forgiveness. On occasion he would make rounds at the Umemori sanitarium for terminally ill tuberculosis patients. It was in the spring of 1950, after a visit to that sanitarium, that something special happened.

"After visiting with patients at Umemori, I packed everything into the jeep and started the drive back to Ehocho parish," he recalled. "I was never good at finding roads, but I drove on anyway, expecting that somehow I would return safely. I was not particularly attentive, being lost in a reverie about the people I had just left."

He was thinking about how desolate they were. In war-ravaged Japan, funds for the care of terminally ill patients were limited. The wait before death was gloomy, bereft of joy and hope. But a few were grateful to be told of God's love. For them, Father Anthony mused, his spirit still heavy at the sight of all that suffering, for them he could help open the gates of heaven.

He was nearing a crossroad now but didn't realize it was there. He was in a wooded area, trees and shrubs crowding to the road's edge, and he saw only the continuous path of the road straight ahead. There was no stop sign, and he barreled the jeep onward to get home.

Still deep in thought, Father Anthony felt a powerful jolt. The jeep, traveling swiftly forward, began to rock dangerously up and down and from side to side. It was like sitting on top of an earthquake. Was it an earthquake? What was happening?

Afraid of braking too hard and turning over, Father Anthony came slowly to a stop. And just in time. No more than fifteen yards ahead, an enormous truck came roaring from a side road that was hidden by the foliage and tore through the place where he would have been.

"If we had collided, the truck would have totaled both the jeep and me," he said. "Spontaneously, I looked to heaven to thank God. I relish the moment still."

But what had gone wrong with the jeep? As his heart quieted from the near miss, he realized that he must have hit something large or, at the very least, blown a tire—a typical occurrence on those roads. Shakily, he got out to look. But there was nothing to see. The jeep seemed perfect—its tires were fine, and he saw no dents or scrapes. And the road was completely smooth, without a rock or obstruction anywhere.

Frowning, Father Anthony got in again and started the engine. Flawless. As he pulled away, the jeep ran smoothly, with no hint of the shaking that had just taken place.

There was nothing wrong with it, absolutely nothing. But something mighty had manhandled it and changed Father Anthony's course. It was then that he realized what had happened and spoke to his guardian angel. "Sorry about that," he said. "And thank you very much."

Later Father Anthony learned that he was not the only priest to have been similarly graced. During that same period, a classmate, Father John, went routinely to a convent near Peking (now Beijing) to say Mass for the sisters there. He knew the route very well; it was a simple straight path. One morning he called a man with a pedicab to take him by that direct route.

Peking was already surrounded by the communists, and the rumble of distant artillery could be heard. "Straight ahead," Father John said to the man operating the pedicab.

"No, sir!" the man said.

Father John was used to bargaining, but this time it was different. The man had already started a roundabout route that would take fifteen minutes longer and cost more. "Straight ahead!" Father John again insisted.

"No!"

"You win." Father John sat back in defeat as the pedicab began its circuitous and seemingly senseless journey.

But the route had not been pointless. For as they traveled, a massive explosion ripped through the air and a bomb made a direct hit on the straight road where Father John would have been. Who can say whether the pedicab operator was an angel or simply inspired by one? But as both priests knew, angels take special care of missionaries.

"What does it feel like at such a time?" Father Anthony asked. "It feels like a pat on the back from God, who says, 'I know you're here, and I like what you're doing. I also have more work that I want you to do. So hang in there! But be more careful!' One does not forget such a time and event."

Father Anthony eventually earned a doctorate and taught in Japan. Later, retired, he wrote books on theology. "I suspect that in heaven, my guardian angel is going to tell me that he already knew all this was coming for me, and that is one of the reasons he made the jeep rock to keep me from being killed," he said. "The episode is etched into my memory. It is a gift I will never forget."

ANGELS ON GUARD

And Elisha prayed, "O Lord, open his eyes so he may see." Then the Lord opened the servant's eyes, and he looked and saw the hills full of horses and chariots of fire all around Elisha.
—2 KINGS 6:17

Perhaps the most fascinating angelic intervention is that which occurs when other people see a figure and the protected one doesn't see anything at all. The Bible offers several examples. The one in the epigraph describes Elisha, God's prophet, seeing the angels clearly but the servant seeing only the opposing army—until his spiritual eyes are opened.

You will read similar stories here. Author Betty Malz gave me the example of her friend Bill (who didn't want his real name revealed). Bill, his wife, and their two children were vacationing at Big Bear Lake in California, near Apple Valley. His wife was cooking on the open fire, and Bill took several photos of the family gathered around it. Then he read the Bible, asking God to protect them and give them a safe vacation.

In a moment, however, their peaceful surroundings were shattered by six men on motorcycles, who seemed to roar out of nowhere. One pulled a gun, demanding that the stunned family put their billfolds and purses on the ground. Terrified, they did so, and Bill, in his haste, dropped his camera, too.

All of a sudden, as quickly as they came, the men seemed to be stricken with fright. Leaving the family's belongings on the ground, they turned, ran for their motorcycles, and sped off. Why had they gone so suddenly, leaving behind the items they intended to steal?

Confused but relieved, Bill's family gave thanks to God for sparing them from a terrible ordeal, then went on to enjoy the rest of their vacation. It was not until they arrived home and had their photos developed that they saw what the bikers had apparently seen that night.

One of the photos clearly shows the form of a white-clad angel patiently standing watch over the family as they sat around the fire.

Louis Torres, a youth minister, was the director of the Teen Challenge Center in Philadelphia. He spoke to Maltz's church congregation one morning and further confirmed the biblical perception of angels as strong soldiers who sometimes remain invisible except to those who need to see them in order to be convinced. In *Angels Watching Over Me* Betty reported this story that Torres told her congregation, about a young woman named Myra.

Myra worked for Teen Challenge at the time Torres did. Since it was located in a rough part of the inner city, she was concerned for the teens who had shown interest in receiving Christian counsel. It was difficult for them to visit the center because on the streets just outside, a group from one of the local gangs repeatedly harassed them. For a short while each evening, Myra was alone at the center, and the gang bothered her as well, banging on the door and shouting obscenities.

One night when the gang appeared, Myra suddenly felt inspired to tell them about Jesus. Knowing the danger, she first prayed for guidance. Yes, she felt sure she had heard the Lord correctly. She opened the door and walked outside.

The gang moved around her, and keeping her voice steady, she spoke to them about Jesus.

Instead of listening to her, however, the gang shouted threats of drowning her in the nearby river. Trying to appear calm, Myra walked back through the door of the center and shut it. They didn't follow her.

The next evening the thugs were back, once again banging on the door and threatening her life. Still believing she should try and reach out to them, Myra breathed a prayer to Jesus. "Lord, let your angels come with me and protect me," she murmured.

Then she opened the door and was about to speak when the gang members suddenly stopped their shouting, turned to look at one another and left silently and quickly. Myra was surprised. Why had they gone?

The gang did not return for several days. Then one afternoon, to the surprise of everyone, they entered the center in an orderly fashion. Much later, after a relationship of trust had been built with them, Louis Torres asked them what had made them drop their threats against Myra and leave so peacefully that night.

One young man spoke up. "We wouldn't dare touch her after her boyfriend showed up. That dude had to be seven feet tall."

"I didn't know Myra had a boyfriend," replied Louis thoughtfully. "But at any rate, she was alone here that night."

"No, we saw him," insisted another gang member. "He was right behind her."

"He was big as life in his classy white suit."[7]

SPECIAL DELIVERY

For God will deign
To visit oft the dwellings of just men
Delighted, and with frequent intercourse
Thither will send his winged messengers
On errands of supernal grace.
—MILTON, *PARADISE LOST*

I first heard of Kenneth Ware through Betty Malz, who profiled him in *Angels Watching Over Me*. The Assemblies of God headquarters in Springfield, Missouri, provided more information. Kenneth Ware was born in Tennessee. A short time later, his father was killed in World War I, and his mother took Kenneth to Switzerland, where she had grown up.

At seventeen, Kenneth became an Assemblies of God minister, going first to Jerusalem and later to the south of France, where he met and married the sixteen-year-old daughter of Max Vinitski, an Orthodox Jew turned Christian and an artist whose portraits hang in the Louvre. Kenneth became known in Paris as a great evangelist, and when World War II broke out, both the Vinitski and Ware homes became havens for Jewish fugitives fleeing to Spain or Switzerland.

As son of an American soldier, husband of a Jew, and supporter of the French Resistance, Kenneth was in constant danger of being imprisoned. Eventually Kenneth, Suzie his wife, and their infant son tried to flee France. Instead, Kenneth was arrested, interrogated, and beaten, but when a German guard discovered he was a pastor, he was secretly released.

Finally reunited with his wife and son in Lausanne, Switzerland, Kenneth tried to provide for them. One Saturday morning in September 1944, however, he found himself without a penny. Suzie decided to pray—specifically. "God, I need five pounds of potatoes, two pounds of pastry flour, apples, pears, a cauliflower, carrots, veal cutlets for Saturday, and beef for Sunday," she said.

A few hours later, someone knocked on the door. Suzie opened it to a man carrying a basket of groceries. The man, between thirty and forty years old, was over six feet tall and strong looking, with blue eyes, white-blond hair, and a long blue apron over his work clothes. He seemed radiant, glowing. "Mrs. Ware," he said, "I'm bringing you what you asked for." He spoke in perfect French, without the usual Swiss accent.

"There must be some mistake," Suzie protested, bewildered. "I have not ordered anything." She called Kenneth.

Kenneth did not think the man looked like an ordinary deliveryman. Perhaps he was the owner of a firm and had gotten the apartment numbers mixed up. "There are twenty-five apartments here, sir. Have you come to the wrong one?" he asked.

The man ignored the question. "Mrs. Ware," he repeated, "I am bringing what you asked for." Then he went into the kitchen and emptied the basket. On the table were the exact items Suzie had requested from God that morning—even the two pounds of pastry flour was the correct brand. The Wares were shocked. "I turned to apologize, to explain that I hadn't a coin to give him, but his look of reproach sealed my lips," Kenneth reported.

Suzie accompanied the man to the door and thanked him; then the couple stood by the window to watch him leave the building—via the only route available. But though Kenneth watched, and Suzie opened the door again to check the hallway, the man never went by.

After the war, the Wares returned to a Paris crowded with refugees. They set up missions and schools and were able to feed, clothe, comfort, and educate the destitute. Eventually, they retired to the south of France.

Kenneth Ware always maintained he would recognize the deliveryman anywhere if he saw him again. He never did. But Kenneth and Suzie were filled with gratitude to the God who would send a personal shopper to fill their needs.

MESSAGE FROM BEYOND

❧

But all God's angels come to us disguised . . .
—JAMES RUSSELL LOWELL, "ON THE DEATH OF A FRIEND'S CHILD"

Sister Mary Dolores Kazmierczak was planning the trip of a lifetime: Rome, then on to Poland. Her elderly father wanted to accompany her, but Sister Mary Dolores was unwilling to extend the invitation. "First, my mother wouldn't fly, and because one of them never went anywhere without the other, I didn't think Dad would be happy on a trip without her," she explained.

The second reason was more awkward. Mr. Kazmierczak had a physical disorder that caused him to lose his equilibrium. This shakiness would come on without warning. How, Sister Mary Dolores wondered, would she manage him on an extensive trip? What if he fell and hurt himself? Her decision was logical, she knew, but she still felt guilty.

However, two months before the trip, in May 1979, Mrs. Kazmierczak died. Now Sister Mary Dolores's father was terribly lonely, and Mary's feelings of guilt worsened. Her father would so enjoy traveling. But her reluctant answer was still no. Taking him anywhere would be too risky.

A few days before she was to leave for Europe, Sister Mary Dolores and her father visited Mrs. Kazmierczak's grave at Holy Cross Cemetery in Calumet City, Illinois. On their way home, they passed a small roadside produce stand. It looked deserted, but Mr. Kazmierczak wanted some fruit, so they pulled in to see if anyone was there.

Two men were running the stand. One, wearing a blue shirt, was behind the counter; the other, in brown pants and a hat, was arranging the tables. Sister Mary Dolores and her father were the only customers there, and none of the four exchanged any comments or greetings.

Mr. Kazmierczak wandered around looking at the displays while Sister Mary Dolores, keeping him in view as always lest he lose his balance, selected some produce. She gave her money to the blue-shirted worker at the cash register, then started toward her father, just a few feet away. It was then that the man in the hat approached her. "It's okay to take your dad on the trip," he told her without any preamble.

"What trip?" What was he talking about?

"The trip you're going on," the man replied. "I just spoke with your mother, and she said it was okay to take your dad. Nothing bad will happen to him."

"How could you have spoken to my mother?" Sister Mary Dolores demanded. "She died this past May."

"Yes, I know," he said.

Sister Mary Dolores looked around in astonishment. She and her father were still the only customers in view. Had her father complained to the man that he was being left behind? Yet the lot was so small—surely she would have seen or overheard a conversation. She could confront her father in front of the stranger, but Dad might be embarrassed or upset. It was better to wait until they were alone.

"Well . . . thank you," she said to the man, who was still standing calmly in front of her, and then she hurried her father to the car.

Once they were on the highway, she broached the subject. "Dad, what did you say to the man at the fruit stand?"

"I didn't talk to him," Mr. Kazmierczak said. "You paid him."

"I'm not talking about the man at the cash register, Dad. It was the other one, in the hat."

"But . . ." Her father looked troubled. "I didn't see a second person. There was only the one man in the blue shirt, behind the counter."

"You saw me talking to the second man. You must have—you were right there the whole time, just a few feet away."

"But I didn't. There wasn't anyone else there."

Sister Mary Dolores stopped talking. She didn't want to upset her father. And slowly she was realizing that something supernatural had just taken place.

During subsequent summers Sister Mary Dolores took her father with her on airplane and auto trips to Arizona and all through the state of Michigan—and he never had a fall. He thrived on the change of scenery and died a fulfilled man at age ninety-two.

"I never worried after the incident at the fruit stand," Sister Mary Dolores said. She knew her mother was looking out for both of them and had sent an angel to tell them so.

THE MAN IN WHITE

How did he git thar? Angels.
He could never have walked in that storm:
They jest scooped down and toted him
To whar it was safe and warm.
—JOHN HAY, "LITTLE BREECHES"

The Durrance family, natives of southwestern Florida, moved to a house in a partially completed subdivision, once farmland. Set apart by side roads, the Durrance house was the only dwelling on their street, and their vast lot was surrounded by woodsy grass, palmetto clumps, and drainage ditches.

Even without a telephone, Debbie Durrance felt comfortable in the isolated brushland, but she was apprehensive about letting her children roam at will. Things could happen—kids could get hurt in places where their cries couldn't be heard. And there had been several reports of rattlesnakes in the area; their pets had even been bitten. "Noise and traffic scare rattlers," Debbie explained, "but they're very much at home in a quiet area like ours."

Still, one lazy Sunday afternoon just before Easter, when twelve-year-old Mark decided to wander the land with his BB gun and his dog, Debbie agreed. She started the dinner dishes, enjoying the peace and quiet of the mild day.

Mark was enjoying the sunshine too. Spying a bird in a clump of palm, he leaped over a drainage ditch for a closer view, landed on something movable—and felt a burst of agony as if his foot had exploded. In horror, he realized that a huge rattlesnake was hanging on to his foot, puncturing his shoe right below the ankle. Mark had never felt pain this intense. And the snake's fangs seemed to be stuck in his ankle! Through a haze, Mark saw his dog growling and snapping at the snake, which eventually released its grip and slithered away.

But the rattler's deadly venom had entered the main vein in Mark's leg, the worst place for a bite. By now, that vein was carrying poison through Mark's body, attacking every system. Mark realized that his strength was ebbing quickly, and he could barely walk. That 150 yards home might as well have been 150 miles. He would die out here—and his family didn't even know he was hurt.

Debbie was putting away the dishes when she heard the front door open and her older son, Buddy, shout, "Mark, what's wrong?"

She heard Mark answer, "I've been rattlesnake bit." She raced to the living room, just as Mark fell to the floor. Pulling off his shoe as Buddy ran for his father, Debbie saw the foot already swollen and purple, and she smelled the same musky odor she had noticed when her pets had been bitten. This was not a simple flesh wound but a venomous snakebite. Debbie began to tremble. Without a phone, they would have to drive Mark seventeen miles to the nearest emergency center. Would there be time? *Not my child, God*, she prayed. *Please, not Mark!*

Her husband, Bobby, raced in and picked up his son. The family ran to their truck and sped down the highway. Mark was already having convulsions, and his breathing grew fainter. All Debbie could do in the silent truck cab was pray.

As they neared the emergency center, however, steam floated from the truck's hood; it was overheating. "Bobby, what are we going to do if it stops?" Debbie asked, but it was already too late. Bobby braked for another car and the engine died. They were in the middle of traffic, but although Bobby leaped from the cab and tried to flag someone down, vehicles just kept going around them.

Then an old compact car pulled over. The driver was a Haitian farmworker who didn't speak English, but the family's frantic actions told him all he needed to know. Debbie and Buddy dragged Mark into the car. "The driver sped off, following my wild gestures, and we arrived at the emergency center a short time later," Debbie said.

At the center, a team attempted to stabilize Mark. "Usually a snakebite could be treated at an emergency center," Debbie explained. "But because the venom in Mark's leg had hit a main artery, he was being poisoned at a more rapid rate and needed special care." By the time an ambulance had been summoned to take him to the nearest hospital in Naples, ten miles away, Mark had lapsed into a coma.

For the next twelve hours, the Naples hospital staff worked on Mark. Debbie and Bobby sensed that the team didn't think their son would survive. Debbie continued to pray.

During the next few days, every part of Mark's body stopped functioning except his heart. The venom bloated him, swelling his eyes so tightly closed that his lashes were barely visible. His kidneys failed. A respirator moved his lifeless lungs up and down. Internal hemorrhaging caused blood to seep not only from his ears, mouth, and eyes but also from his pores; he required transfusions of eighteen pints of blood before the nightmare had ended. There was a 90 percent chance he would lose his leg, and it swelled so large that eventually the doctors slashed it from top to bottom to relieve the pressure. Every new symptom was worse than the last.

Debbie sat for hours by his bedside, praying aloud and talking to her son. "I hoped Mark might hear my words to him and to God," she said. "I wanted him to know that I believed he would live."

Miraculously, Mark began to improve. Gradually he emerged from the coma and began writing to his parents on a tablet. Then one day the doctors took him off the respirator. And though his voice was scratchy, Mark began to tell them of his ordeal.

"It was a rattler. It stuck on my shoe and wouldn't let go."

"But where were you?" Mark's father wanted to know.

"Out in the fields, next to the ditch."

"But that's at least 150 yards!"

"He must have been much closer," one of the doctors said, shaking his head. "Mark could never have walked that far. There was too much venom in his system—he would have been unconscious right away."

And there were the thirteen steps up the front of the house to the living room. How had this terribly wounded boy managed to climb them?

"The man in white helped me," Mark explained.

"Man? What man?" Debbie asked.

"The man. He was just . . . there. When I knew I couldn't make it to the house, he picked me up and carried me."

"What did he look like?" Debbie felt a tingle on the back of her neck.

"I never saw his face, only from his shoulders down. But he had on a white robe, and his arms were real strong. He reached down and picked me up, and I was hurting so bad that I just sort of leaned my head on him. I felt calm."

"Did he say anything, Mark?"

"He talked to me in a deep voice," Mark answered. "He told me I was going to be real sick but not to worry. Then he carried me up the stairs and I didn't see him again."

A man in white. Debbie didn't know what to say. Had her son dreamed the whole thing? But how had he gotten home?

Mark was in the hospital for nine weeks. Later he had numerous grafts to rebuild the muscle and tissue at the back of his leg. But doctors expected him to suffer no permanent damage.

"While Mark was recovering, he told me that he was sure his granddaddy Durrance had been with him in the hospital emergency room," Debbie says. "There's an old custom in Georgia that if you walk a newborn baby around the house three times, the baby will be like you. Granddaddy Durrance had done that with Mark, and the two had always been close."

But Mark's grandfather had died some time before the accident, and Debbie reminded Mark of this. "But he was right there with me, Mom," Mark insisted. "I know he was."

Of course! Granddaddy Durrance must have been the man in white that Mark dreamed of seeing.

But Mark was firm. "No, Mom, that wasn't Granddaddy. And I didn't *dream* about the man in white. He was real."

Mark's experience touched many people. The Durrances had a thank-you note to the Haitian farmworker published in the newspaper. They never found him, but their note inspired readers to think about their own responses to people in trouble. Debbie worked as a hairdresser, and because the family received so much publicity at the time, customers occasionally recognized her and she was able to tell them of her belief that God does indeed answer prayer. She also visited other snakebite victims to comfort and encourage them.

Since that traumatic time, Mark has lived the life of a typical young man, except for one difference: the awareness that something very special happened to him out in that Florida brushland. Mark Durrance passed through the valley of death as few people ever do—and had an unforgettable Easter awakening.

SCALING THE HEIGHTS

But if these beings guard you, they do so because they have been
summoned by your prayers.
—SAINT AMBROSE

Can angels rescue us even when we never see them? Even from something as commonplace as weather?

On a very stormy and blustery morning, seventy-nine-year-old Anna May Arthur was climbing the steep steps of a cathedral in her native Ireland. She knew she should have used the front staircase, which provided a railing and some shelter, but she had cut through the churchyard, and the back flight was handier.

As she climbed, the wind buffeted her and she felt unsteady and vulnerable. Since most churchgoers entered from the front, there wasn't a soul around to help her stay upright, no one on whom to lean. "I envisioned losing my balance, falling backward, and cracking my poor head open," Anna May related. "I wondered if anyone would even find me."

The forty steps were starting to feel like four hundred. As the frail woman approached the top, her fears came to pass—an especially strong gust caught her and she started to tumble backward.

Instinctively Anna May appealed to heaven, crying, "Oh, my guardian angel, save me!" Immediately she felt two strong hands on her back, pushing her forward and erect.

"I really wasn't surprised," Anna May says. "In fact, it crossed my mind that when I turned, I would actually see a heavenly being in white! What did one say to one's angel? I wondered."

But when Anna May turned, she saw a neighbor holding her upright. She had known Thomas Hillen for years and was aware that he suffered very bad heart trouble. Because of his debilitating illness, Thomas always walked at a snail's pace. Had he risked his own health to save her?

"As I came in the yard, I saw you sway and start to go backward down the steps," Thomas told Anna May.

"But, Thomas, how did you get up here so fast?"

"That's just it! I don't know!" His face was bewildered. He had been at the church gate, at least forty paces from the bottom step, when he saw Anna May lose her balance at the top of the flight.

And suddenly he was there too, across the courtyard and up the steps, right behind her. "I don't remember crossing the distance. I—I seem to have been carried," Thomas told her. "And yet, that would be humanly impossible."

Shocked, Anna May looked at him more closely. He was not even winded. How could a heart patient—or even a long-distance runner—have covered that span during the split second when Anna May began to fall and called to her angel? She looked around, but there was still no one within sight, no one who might have helped in some way. She and Thomas had been the only ones in the churchyard.

Confounded, the two discussed the event for a while, looking for logical explanations, then went into church to give thanks. "I had always been aware of my guardian angel, in a vague kind of way, but nothing as positive and dramatic as this has ever happened to me, before or since," Anna May said. "But then, there are always those little 'accidents' where one feels one is fortunate to have escaped injury. Is such a thing always a coincidence?"

Anna May has left the answer to others.

⸎

Diane Barnard (not her real name) doesn't believe in coincidences either. She remembers a very special Christmas Eve when she asked for help—and received it.

Snow had been falling all that day in Rittman, Ohio. The white covering was almost a foot deep, and although it looked beautiful, driving in it was virtually impossible. For twenty-three-year-old Diane, however, walking was just fine. Even though she lived more than a mile from church, she was so happy to be going to midnight services that she didn't mind the trek, or the fact that she would have to travel alone because her husband would stay home and care for their toddler. Christmas was just the very best time of year!

At about 11 p.m., Diane said good-bye to her husband and set out. Although the drifts were quite high in places, the journey was downhill, and she got to the church with time to spare.

The festive and beautiful ceremony ended just before 1:00 a.m. Diane hadn't encountered neighbors or friends who might have given her a ride home, so she started her hike. But getting *up* the hill was a far different matter from going down. Each step now seemed deeper and more difficult than the one preceding it, and her path was both dark and deserted, with no homes nearby. Diane's breathing came in small gasps as she plodded onward. Oh, she was tired! And as she passed a barren wooded area, she became even more alarmed.

"My feet were getting heavier with each step, and I started to realize that I was in trouble," she said. "There was a distinct possibility that I actually wasn't going to make it home—I was just too cold and weary. Would my husband wake up and realize I was missing? Would anyone find me here, or would I fall and freeze?" Her joyous excursion was rapidly turning into a nightmare.

Diane looked at her watch: 1:15. There was still a long way to go to reach warmth and safety, and her strength was at an end. She gazed at the star-studded Christmas heavens. "Oh, God, I'm so afraid," she blurted. "Help me to get home!"

Suddenly Diane heard beautiful music—and felt herself floating on top of the snow, as if she were in a dream. What was happening? Was she freezing? Was this how it felt to die?

No. She was in front of her house. But how could this be? Diane blinked, looked at the familiar landmarks, then at her watch again. It was 1:20. And yet she had no memory of moving since she had prayed. Certainly five minutes had not elapsed. Nor would she, in her exhausted condition, have been able to scale the steep hill looming in front of her. She had been ready to lie down in the snow and give up. And yet she was safely home and feeling exultant.

The young mother entered her quiet house and, still wearing her coat and boots, sat in a chair and looked at the winking Christmas lights. "I don't remember how long I sat, but I knew something strange had happened to me, and I was afraid even to admit it to myself."

"But I've come up with no other explanation in all the years since then. I think it was an angel, commanded by God to carry me safely to my front door." A member of the heavenly host, perhaps, leaving his duties on a Bethlehem hillside to touch a young woman in Ohio.

These women both *asked* for help in dangerous situations, tapping into an invisible source of strength and grace. "Perhaps angels won't intervene unless we ask them," said one respondent. "But we should—most of us need all the help we can get!"

THE FLUTTER OF WINGS

Writ in the climate of heaven, in the language spoken by angels.
—HENRY WADSWORTH LONGFELLOW, "THE CHILDREN OF THE
LORD'S SUPPER"

In the early 1960s, Lee Ballard, a missionary linguist, was sent by the Summer Institute of Linguistics to a remote village in the Philippine Islands. His job was to lay groundwork for the eventual task of transcribing Ibaloi, a completely oral language, into written form.

It's difficult to imagine societies that can't write their words. We take our inscribed languages so for granted that we forget that, for some cultures, sound is still the only means of communication.

And that's the talent of linguists—to reframe those sounds into something readable. They do this first by immersing themselves in the spoken words. Gradually they describe a sound system, analyze its grammar, begin a dictionary, collect folklore, tape dialogue—all aimed at ultimately inscribing speech. Lee Ballard's group had a second agenda as well: after developing text, they hoped to translate the Bible into Ibaloi for the villagers.

The institute had selected this particular village because no one there spoke English and Ballard could immerse himself in the language. On the night of this incident, he had been there five months. Ballard told his story originally in the May 1986 issue of *Dallas* magazine:

He told me his name was Pug-Pug. And of course I believed him. More than a year was to pass before I learned that "pug-pug" in his language meant "amputated." Maybe he told me Pug-Pug was his name because he knew it would be easy for me to remember. He wanted me to tell my neighbors his name and have them laugh and tell me no one was named Amputated and shrug it off as a joke. He knew it would make me think.

You see, as I look back on the incident and weigh the alternatives, I think Pug-Pug was an angel.

Pug-Pug came to visit on a night of chilled splendor. From my bench on the front porch I could see far off down the valley, past the tall banana trees and dull thatch of the village houses to the mountainside rising from the river with its sheer rocks glistening white in the moonlight. Only an occasional baby's cry or the bark of a dog broke the absolute still of midnight.

But I was not sitting there to absorb the view. My thoughts played and replayed the disheartening hours of my supervisor's visit just completed. He had come to the Philippines to measure my progress in learning the local language—and I had not even understood when a villager said my supervisor needed a haircut! I knew so many hundreds, even thousands, of words and phrases, and yet I was unable to handle conversation. I was deeply discouraged.

That is when Pug-Pug appeared. His boots clacked on the wooden ladder leading up to my porch, and I heard him say in deep raspy tones, "Iyayak ali" (I am here), the local equivalent of "Hi."

As I look back, several things were strange about his arrival. For one, tribal people rarely go out at night and never without a pitch-pine torch. Even the most sophisticated fear the *ampasit*—spirits that are said to live in rocks and trees. More remarkable was the fact that no dogs warned of his arrival.

In the surprise of that moment, I was aware only that his appearance and manner were different. He was forward and assertive in a place where shyness is a strong cultural value. And he wore boots and a heavy wool overcoat in a barefoot society where people wrap themselves in blankets.

I followed local etiquette and tried to make small talk. "Where have you come from?" I asked.

In return, he spoke directly. He told me immediately his name, that he had come from Baguio, where he worked for Benguet Consolidated Mining Company as an *osokiro*, a "tunneler." He volunteered his relationships in the village and his mission. He was looking, he said, for treasure—the millions in gold reportedly taken from the Philippine treasury by the fleeing Japanese in 1945. He thought it might have been stashed in a cave between our village and the town on the other side of the mountain.

We talked for an hour or more. I had read accounts of the war in our area, but he told me much more than I knew. Not only that, but the entire conversation was in the tribal language—and I understood!

As we talked, I waited for this stranger to tell me why he had come to my house. But he never did. At one point in the conversation he stood up and said, "Ondawakda" (I am going now). He stepped quickly down the ladder, passed under the elevated porch, and disappeared into the coffee grove.

In the morning, I joined four or five men as they sat on a wall next door, warming themselves in the day's early sunshine. I told them about my night visitor. When I came to his name, they smiled. Then, one by one, their faces creased and cracked into knee-slapping laughter.

"What did he look like?" asked one, wiping a tear from his eye. He wanted to know who had played such a wonderful trick on me.

"He was big," I said, "with a long thick coat and boots. He said he was Aloto's brother. He said he works in the mines."

"Does Aloto have a brother in the mines?" one man asked the others. "Or even a second or third cousin?"

"Aychi met" (emphatically not), they all said. I heard one of the men whisper to another, "Who probably was it?"

Who was it indeed? I have no idea. But I do not think his mission in our valley was to hunt treasure. I think he came because I was discouraged. And if I am right, he was successful. For his visit that night marked a turning point in my career. The success of that night's conversation gave me the confidence I needed to succeed. Discouragement vanished into the night with Pug-Pug.

Have you ever been visited by Pug-Pug, in one of his many guises? Maybe not.

But then . . . how do you know?[8]

"Had I been there only for business reasons, I doubt Pug-Pug would have come to comfort me," said Ballard years later, when he was living and working in the Dallas area. "But our organization had a special motive, and perhaps that was why my work was graced in such a unique way." By the mid-1970s, both the New Testament and a series of hymnals had been written in the Ibaloi language. And when Ballard later returned to the area as a tourist, a villager referred to him as "the man who gave us books." Pug-Pug provided something far more valuable than gold to the villagers—and to one gifted linguist.

BRIAN'S ANGEL

Angel of God, my guardian dear
To whom God's love commits me here;
Ever this day be at my side,
To light and guard, to rule and guide.
—TRADITIONAL CATHOLIC PRAYER

Zena Marie Anagnostou was the youngest in a family of seven, living in Antioch, California. She was a high school sophomore when her married sister, Rene, had her first baby, Brian. "My mom and I took care of him when Rene went back to work," Zena explained. "His bed was in my room, and he occasionally stayed overnight. We got to be very close."

Everyone who knew him agreed that Brian was the all-American boy. He had a zest for life and seemed to like everyone. As he grew, he became a class leader and a straight-A student.

Although the entire family was close, with cousins, aunts, and uncles all keeping up with one another's news, Zena and Brian had a special bond. "I took him and his younger brother, Sean, everywhere, to church, movies, walks around the lake," Zena remembered. "The boys came to visit me at college. We collected cans to recycle for their savings accounts. We talked about everything, all our dreams and thoughts."

One day when Brian was eleven, Zena was working the evening shift at the medical-records office at Roseville Hospital. Her sister Theresa came to break the news: "Zena, there's been an accident. It's Brian . . ."

"Brian! What happened?"

"He got hit by a bus on his way home from school." Theresa started to cry.

Zena stood in shock. It couldn't be happening. Was he a patient here? She'd have to go up to his room right away. "Theresa, where is he? Is he here, in emergency? How bad is it?"

"He didn't make it. Zena, he's dead."

Zena refused to believe it. Even as they drove to the morgue, she couldn't comprehend such a loss. But slowly she was forced to accept the unthinkable. Brian had gotten off his school bus, heard the city bus coming up behind, and waited by the side of the road for it to pass. The city bus had cut back in front of the parked school bus, catching Brian and dragging him to his death.

Brian's death devastated the family. Zena seemed to walk in a fog. God would get her through it eventually, she knew, but right then the pain seemed unbearable.

Because Zena worked the evening shift at the hospital, she often came home at two or three in the morning. One Sunday shortly after Brian's death, although she usually accompanied her family to the 8:00 a.m. Mass, Zena left word that she would sleep late and attend noon services by herself.

The church was sparsely occupied when Zena arrived, and it was very hot. She usually sat in front, so she went to the second pew, which had only one occupant, a boy about twelve. Even before Zena reached the pew, the youngster had gotten to his feet and stepped out into the aisle to let her in. Zena slumped dispiritedly in the center of the pew. Some elderly ladies were sitting right behind them.

As the Mass progressed, Zena noticed that the young boy was reciting the prayers perfectly. Not only was he saying the people's responses, but he was also murmuring the priest's part, words that usually do not appear in the prayer book. "He just glowed with peace, and he was so pleasant to look at. He sang all the songs in a beautiful voice, without using the songbook," Zena said. Her sorrowing spirit began to lift. "I wanted to tell him how pleased I was to see a young person so tuned in to Mass." She decided she would compliment him when services were over.

In many Catholic churches, people hold hands while reciting the Lord's Prayer, and when that time arrived, the boy came smiling to Zena and took her hand. His hand was very warm and comfortable in hers. Zena felt a serenity seeping into her, like a balm soothing her raw emotions.

Holy Communion followed, and the people arose, pew by pew. Zena exited her pew, and the boy stepped back so she could precede him to the altar. She received communion, stepped aside for a moment, "and out of the corner of my eye, I saw the boy receive communion next." She began walking back to her pew, but glanced behind her, just to keep him in view.

But the boy was no longer there. In fact, although Zena had a clear view of all three nearby exits—and he couldn't have reached any in the few seconds that had elapsed—he had simply disappeared. Quickly she scanned the aisles, but there was no sign of him anywhere.

At the end of Mass, Zena was still thinking about the boy. Odd that someone so obviously reverent would leave Mass before it ended. Had the heat made him ill? She followed the elderly ladies down the aisle and out into the sunshine. "You didn't happen to notice where that boy went," she asked them, "the one who sat in front of you during Mass?"

The ladies looked at one another, then, puzzled, at Zena. "There was no boy in front of us, dear," one told her gently. "You were alone in the pew."

Brian's family has been comforted ever since. Surely his guardian angel had sent Zena a signal that all was well.

UNSEEN PROTECTORS

*A shiver runs down your spine when you realize it is not our
imagination. Something is watching us out there.*
—SOPHY BURNHAM, *A BOOK OF ANGELS*

How many times are we kept from danger by an unseen guardian? Some people are fortunate enough to know. In 1960, the well-known Dr. Norman Vincent Peale preached a sermon that included a story about an Episcopal minister in a Southern town who stood up to Sam, a political boss, and was able to defeat a plan of his. "I'm going to kill that minister," Sam told several of his friends after the meeting.

Friends alerted the minister and offered to walk home with him, past a dark wood. But the minister waved away their concerns. "The Lord will be with me," he told them, and he walked home alone in safety.

Years passed, and on his deathbed, Sam sent for this minister. "Reverend, I meant to kill you that night," he said. "I was in the woods with a club."

"Why didn't you?" the minister asked.

"What do you mean—why didn't I?" Sam asked. "Who were those two big men with you?"

"There were no big men with me," the minister protested. "Yes, there were," Sam said. "I saw them."

Several writers told of similar events. Suzanne Vecchiarelli of New City, New York, was visiting a friend in the hospital and had brought her a copy of a book about angels. When the friend's roommate saw the book, she became very emotional and told the women a story about her cousin Stacey (not her real name).

Stacey, then in her midtwenties, lived in a poorer section of Brooklyn, New York, an area with many tenements. One night, on her walk home from work, Stacey saw a man ahead of her, loitering against a building. Stacey had an immediate feeling of fear; there had been some recent muggings in the neighborhood, and she sensed the man was up to no good. But she had no choice—the only way to her apartment was to pass him.

"Guardian angel, protect me," Stacey murmured. "Be right beside me now and save me from harm."

With an outwardly confident stride, she looked straight ahead and went by the man. She could feel him looking at her, but he did nothing. It was all Stacey could do to keep from breaking into a run, but, with her heart pounding, she managed to continue walking calmly until she had reached the corner. Then she raced the rest of the distance to her apartment building, ran up the stairs, and breathlessly locked the door behind her. It took a while for her to calm down. For some reason, she felt she had escaped a great danger.

A short time later, Stacey heard police sirens and, looking out her window, saw flashing red lights. Something was going on nearby, an accident or another mugging.

On her way to work the following day, she saw a neighbor. "What was all the excitement about last night?" Stacey asked.

"A rape," the woman told her grimly. "Just after six o'clock."

Stacey's mouth dropped. The rape had occurred on the very spot where she had passed the loitering man, just *before* six o'clock. What if he was the rapist? She had gotten a good look at him. Perhaps she could help the police with a description.

When she phoned, however, she discovered that the police already had a suspect in custody. "Would you want to try to pick him out in a lineup?" the officer asked her. "Your testimony could help place him at the scene."

Stacey agreed. That night she identified him as the man she had passed on her way home. "Why didn't he attack *me?*" she asked the officer. "After all, I was just as vulnerable as the next woman who came along."

The policeman was curious, too, and he agreed to describe Stacey to the suspect and ask him if he remembered her. Stacey never forgot his answer.

"I remember her. But why would I have bothered her?" the rapist asked. "She was walking down the street with two big guys, one on either side of her."

TENDER TOUCHES

❧

There was a shift of stars, a glimmering of blue light, and he felt himself
surrounded by blueness and suspended. A moment later he was
deposited, with a gentle bump, upon the rocks.
—RAY BRADBURY, "THE FIRE BALLOONS"

The touch of love can be subtle, just a hint that someone else is there to help, just a small whisper or caress. Or it can be something physical but invisible. In some cases, this touch is firm, almost a grip—but with nothing seen, nothing "proved."

❧

Jean Biltz was expecting her fifth child in a few months. On a cold spring morning, she awakened in her Wichita home early and, after making the coffee, went outside to see if the milkman had made his delivery.

During the night, the back porch had become glazed with ice, and as Jean stepped onto it, both her feet slipped out from under her. There was no railing on the stoop, nowhere to catch hold and keep herself from tumbling down the stairs. Almost in slow motion, Jean saw herself falling . . . falling . . . perhaps losing her unborn baby.

Then all of a sudden, two strong arms caught Jean and stood her up straight against the door. Thank heaven her husband had awakened early and was at the right place at the right time! Her grateful heart still pounding, she turned to him.

But there was no one there at all. The door stood open, the kitchen beyond was empty, and even the snow-covered yard was silent, except for a little sigh in the wind.

Jean's baby was born strong and healthy and grew up to be the father of eight.

Someone touched little Tess with the same degree of protection. She and a friend had been playing in a Tennessee yard, and it was time for Tess to go home. Saying good-bye to her playmate, Tess ran toward a backyard precipice and took a flying leap across it, as she usually did when going home. But although her feet definitely left the ground, she felt hands on both her arms pulling her firmly back, and she landed on *this* side of the ravine.

What was going on here? Puzzled, the child backed up and ran again, trying to jump the chasm a second time. Again the hands caught her, held her, then set her gently down. Her playmate had gone in to dinner, and there was no one anywhere in view.

Perplexed, Tess walked to the edge of the ravine and looked across. There, coiled in the exact spot where she would have landed, was a rattlesnake.

The "tender touch" was even subtler for Emily Frank-Pogorzelski. It was early evening—a fatiguing and frustrating period of the day for all mothers—and Emily was preparing dinner. Diana, her toddler, was riding her toy horse around the kitchen. Several times Emily almost tripped over Diana and her clackety toy. Emily's patience wore thinner by the minute. Finally, in exasperation, she reached down to give the horse a hard push, to roll her daughter away from her. "Suddenly I felt my whole arm stop in midair, as though it met some sort of invisible block," Emily recalled. "I didn't feel another hand or a grip, but actual paralysis, which extended from my shoulder all the way down. I was aware that the power (or lack of it) was coming from something outside myself." Nor did her arm feel asleep or tingly; she could move it anywhere *except* toward Diana's horse.

Emily looked up, bewildered. And in one of those microseconds that seems eternal, she realized that the cellar door was open. Had she pushed Diana, the little girl would have shot across the floor, through the door, and down the steps to the stone floor below.

⁂

Mary Stebbins, another young mother, was also having an aggravating day, and her anger over a situation with some noisy neighbors was threatening to get out of control. Irritated, she huffed out of her bedroom and stomped down the hallway toward the kitchen. In her path was the open door to the basement, blocking her way. "As far as I can remember, none of the family was in the kitchen. In fact, I thought the area was deserted," she told me.

Wanting to vent her anger, Mary reached out to give the basement door a satisfying slam. But, oddly, a strong pressure prevented her from doing so. The pressure seemed like a mass of invisible matter, a pillowy sort of "something" that gave an inch or two with the force of her hand. But then her hand seemed to encounter *another* block, which thrust it back. She simply could not finish the push.

Puzzled, Mary looked around the door and gasped. There was her two-year-old daughter at the top of the basement stairs. Had Mary slammed the door, it would have smacked the baby, and the child most likely would have plummeted down the stairs to the cement floor.

In every case, the recipients felt "trembly" as they realized what *could* have happened, then elated that everything was all right. Emily experienced an additional emotion: reassurance. "It was as if the wonderful being who stopped me from making a grave mistake was saying, 'Okay, you were impatient, but so what? Don't dwell on it. Go on from here.'"

"I don't know if the being was my angel, my child's angel, or a combination," Emily said. "But there are times when I feel a loving spirit so close behind my right shoulder that I could touch her with my fingers. We are fortunate to have such spirits helping us—and sometimes saving us from ourselves."

A Tiny Piece of Heaven

I want to be an angel
And with the angels stand,
A crown upon my forehead,
A harp within my hand.
—URANIA BAILEY, "I WANT TO BE AN ANGEL"

Most adults don't see an angel that resembles the typical rendition in art. Children, however, seem to connect with the winged and haloed version.

One mother and her little daughter were walking down the street when, a few feet from a wall, the child stopped. The mother urged her on, but the child seemed rooted to the spot. Suddenly there was a great crash. The wall had fallen. Had they gone on, they undoubtedly would have been crushed to death. Pale with fright, the woman asked her daughter why she had stopped at that precise moment.

"Didn't you see that beautiful man, dressed in a long white gown, Mommy?" the child asked. "He stood right in front of me so I could not go on."[9]

Jesus had special things to say about children. He wanted them to be able to come to him freely, unhindered by adults, because their innocence and pure hearts are what the kingdom of heaven is all about (Mark 10:14). Perhaps this is why little ones seem able to cut through the spiritual barriers we adults so often construct, and see a tiny piece of heaven. But when it happens, we adults still find it hard to believe.

That was the reaction of Laura Leigh Agnese of Bethpage, New York. Her then three-year-old son Danny was by all accounts an especially nice child, caring and honest, although he loved telling—and embellishing—stories. He also had his share of accidents.

One morning, Danny tore across the living room floor and tripped. A horrified Laura Leigh watched him, almost in slow motion, hurtle headfirst toward the sharp corner of a table. She took several steps, knowing already that she was too late to break his fall.

But Danny didn't hit the table at all. Instead, he seemed to stop in midair. Within a few seconds, he stood straight up again and ran on.

Puzzled, Laura Leigh replayed the scene in her mind. Yes, he had certainly been falling straight toward the table, and a three-year-old tumbling at that speed wouldn't have enough control or agility to twist away. Nor had she noticed Danny trying to catch himself. Yet he had somehow stopped falling. The episode defied the law of gravity!

By the next day, Laura Leigh had forgotten the incident until Danny, absorbed in play, looked up at her. "Mommy? I saw a beautiful lady. With wings."

"Really, Danny?" Laura Leigh smiled. His stories were so imaginative. "What is the lady like?"

"She's nice," Danny said matter-of-factly. "She caught me yesterday so I didn't hit my head against the table."

Laura Leigh felt a chill. "Did the lady say anything?"

"Uh-huh. She said she was going to watch over me and keep me from getting hurt."

Danny went back to his toy, but Laura Leigh was lost in thought. "Danny was so little that my husband and I hadn't really taught him about spiritual things," she said. "We had told him about God, but we hadn't mentioned angels—we didn't know much about them ourselves." He'd had no exposure to angels through preschool, church, or television either, at least not that she knew of. "Now Danny was telling me about a beautiful lady, and it seemed a perfect answer to an unexplainable event."

Yet Laura Leigh found it hard to believe her son. Children that age had trouble separating fact from fantasy, didn't they? And yet, he had seemed so certain.

When her daughter was born, Laura Leigh had placed a print of a cherub over her crib. Now she went and got it. "Did your beautiful lady look like this, Danny?" she asked.

Danny looked at the picture of the baby angel, then at her. "No, Mommy. That isn't a *lady*."

Laura Leigh didn't want to mention the word *angel*. "But it has wings. Don't they look just a little bit alike?"

Danny shook his head firmly. Although he usually enjoyed telling stories, this was different. Obviously, to him, the lady had been real.

Confused, Laura Leigh phoned her sister-in-law Roseann Sciaretta. Not only was Roseann a faith-filled woman, able to reassure Laura Leigh that angels were wonderful, but she also knew Danny very well. "Danny wouldn't lie about a thing like that," Roseann said. "But let me try something."

The next day, Roseann brought a picture card of a guardian angel to Laura Leigh's home. The angel looked female and had large wings coming out of her shoulders. "Take a look at this, Danny," Roseann said, giving her nephew the picture.

Danny's eyes instantly lit up. "The lady!" he said, smiling. "Look, Mommy, that's the lady I saw! She's the friend that's going to watch over me! Can I keep this?"

Danny never mentioned the beautiful lady again, and even a few years later he had forgotten the incident. But he continued to grow into a remarkably kind and gentle boy who was particularly interested in spiritual things. He kept the angel picture on his mirror for years.

THE LIGHT OF LOVE

Because He is love in its essence, God appears before the angels . . . as a
sun. And from that sun, heat and light go forth; the heat being love and
the light, wisdom. And the angels [become] love and wisdom, not from
themselves but from the Lord.
—EMANUEL SWEDENBORG, *ANGELIC WISDOM*

Since angels are creatures of God, who is the light of the world, a glow or even a flash of brilliant light is another signal of their presence. Malcolm Muggeridge, writing in *Something Beautiful for God*, the story of Mother Teresa of Calcutta, recounted an episode when the British Broadcasting Company was filming a documentary about her. The script called for some scenes within Mother Teresa's Home for the Dying, but it was dimly lit, with small high windows, and the photographer was certain that filming could not be done there. It was decided to try anyway, but just so the visit would not be a complete loss, the photographer also took some footage outside in the sunny courtyard.

When the film was processed, the part taken *inside* was bathed in a beautiful soft glow, whereas the part taken in the sunny courtyard was rather dim and confused. The film was checked and found to be perfectly adequate. Such a thing should not have happened.

"I am convinced that the technically unaccountable light is, in fact, supernatural," Muggeridge wrote. "Mother Teresa's Home for the Dying is overflowing with a luminous love, like the halos artists have seen and made visible. . . . I find it not at all surprising that the luminosity should register on a photographic film."[10]

⚬◈⚬

This light of love is more common than we realize. Consider Chad and Peggy Anderson, who on a cold predawn Saturday were already bustling around the kitchen in their Antioch, Illinois, home. Peggy, a nurse, was due to work the 7 a.m. to 3 p.m. shift at McHenry Hospital. And as any working woman knows, it takes plenty of time to get up, dressed, and out the door. As he usually did when Peggy worked a Saturday shift, Chad would be caring for the Andersons' two sons as well as two preschool grandchildren who were living with them. Now, though, as he glanced outside, he frowned and said, "It's snowing, Peg."

Peggy peered out the kitchen window. "Not heavily."

"No. But I think you ought to drive the Lincoln rather than your little Chevette. Just in case."

"Well . . ." Peggy wasn't especially nervous in snow, but the hospital was twenty miles away, and she had to cover a rather zigzag, mostly rural route. The big car would be safer, so she decided to take Chad's advice.

The cold white blanket made everything look fresh and new, and, although Peggy seemed the only traveler on the road, she was actually enjoying the ride—until she hit a curve on a bridge about eight miles from McHenry. The snow-covered pavement was slicker than she had assumed, and with the frozen marsh some thirty or forty feet below, Peggy attempted to slow down. Instead, the big car swerved and went into a 360-degree rotation. Peggy tensed immediately, trying frantically to remember what one was supposed to do to straighten a spinning car. But it was too late. She had lost control, and the Lincoln was obviously going to plunge through the guardrail into the marsh below—there was nowhere else for it to go. Would she drown in a watery prison? Her little boys—what would become of them? "Oh, God," she called as the Lincoln veered toward the posts, "help me!"

There were no other vehicles in view, and Peggy's headlights were still the only illumination. But suddenly, in the dawn's semidarkness, a warm glow lit the spinning car's interior. At the same time, Peggy was filled with indescribable reassurance. The light warmed her, bathing her in contentment, and it was simply . . . heavenly. She knew—without exactly knowing *how* she knew—that there was no reason to be afraid.

And yes, the car was still going—but somehow approaching the end of the bridge without crashing through the rail, now rolling down the side of the steep thirty-foot ditch to the marshland below, now, unbelievably, slowing in a small clearing. It came to a stop. The light immediately went out.

"I sat in the car in amazement, just praying and praising God for a few minutes," Peggy recalled. "Then I got out and made my way up to the road."

The highway was still empty, but Peggy saw one house—the only one in view—all lit up and looking warm and inviting. The man who lived there was extremely hospitable and concerned about Peggy and her near miss. She phoned the hospital and her husband, blurting out the story as if she could not believe it herself. Chad sent a tow truck and came to fetch her in their little car, filled with children—and joy.

"Nothing like this ever happened to me before, and nothing quite as marvelous has happened since," said Peggy. "But the experience gave me a deeper understanding of what total trust in God is all about." She still likes to tell people about the day an angel met her on a bridge—and gave her a glimpse of heaven.

ANGEL IN THE ANDES

An angel stood and met my gaze,
Through the low doorway of my tent;
The tent is struck, the vision stays—
I only know she came and went.
—JAMES RUSSELL LOWELL, "SHE CAME AND WENT"

Born in 1900, Dr. Raymond Edman was a missionary, lecturer, professor of history, and, for twenty-five years, president of Wheaton College in Wheaton, Illinois, the alma mater of the Reverend Billy Graham and many other well-known Christian leaders. Dr. Edman wrote nineteen books and edited the *Alliance Witness*, but was probably best known for his deep devotion to God. "He was a mystic in the finest sense of the word," Billy Graham eulogized at Edman's funeral in 1967. "Part of his life was always in heaven."

Dr. Edman believed firmly that angels are involved in the world and that occasionally their work requires appearance in human form. During these times, "nothing about their dress or speech would make them different from others present," he said. "Only the discerning heart understands, and usually long afterward, that the stranger who helped at a moment of emergency was really one of God's angels." As an example, in the *Wheaton College Bulletin* Dr. Edman offered an experience of his own.

From 1923 to 1928, Edman and his wife were young missionaries in the Andes region of Ecuador. They lived on the outskirts of the city, where they could reach both the Spanish-speaking citizens as well as the shy, suspicious indigenous people who passed their door on the way to market.

But their assignment was difficult. "The people were unfriendly, and some were fanatical in their bitter opposition to our presence in their city," Edman recalled. "On occasion, small crowds would gather to hurl insults as well as stones. The Indians from the countryside were especially timid about being friendly with us because of intimidation by the townspeople. As a result, it was often difficult for us to shop for the bare necessities of life—fruits and vegetables, or charcoal for the kitchen stove." Perhaps more burdensome than physical hardships was the loneliness. The young couple was never fearful, but with a complete lack of a support group—of even one encouraging friend in this unfamiliar land—their emotional isolation must have been intense. And because they knew that some stranger might harass them or get into their house to steal, they kept the gate of their high iron fence locked at all times, probably adding to their sense of disconnection.

The couple often fed hungry strangers or attempted to buy necessities from passing indigenous people, and one noon as they ate on their patio at the back of the house, they heard a rattling at the gate. When Edman went out with the key, he saw a barefoot woman standing on the other side of the gate, one hand inside the bars knocking on the chain with the padlock. She wore beads and the large heavy hat of the mountain women, along with a dress of coarse woolen cloth and a brightly colored homemade belt. On her shoulders were a bundle and a blue shawl, but she did not appear to have merchandise or food to sell. Edman hadn't seen her before.

As he approached, she began to speak softly in the mixture of Spanish and Quechua typical of the people who lived close to town. Pointing to a Gospel verse the Edmans had posted on the porch, she then asked, "Are you the people who have come to tell us about the living God?"

Edman was startled. No one had ever asked him that. "Yes," he answered. "We are."

The woman then raised the hand that was still inside the gate and began to pray—for blessings upon the couple's house, for their courage to follow God's guidance, for joy in the task. Finally, she blessed Edman, withdrew her hand, smiled at him, eyes shining, then bowed and turned to go.

He had been so taken aback at her friendly support that he was speechless. Then, realizing that it was hot and the woman should be invited inside to eat and rest, he quickly unlocked the gate and stepped through to call her back. In the time elapsed, she could not have gone more than five or ten yards in any direction. But she was not there.

"Where could she have gone so quickly? It was at least fifty yards from our gate to the corner of the street, and there was no opening along that stretch." Edman ran to the corner—assuming that if she had gotten that far, he could surely see her—but again, no woman, no passages into which she could have slipped. He went to the nearest open gate and asked two men repairing a wheel if a woman had passed or come in.

They both looked up. "No, sir."

"I mean *just* now."

"Sir, we have been here for an hour or more," one answered, "and no one has entered or left during that time."

Edman hastened back to the corner, but there was not a soul in sight.

Thoughtfully, he returned home and told his wife about the matter.

For the next several days, Edman remained strangely moved and peaceful concerning his formidable assignment. There seemed to be a sweet and indefinable aroma surrounding him, something that did not come from the flowers in his garden. It was only later that he gradually pieced together the meaning of it all. "I began to understand that the Almighty had none of his earthly servants at hand to encourage two young missionaries, so he was pleased to send an angel from heaven," Edman concluded. "Over the many years since then, during all of life's deep testing, there has remained the glow of God's blessing, pronounced by someone who looked exactly like an old Quechua woman."[11]

THE HANDS OF A COMFORTER

Who does the best that circumstance allows
Does well, acts nobly; angels could do no more.
—EDWARD YOUNG, *NIGHT THOUGHTS*

Millions of people watch the wholesome family fare on cable television's Eternal Word Television Network. The unlikely founder of EWTN, Mother Mary Angelica, was a Catholic cloistered nun who, with a handful of other sisters, two hundred dollars, and absolutely no knowledge of television ("Okay," Mother Angelica conceded, "so I did know how to turn one on") became the only woman in religious television to own a network. (Mother Mary Angelica died on Easter Sunday, March 27, 2016, at age ninety-two.)

Visitors to the EWTN complex outside Birmingham, Alabama, cannot help but be impressed with what God and this nun accomplished. A monastery, network facilities and satellite dish, a print shop,and a chapel stand incongruously in the midst of the Protestant Bible Belt. When Mother Angelica believed in 1981 that God was calling her to begin a media ministry, she simply did so, and everything else fell into place.

Mother Angelica didn't take herself too seriously, which was probably why viewers chose her twice-weekly show, *Mother Angelica Live* as their favorite. Although it featured a studio audience, call-ins from across the country, and popular guests, the show was sometimes less than polished. Sets occasionally collapsed, for example, and Mother Angelica was prone to fits of giggles and witty asides.

Despite her grandmotherly image, she was firm and no-nonsense in her views on morality yet quick to encourage and express compassion. Often, she ministered on the air to anonymous callers, counseling a distraught divorcée, gently scolding a drug addict, bringing God's healing "to those who, perhaps, can't reach out any other way."

"I want to be a thorn in people's sides," she once admitted. "I want to challenge them; I want to be another John the Baptist who says, 'Get with it!'"

Relatively few viewers know, perhaps, that Mother Angelica, who was born Rita Rizzo, had a rough childhood. After a bitter marriage, her parents divorced when Rita was six. Little Rita was poverty-stricken, vulnerable, and, because of her mother's divorce, ostracized within her Canton, Ohio, church community. Nor was she particularly impressed with the nuns. "I remember sitting in church watching them pray and vowing I would never be among their ranks," Mother Angelica said. "Their facial expressions were sour, their headpieces too large—I was convinced they were the most unhappy people I'd ever seen." Then one day she experienced a moment of grace, a touch meant especially for her.

Mother Angelica told the story often. When she was about eleven years old and feeling especially lonely and sad, she was walking downtown one evening, oblivious to everything around her. "I started to cross a busy street, then heard a woman's shrill scream behind me." Rita looked back, expecting to see someone in trouble and instead realized that a car was speeding toward her, the headlights shining in her eyes. There was no time to get to the safety island. Rita froze, closed her eyes, and waited for the fatal impact.

Instead, she felt two strong hands lift her high in the air. A moment later, she blinked and looked around in disbelief. She was standing on the sidewalk!

A crowd gathered. Onlookers had expected to see a terrible accident and a child's crumpled body. Instead, they found a healthy, but quite frightened, girl. To them, it appeared that she had definitely been hit, then hurled aside by the force of the collision. They were completely mystified at her lack of injuries.

A bus driver who witnessed the event from his higher perch later reported, with disbelief, a somewhat different scenario. He insisted that Rita had jumped or somehow been catapulted high into the air, easily clearing both the safety island and the onrushing auto. Such a feat seemed impossible, and the man was dumbfounded.

As soon as she got home, Rita told her mother what had happened, and both of them gave thanks for this rare moment of joy. Somehow they understood that, despite their hardships, they were being guided and cared for.

That was the beginning of Rita's confidence in angels. When she entered the Poor Clares convent, she chose a new name that would honor them. Later she founded (and named) Our Lady of the Angels Monastery, where she lived and wrote books, and from which she directed her television network. Her long, fruitful life was a testimony to the power of faith.

Mother Angelica never forgot that extraordinary moment when she felt the hands of a comforter and knew that God's love would never fail.

BEDSIDE COMPANION

What know we of the blest above
But that they sing, and that they love?
—WILLIAM WORDSWORTH, "SCENE ON THE LAKE OF BRIENZ"

It was Labor Day weekend, and Sandy Smith (later Waters) would soon be leaving for her first year of college. Her mother had died the previous spring, and Sandy was still raw over the loss, apprehensive about the transition from high school to a university. She and her friend Bobbie decided to drive to Hocking Hills State Park in southern Ohio to camp—a "last fling" before saying good-bye to summer.

The girls were on Interstate 23 when Sandy, who had a heart condition, experienced some angina pain. "I swerved over the gravel on the roadside," Sandy recalled. "Then, trying to turn back, I swung the wheel too far. The car flipped and rolled over several times down a small hill." Sandy was sure she was going to die. "I saw the whole scene in slow motion, just like other survivors have mentioned. But I fainted before the car stopped."

Miraculously, only Sandy's nose was broken, but blood was everywhere. Bobbie, who had remained conscious, managed to wedge open the passenger door and stumble up to the highway, where she flagged down a trucker.

When Sandy awoke at Grady Memorial Hospital, she was in a bed in a secluded alcove. How badly was she hurt? Was Bobbie all right? She looked at herself, shocked to see dried blood all over her clothes and arms. Filled with loneliness and fear, she started to cry.

"All I wanted was my mother," Sandy said. "I cried out for her to come and hold me. But she was dead, and no one came."

Sandy fainted again, and the next time she awakened, there was a person sitting next to her, stroking her hand in the most comforting way. "I'm not positive it was a woman, and it hurt too much to turn my head, but I could tell that she had long, almost-white hair and pale skin," Sandy said. "Her clothing was white too, but I couldn't see if she was wearing pants or a skirt."

With the soothing sensation of a protective hand on hers, Sandy calmed down. A noise seemed to be coming from the figure, a fanlike whirring but deeper, like the beating of thousands of birds' wings. Sandy felt an overwhelming sense of peace and love. The love actually seemed to flow from the noise the figure made, filling the lonely room.

"The noise sounded like a song, not in a conventional sense, but almost like millions of voices blending together in the most extraordinary tones . . . This is difficult to discuss. I know it was not a psychological experience. Nor was I hallucinating because I had been injured. I felt it was a supernatural being who had come to comfort me. And I had a serenity so profound that it was impossible to explain."

As the figure hummed, Sandy fell into a restful sleep, and when she awoke for the third time, a nurse was washing her face. Sandy assumed the nurse was her figure in white. "When you finish, could you hold my hand?" Sandy asked. "Like you did before?"

The nurse looked puzzled. "No one's been holding your hand," she said.

"Yes, a blond lady in white did," Sandy said. "I thought it was you. Didn't you sit next to me and sing?"

"I wouldn't have had time," the nurse explained. "It's Labor Day weekend, and we're extremely short of help."

"But someone . . ." Sandy began.

"It must have been a dream," the nurse said, trying to soothe her. "You see, I've been right outside this alcove ever since they brought you in, and no one's been near you. Everyone in the emergency room has been caring for your friend and the other patients. And there are no fair-haired nurses on duty today."

Sandy didn't ask again. She was beginning to realize that her visitor had been someone out of the ordinary, perhaps sent at a time when she was so emotionally overwhelmed, so needy for her mother, that only a special being could bring the consolation she needed.

"It was a pivotal point in my life," Sandy said, years later. "I was going through a spiritual rebellion, questioning whether there was a God, reading a lot of philosophy. My visitor changed the way I thought about religion. She also restored my faith that life could be good again, despite my mother's death. The tranquility she left with me remained for a long time."

Sandy experienced many moments of joy after that experience. Only rarely did she reach this indescribable peace—and when she did, she knew her angel was near. One significant moment was the morning of her wedding day, when she heard the familiar humming noise fill her room.

"This must be how we'll feel in heaven," Sandy said. She developed a real affinity for angels and has looked for them everywhere. "I suspect I've come across others, even if I didn't recognize them. And I'm certain I'll meet my special comforter again."

TWICE BLESSED

Praise the LORD, *you his angels,*
you mighty ones who do his bidding,
who obey his word.
—PSALMS 103:20

I'm not especially holy," most of us would conclude. "Spirits wouldn't appear to *me.*"

Yet we ought not to second-guess these blessed helpers. After all, if their job is to minister to humankind to bring us closer and closer to God, why would anyone be exempt?

Bob Lessnau was raised in a Christian home but had given up trying to please God by the time he was sixteen. "As a typical adolescent, I figured I was always offending God with one sin or another," Bob explained. "I decided to put religion behind me."

Bob served in Vietnam, returned to Michigan, became a telephone repairman, married, and had three children. "During those years I began to reflect on the close calls I'd had in Vietnam. I'd felt protected then, and thought maybe I ought to reevaluate my relationship with God. Even a dunce could see that not only was God *not* looking for an excuse to toss me into hell, but he was doing everything he could to keep me alive so I could come to my senses!"

Bob hadn't gotten around to acting on his good intention on the day he entered the Big Boy on Biddle Street in Wyandotte, Michigan. The restaurant was busy but not crowded, and Bob had a good view of his surroundings. He sat at the counter and ordered lunch. No one he knew was in the restaurant, and strangers were sitting on the stools on either side of him.

Bob didn't see anyone approach. But suddenly he felt someone tap him on the shoulder. He swung around on the stool to see a scholarly looking man in a suit.

The man looked at Bob. "I want to see you in church," he said. Although he wasn't shouting, his voice could certainly be heard by everyone in the immediate vicinity.

Bob was dumbfounded and embarrassed. When he recalled the story, he said, "Why me? Although I wasn't going to church at that time—and was still smoking pot and behaving in less-than-holy ways—I wasn't wearing a sign announcing any of it. I decided the guy was some kind of nut soliciting for his church. But I didn't live in Wyandotte, and I told him so."

"I didn't say *what* church," the man replied. "I said I want to see you *in* church."

Bob swiveled away for just a few seconds, to mull over the strange comment, then turned back. "I wanted to ask him how he knew I wasn't going to church." But the man was no longer behind Bob. In fact, Bob couldn't see him anywhere. He had turned away for only a few seconds—the stranger couldn't have made it to the door in that time, "not unless he had broken into a run, which certainly would have attracted the attention of the customers." But he was gone.

Everything else was just the same. People kept eating and talking. Those on either side of Bob seemed not to have noticed or overheard anything peculiar. Had Bob been the only person in the restaurant to see and hear the visitor?

That night, Bob discussed the incident with his wife, Sandy. "We decided that if God wanted us in church so much that he would go to all this trouble, we ought to give it some thought." The couple worried that their noisy preschoolers would bother other worshipers, but they joined an Assemblies of God church anyway. Bob decided to give up marijuana. He found his spiritual life flourishing, and he and Sandy developed a fellowship with other couples.

They needn't have worried about their little ones. "The children were fine. They sat there obediently, week after week," Bob recalled. "Just like little angels."

But God hadn't finished with Bob. Several years later, he was in his driveway, working on a friend's 1971 Dodge Dart. The car was facing up a slight incline. Bob was lying under it in the gas-tank area, his feet pointing toward its front. His friend had gone to the store to buy a replacement part.

"I had forgotten that removing the drive shaft gives you, in essence, four free-wheeling wheels," Bob explained. "Though the car was set in 'park,' it started to roll backward."

Bob attempted to scurry out from under the car. He almost made it, but the front wheel caught his left foot, pinning it by bending it forward toward the shin. His heart dropping, Bob saw that the slant in the driveway was enough to make the car roll but not enough for the wheel to complete its revolution over his foot. He was stuck.

Pain exploded in waves. His foot felt as if it were being crushed into bits.

Alerted by his shouts, Sandy and a neighbor woman came running. "We'll lift the wheel, Bob, and then you can get out!" Sandy cried.

But their efforts only made matters worse. Because of the incline, every time the women tried to shift the tire, they only pushed it farther up, resting even more weight on Bob's whole leg. If the wheel could have turned completely over the foot, Bob could have gotten free, but it wouldn't move far enough.

Soon there were at least seven other neighbors surrounding him. Some tried the same type of lifting, to no avail. "Everyone should have pushed the wheel from behind," Bob says in retrospect, "but none of us was thinking clearly." It seemed as if he would be trapped forever. Through a haze of pain and fear, Bob cried out, "God, help me!"

Immediately, Bob saw a large man running toward him. The man reached the front of the car and quickly lifted the bumper high enough to raise the entire chassis off Bob's foot. Bob groaned in relief and rolled free.

Everyone crowded around. "Are you okay?" someone asked. "Should we take you for an X-ray?"

"No." Experimentally, Bob wiggled his toes and flexed his ankle. The foot had no apparent injury. "It feels fine," he told his relieved neighbors, getting up slowly.

Then Bob looked around for the large man who had so effortlessly lifted the car. "I was beginning to realize just how strong he would have had to be. Allowing for the 'springiness' of the car springs, lifting a car ten or twelve inches would still leave a tire on the ground. You'd have to lift it a lot higher than that to get a wheel completely off a foot. And there was no one else lifting on that side when he came."

Bob could find no large man to thank. And no one remembered seeing him dash to Bob's aid. "The tall guy, the one who came running across the lawn?" Bob asked everyone, but was rewarded with stares and head shaking. "There was no one here but us," the neighbors insisted, "and we would certainly have noticed a stranger." Nor did Sandy remember seeing anyone she didn't know.

There were no service vehicles around, no deliverymen or any outsiders on Bob's street that afternoon. No one had seen a car stop. More significantly, no one had seen or heard a car leave. There just wasn't any explanation as to why the car had suddenly moved off Bob's foot. Any logical explanation, that is.

"I'm ninety-nine percent certain that he was an angel, because of the timeliness of his approach, his extraordinary strength, and his quick vanishing act," Bob said. In fact, even though the muscular stranger bore no resemblance to the bookish messenger in the Big Boy restaurant, Bob believes they could have both been sent from heaven.

Why isn't Bob 100 percent sure? "Maybe because it leaves room for faith," he explained. "I have a choice. I can write these experiences off to good luck. Or give God the credit."

Bob chose God.

HE WILL SEND ANGELS

How many angels are there?
One—who transforms our life—is plenty.
—TRADITIONAL SAYING

There are many points of view about guardian angels. Some people who have studied what various texts and traditions say about angels believe that each of us may have two. But in telling the following story, Hope Price, of Portland, Oregon, obviously believed that one was indeed plenty.

If it is true that each of us has a guardian angel, then mine has been seen three times that I know of—each time by a different person.

My mother, Minnie Metcalf Miller, said that when I was three weeks old, and very tiny because I was premature, she was awakened in the night by a beautiful young girl bending over her.

Mother somehow understood from this beautiful visitor that her new baby, asleep in the next room, needed her. Mother also seemed to know that she would be facing a long ordeal, so she dressed carefully and went in to me. She found me blue in the face and struggling for breath.

There followed a long battle with pneumonia in which Mother did not have her clothes off for several nights. She said the beautiful girl was there beside her every minute of the fight with death.

A kind neighbor also saw the girl and asked my mother, "Who is the beautiful lady staying with you since the baby has been so sick? I see her come out on the front porch sometimes." The beautiful lady disappeared when I was completely out of danger.

Years later, in 1934, she returned to rescue me again. I now had small children of my own and had just gotten a divorce. I had been told by my doctor that I must have a serious operation, and an intensely religious woman named Lude was doing my housework. She was to stay with my three young children while I went to the hospital.

However, Lude seemed dissatisfied with conditions in our house, as she was used to working in wealthy households with other servants. One afternoon, as Lude entered the room with a vacuum cleaner, a cat, who was calling on my cat, jumped through the window, breaking the glass. This was the last straw for Lude. She gave notice rather sulkily, saying she would leave in the morning as she simply couldn't stay on.

I wondered what I would do! I couldn't leave three little children alone in the house while I was in the hospital. I finally decided I would have to call the doctor the next morning and tell him I could not have the operation.

However, early the next morning Lude entered my room fairly beaming with good humor. She was wearing a white uniform. "Breakfast is ready." She smiled.

"Why, Lude, how nice of you to get breakfast before you go," I said.

"Mrs. Price," Lude replied, "I've changed my mind. I'm not going. I had a vision last night. A beautiful young girl, an angel, came flying in to my bedside through that window the cat broke. She was all in shining white and surrounded with light. It lit up my whole room. She asked me not to leave you because you needed me. I'm going to stay just as long as you need me."

So I went to the hospital comforted by the thought that the children were safely watched over by Lude.

In each case, the angel was seen by a kind person with a good deal of spiritual understanding. They were the kind of persons able to see angels, obviously.

The lovely angel seems to appear when I need her most. I hope she always will. Perhaps someday I will see her myself.[12]

CALLERS IN THE NIGHT

Angels, as 'tis but seldom they appear,
So neither do they make long stay;
They do but visit and away.
—JOHN NORRIS, "TO THE MEMORY OF HIS NIECE"

Angels do many things for us, but one of their primary jobs is to bring help just when we need it most. I read of an incident involving a Philadelphia neurologist, Dr. S. W. Mitchell, who was awakened after a tiring day by a little girl knocking on his door. The child, poorly dressed and deeply upset, told him that her mother was sick and needed a physician.

Dr. Mitchell followed the child through the snowy night and found the mother desperately ill with pneumonia. After arranging for medical care, he complimented the sick woman on the intelligence and persistence of her little daughter. The woman looked at him strangely and then said, "My daughter died a month ago."

Dr. Mitchell, amazed and perplexed, went to the closet and opened the door. There hung the coat worn by the little girl who had led him to her mother. Despite the wintry night, the coat was completely dry.[13]

And then there is the account of Father O'Keeffe of Cork, Ireland, who was summoned by a handsome young man to attend a woman who was dying. The priest followed the man into a poor section of Cork in which nothing could be seen but ramshackle stables. "Where on Earth is this person to be found?" he asked his guide.

"We are near the place now, Father," the young man said, and instantly disappeared.

The priest was astonished and at a loss until he heard groans nearby and found a young woman dying on a dunghill. She told him that her family had been well-to-do and she had attended a convent school where the sisters had told her to call on her guardian angel if she was ever in need.

The woman had gone on to live a wretched, debauched life and now, abandoned and left to die alone, she had remembered her early teaching and had begged her guardian angel to bring her a priest.[14]

<hr>

I learned of a similar incident in Chicago. In the late 1870s, Father Arnold Damen of the Society of Jesus founded Holy Family Church, which still stands just west of the University of Illinois's campus on Roosevelt Road. Father Damen was an outstanding preacher and traveled extensively. He also developed a large altar-boy society in Holy Family parish. Through the latter days of the nineteenth century, hundreds of Chicago youths were taught to assist the priests at Mass.

Years passed, and Father Damen aged and slipped into semiretirement. On one especially raw and windy night, two young boys came to the Holy Family rectory, where Father Damen lived, and rang the bell. Their grandmother was terribly sick, they explained to the porter when he answered the door, and she needed a priest to prepare her for death.

"It's too cold and rainy tonight," the porter told the youngsters. "We'll send a priest in the morning."

But Father Damen had heard the bell ring, and he went to the boys. "I'll go with you at once," he told them. "Come in and get warm while I go to the church for Holy Communion."

Father Damen followed the boys through the cold and desolate streets. They led him at last to a far corner of the parish, over a mile from the rectory. "She's up there in the attic rooms, Father," said one, pointing to a dilapidated building.

The priest ascended the narrow, dark stairs. Indeed, the door on the top floor was open. Entering the darkened apartment, he found an elderly woman, ill, cold, and close to death. Quickly, he anointed her and gave her Holy Communion for her journey into eternity. "Father," she whispered as the blessing was finished, "how did you happen to come? Only a few neighbors know I've been sick, and none are Catholic."

"Why, your grandsons brought me here to you," the priest explained.

The woman closed her eyes. "I had two grandsons, Father," she said, "and they were altar boys at Holy Family Church. But they both died, many years ago."

Were the little messengers angels? Father Damen believed so. And to mark this heavenly visitation, he had statues of two acolytes, holding candles and facing each other, placed high on either side of the entrance to the church's sanctuary, where they still stand.

A Voice from Beyond

The angels . . . regard our safety, undertake our defense, direct our ways, and exercise a constant solicitude that no evil befalls us.
—John Calvin, *Institutes of the Christian Religion*

Margaret walked the dog every morning; her husband, Paul (not their real names), did so at night. There was a small park across the busy street in front of their house, and Paul usually took the dog there. He was a reserved man who enjoyed solitude and rarely showed his emotions.

At about nine one April evening, Paul and the dog started out on their customary jaunt. "I'm never in the garage after dinner," Margaret related. "But that night, I happened to go there for something. The garage door was open, and even though it was almost dark outside, I had a perfect view of Paul going down our driveway to the sidewalk."

Paul had to wait a few moments until there was a break in the traffic. While he was standing there, Margaret heard a voice calling. "Paul!" it said. That was all. "It was a male voice, the kindest-sounding voice I'd ever heard," she said. "There was shrubbery alongside our driveway, and I assumed our next-door neighbor, hidden from my view by the garage wall and the foliage, was calling Paul. But I knew his voice, and this wonderful voice was not his. A second later I remembered that the neighbor wasn't home."

Paul did not appear to have heard the voice. Maybe it had been her imagination. Or the sound of the wind? But there was no wind. Someone in a passing car? But the voice had been coming from her direction, as if the caller was near. Puzzled, Margaret wondered what, if anything, she should do. Again, as her husband started to step down from the curb, the kind voice called his name.

"Paul!"

Now Margaret saw Paul stop. Had he heard the voice this time?

Incredibly, a large tree in the park started to fall. Down it came, almost in slow motion, until, with a loud crash, it came to rest across the park path, its highest branches practically lying in the street. The tree had fallen on the very spot where Paul always walked, where he would have been at that moment had a voice not delayed him. Stunned, Margaret stared at the tree. Paul, in his usual unemotional manner, crossed the street, went around the tree, looked at it for a moment, and continued on his way. But by the time he returned, he'd had a chance to think.

"Someone called my name," he said to Margaret. "It happened twice. Did you hear the voice?"

"Yes. I wondered if you had."

"But there wasn't anyone around. Unless you saw someone."

"No, I didn't," Margaret told him. "And from the garage, I would have had a good view." They looked at each other.

"Well, then," Paul said in his usual calm fashion, "it had to have been my guardian angel."

Margaret replayed the episode in her mind many times, and her husband told several neighbors and relatives about it. But neither of them ever found anyone to thank.

MASTER BUILDERS

❦

What's impossible to all humanity may be possible to the metaphysics
and physiology of angels.
—JOSEPH GLANVILL, *THE VANITY OF DOGMATIZING*

In the mid-1800s, a courageous little band of Catholic nuns journeyed by paddle-boat and covered wagon from Kentucky to sun-bleached Santa Fe, New Mexico, to establish a school. Their new surroundings felt desolate. Most of the people in the area were Native American or Mexican. While the Sisters of Loretto learned the Spanish language and became acclimated, they lived in a tiny adobe house. Over time, Mexican carpenters built them a larger convent, a school, and an adobe chapel.

Eventually the little church became too small for the burgeoning community, and in 1873, work began on a larger stone building. In honor of their founding bishop's French background, Loretto Chapel would be the first Gothic structure west of the Mississippi. Impressively large by southwestern standards, it would measure some twenty-five feet by seventy-five feet, reach a height of eighty-five feet, and have a choir loft at the rear.

The work progressed well until it was nearly finished—and the sisters realized that a formidable error had been made. There was no way to climb from the chapel floor to the choir loft. A staircase had been inadvertently left out of the plans. Mother Magdalen, superior of the group, consulted several expert carpenters, but their verdict was the same: a staircase was impossible. The loft was exceptionally high, so an ordinary passageway would take up too much room. There were only two alternatives: climb to the loft via a ladder, which few of the sisters could imagine doing, or tear the whole balcony down and rebuild it, which would be a financial disaster.

In typical faith fashion, the sisters decided to take no immediate action and simply to pray and wait. They made a novena, a nine-day prayer, to Saint Joseph, the patron of carpenters, and asked for a workable—and, one would presume, inexpensive—solution.

On the last day of the novena, a gray-haired man approached the convent, leading a donkey and carrying a tool chest.

"I've heard about your problem with the chapel," he told Mother Magdalen. "Would you let me try to build a staircase?"

"By all means," Mother Magdalen responded. She must have wondered how he could do it. According to later reports, the man had only a hammer, a saw, and a T square. There is no evidence that he ordered any wood, either, but some witnesses reported seeing tubs of water sitting around, filled with pieces of soaking board.

Accounts differ as to how long the work took—some say six to eight months—but eventually the man disappeared. Mother Magdalen went to pay him, but he was nowhere to be found. Nor did the local lumberyard have knowledge of the project or any bill for materials. To this day, there is no record that the job was ever paid for.

But what a job it was! For when the sisters went to inspect the chapel, they found a graceful spiral staircase linking the loft to the first floor, cleverly designed to take up a minimum of space. It is constructed only with pegs—no nails. Each stair is made out of several pieces and is perfectly curved and fitted. The unit makes two complete 360-degree turns, but because it has no supporting center pole or anchor for the sides of the treads, it should have long ago collapsed. Experts have failed to identify the wood, but it is definitely *not* a variety native to the New Mexico area. Where did the carpenter get it? With the exception of some brief modifications and an added banister, the staircase remains today as it was completed over one hundred years ago, a marvel of design unexplainable to the many architects, engineers, and construction experts who visit the site.

The sisters, of course, remain mum on *who* the considerate contractor was; it would be speculation at best. But he left behind a holy place, and their community is forever grateful.

⁂

A similar event took place in Covington, Kentucky. In 1938, the Reverend Morris Coers and his wife had traveled to the Holy Land, where they were deeply moved by a visit to a tomb reputed to be the authentic burial place of Jesus. Someday, Reverend Coers decided, he would build a replica of that sepulcher in America. It would be a sacred spot for people of all faiths who could not afford to visit the Holy Land site.

By the mid-1950s, Reverend Coers was a minister at the Immanuel Baptist Church in Covington, and he shared his dream with the congregation. The plan received enthusiastic support, and Reverend Coers found the perfect setting: a beautiful hill overlooking the Ohio River. Although the owner at first balked at selling the property, he eventually agreed. People from all over Covington contributed, and plans expanded to include a reproduction of a first-century carpenter shop, a chapel, and a bookstore. Coers named it the Garden of Hope.

The tomb and garden had been completed—and churches were already holding devotional services on the patio in front of the sepulcher's entrance—when difficulties developed. During the winter of 1958, the hillside began to give way, causing expensive landscaping, walkways, and the patio itself to slip downward.

"The following summer, the church borrowed forty thousand dollars to sink cement pilings into the earth and pour tons of concrete onto the base of the hill," recalled one longtime parishioner. Workers rebuilt the patio and shored it up with more concrete.

But during the following winter, the entire area, including the patio, slid all the way to the bottom again. Distinguished engineers came to evaluate the church's predicament, but their verdicts were the same: the Garden of Hope could not be safely constructed on this site. However, there was no money left to begin elsewhere. "It was heartbreaking," Morris Coers's widow said later. "The Garden of Hope had been a dream come true for Morris, and it looked impossible."

On a hot August day in 1959, several church members stood in the garden, dispiritedly surveying the situation. What could they do? Take out more trees? Rebuild? Pour even more concrete at the hill's base? Or should the project be abandoned?

No one took notice of a stranger making his way through the garden until he stood in front of them. "I'm looking for Reverend Coers," the man said.

The others looked at him. He was huge, surely over three hundred pounds, and wearing bib overalls. Someone ran and got the minister.

"Hear you have a landslide going on here," the large man began.

"We do," Reverend Coers agreed. "The earth down there is full of concrete and steel pilings, but nothing seems to keep the hill—and everything on it—from sliding."

"Show it all to me," the man suggested.

Reverend Coers, impressed with the large man's dignity and air of quiet confidence, did so, while the rest of the men continued talking and wandering around. But when the minister returned from the brief tour, he was excited. The man in the overalls, it seemed, was an engineer who had experience with railroad construction, particularly in the mountainous areas of the West. "He told me to write everything down, and I did," Reverend Coers told the others, waving sheets of paper. "We apparently need workmen to construct a certain kind of wall, like railroads use, to retain hillsides." Reverend Coers was filled with rekindled enthusiasm and joy. No one noticed that the man in the bib overalls had disappeared.

Workmen were hired, and the retaining wall was completed ahead of schedule. But would it hold?

Winter weather arrived, with an onslaught of cold rarely experienced in Kentucky. Freezing and thawing was almost a daily routine, and Covington held its collective breath. The wall could not have been tested more severely. But not a foot of dirt moved, despite the elements.

Today the Covington hillside has become a popular pilgrimage spot, and the chapel is busy with weddings, worship services, and seminars. The tools in the carpenter shop are many centuries old and were donated by Israel's prime minister David Ben-Gurion. A piece of the Wailing Wall, a flag from Egypt, and a stone from the hillside on which Christ preached the Sermon on the Mount mingle with stained glass and statues donated by churches of various denominations; the project is truly an ecumenical venture.

Few visitors, perhaps, notice the retaining wall, although an occasional engineer marvels at its unique structure and design. But no one can explain who was responsible for it. The considerate contractor never submitted a bill to the church board. Nor was he a member of any engineering fraternity or listed among the certified engineers in the United States or, despite his imposing appearance, ever seen in the area again.

But, like the spiral staircase in Santa Fe, the wall speaks silently but powerfully of things unseen.

Julia's Visitor

*He heard an odd noise, as though of a whirring . . . and when he
strained for a wider view, could have sworn he saw a dark figure born
aloft, on a pair of strong black wings.*
—Bernard Malamud, "Angel Levine"

Eleanor Duffin of Justice, Illinois, shared a story handed down to the family by her mother, who was born in 1884.

A conscientious woman, Julia Zulaski devoted much time to teaching her children about spiritual matters. In the mornings, before she dressed Eleanor and her three siblings, Julia would help them ask their angels to keep them safe. At night, Julia would tuck the children into a large double bed, turn off the light, then kneel in the semidarkness and pray for them.

"Since we four had been born in less than four years, we were all little and fit two at each end," Eleanor said. The children felt snug and safe, watching their mother pray beside them.

One night, after Eleanor and her siblings had fallen asleep, Julia remained on her knees in the darkened room. As she prayed, she noticed that the bedroom wall that held a window was beginning to glow. Was there something shining outside? Before she could get to her feet and investigate, the wall became luminous, more intensely bright.

Then the startled young woman saw a large angel fly through the closed window. He looked strong, powerful, and just like the pictures of angels Julia had seen in books. For a moment, he seemed to hover protectively over the bed where the four children slept. Then, as Julia watched in awed silence, he flew across the room and out through the other wall, and the room darkened once more.

"My mother didn't tell me about this until I was a teenager," Eleanor said, "and once she had told me, she never mentioned it again." It was as if such a memory was too precious to put into words, especially if others could not comprehend its majesty and meaning.

Julia Zulaski had a happy life, spending much of her time in cheerful service to others. Perhaps she knew that she had little to worry about. Her angel, after all, was nearby.

THE GRAY LADY

In this dim world of clouding cares,
We rarely know till 'wildered eyes
See white wings lessening up the skies,
The angels with us unawares.
—GERALD MASSEY, "BALLAD OF BABY CHRISTABEL"

Angelic rescues are sometimes dramatic. But they can also come softly, in such a tender manner that the one being helped is unaware of the supernatural aspect until some time has passed. Jean Doktor of Oceanside, California, knew this very well.

In 1980, Jean's husband, John, was struck by a strange illness. He had been a healthy sixty-year-old, jogging every day. But after returning from a business trip, he ran a mild fever, which soon soared to 105 degrees. John's physician gave him antibiotics, but by the next day the fever had not broken and John was acting strange. "Whenever I spoke to John, I seemed to hear two voices in his response," Jean recalled. One was the familiar tone of her husband, then vague and wandering. Seemingly underlying *that* voice, however, was another, this one deep and comforting, which Jean seemed to hear saying, "You will get through this, John." Jean called the doctor again, reporting not only the symptoms but the two-voiced phenomenon. "He must be hallucinating because of the high fever," the doctor told Jean. "Get him to the hospital right away."

Jean did, and although the diagnosis was pneumonia, John soon rallied and was sent home. But the strange symptoms reappeared, and by the time John had been rushed again to the hospital, he had fallen into a semiconscious state. "The doctor told us that John could hear our voices but could not respond to us—instead, he would repeat every word we said to him," Jean said. "It was a nightmare. My healthy, reliable husband was failing right in front of me."

During the next few days, John faded in and out of awareness. Four specialists entered the case. They took spinal taps and blood cultures, even checked the possibility of chemical poisoning, but remained baffled. Nothing seemed to work—and there was nothing more to do.

By Saturday night, the Doktors' three grown children had gathered in their father's room, shocked at his deteriorating condition. Jean wept quietly with fear and exhaustion. It seemed obvious that John was slipping away from them, and she could do nothing at all to help. "Please God," she prayed, as she held John's limp and unresponsive hand, "let me keep my husband. I need him . . . I love him . . ."

On Sunday morning, Jean was alone in the room, watching John's drawn and pallid face. There was a knock, and she rose to face an elderly lady dressed stylishly in gray silk, her white hair beautifully arranged. She was carrying a little gold container holding communion hosts, and Jean assumed she was what Catholics term a "lay minister," someone who brings the Eucharist to hospital patients. "Get Brother John on his feet," the woman told Jean in a firm but friendly tone.

Brother John? Who *was* this person? Jean was sure that a lay minister would never interfere with a patient's routine. "That's impossible," she protested. "My husband can't move."

"He needs to stand up," the "gray" lady repeated in a gentle but reproving tone. Jean was irritated at the woman's high-handedness. What if the floor nurse came in and found them disturbing John? Yet Jean also felt compelled to obey this brisk but oddly reassuring stranger, so much so that she suddenly reached for her husband and pulled him to a sitting position. The woman looked on, composed and quiet.

John was groggy, but he didn't protest Jean's efforts, and somehow, with her support, the two of them stood swaying. Then the gray lady gripped both their hands, and waves of cold electricity shot through Jean.

"We earnestly request the healing of Brother John," the gray lady murmured, "and may the love of Jesus touch him. May he be instantly healed."

She placed the wafer on John's tongue, snapped the little gold box shut, turned, and briskly left the room. Jean helped John into bed, where he immediately fell into a deep sleep.

That had been an odd episode, Jean mused. She was fortunate that hospital personnel hadn't caught her dragging John out of bed! But it had been nice of the nurse to break the rule about no visitors for John. Grateful, Jean popped her head out the door. "Thanks for allowing John to have communion," she told the nurse sitting at the desk. "The lay minister just left."

The nurse looked at her. "I've been sitting here for the past twenty-five minutes," she replied. "I didn't see anyone leave your room."

Puzzled, Jean approached a woman at the door of the next room. "Did you see anyone coming out of our doorway?"

"No." The visitor shook her head. "And I've been standing here for at least half an hour."

Jean checked all the rooms on the floor, then went to the waiting rooms and reception area. The gray lady had not registered at the desk. There had been a group of Catholic men bringing communion to the patients, but no woman of any age or description was among them. Exasperated, Jean gave up. It was peculiar but best forgotten, especially since John seemed to suffer no ill effects.

John slept all day, and at four thirty that afternoon he abruptly sat up in bed. Jean went cold with apprehension. Was he hallucinating again? But no. "Are the kids waiting in the foyer?" he asked her.

"Yes. Would you like me to get them?"

"No. I'll get dressed and walk down to visit with them."

"Absolutely not!" Jean gasped. "You're terribly sick—you'll be even worse after all that exertion."

"I feel just fine, honestly," he told her.

Jean looked closer. John's waxen complexion had turned rosy; he looked better than he had in weeks. Relenting, she helped him into slippers and robe. The look of relief and joy on the children's faces when they saw him confirmed Jean's own suspicions: her husband was going to get well.

The doctor examined John thoroughly the following morning and was completely mystified. "John's fever is gone, his eyes are clear, and he might as well go home, as there isn't a sign of any illness," he told them. "I simply can't explain it." Jean saw no reason to mention the gray lady, not to a doctor of medicine. But John returned to normal activity within two weeks, and no such illness ever recurred.

For a long time, Jean resisted the idea that their mysterious visitor had been an angel. Didn't angels appear in white shining robes, wearing gold halos? By contrast, her gray lady had been efficient, no-nonsense, detached, and completely in control of the situation. "She commanded firmly, prayed firmly, and after finishing her mission, vanished firmly," Jean said. "She was the most unangelic spirit I could ever imagine."

And yet, who could doubt the wondrous healing that had occurred? And hadn't there been comforting signs all along the way, evidence that she and John were not alone in this ordeal? Hadn't she even heard that "second voice" reassuring her? "I think many people experience these special touches," Jean said, "but we're afraid others will ridicule us if we talk about them. But I was there, I saw the change in John, and now I consider life a loving gift."

Nor will Jean forget the fervent prayer she whispered during the crisis of illness. "Please, God, let him live . . . I need him . . . I love him . . . Send me a miracle . . ."

God did—and a messenger to bring it.

Rescue on the Tracks

'Tis only when they spring to heaven that angels
Reveal themselves to you.
—Robert Browning, *Paracelsus*

Carol Toussaint was driving her large station wagon across Arlington Heights, Illinois, at around 5 p.m. one hot summer weekday. She was going to pick up one son from his guitar lesson, and her other youngsters, Dave and Katie, were in the backseat. It was past the time when she should have started dinner, and her mind was on getting home as soon as possible.

The traffic light was green. Carol turned left off the busy highway up a little incline and onto the railroad tracks that intersected the downtown area. But before she could complete her turn and travel through the railroad crossing, her engine died abruptly. She was stuck—blocking several lanes, with her front wheels resting in the track grooves.

Carol tried again and again to start the car, but the ignition wouldn't catch. The traffic light changed, cars began to honk, brakes screeched as rush-hour travelers attempted to go around her and avoid plowing into one another. Dave and Katie, hot, confined, and sensing their mother's distress, started to complain. It was a driver's worst nightmare.

Suddenly a young man wearing a white shirt and tie loped casually over to Carol's open window. Dave, then only about five, thought the man got out of a small brown car before approaching them.

"Did you know that you're in danger here?" the man asked softly, with an air of complete peace and tranquility in the midst of the rapidly snarling traffic.

"I sure am," Carol responded. "My husband's going to kill me for being late and not having dinner ready! If one of these drivers doesn't do it first."

"No, I didn't mean that," the young man went on. "There's a train due through here in about half a minute. I'm going to have to move the car for you." Carol had forgotten that at this time of day commuter trains whizzed through the crossing at frequent intervals. Some stopped, others didn't. And yes, now she noticed that there were several people standing at the station a block or two away. But even if a coming train was due to stop, it couldn't avoid hitting her—at this point it would still be traveling too fast.

Carol was never sure what she did next—she was in such a panic that she couldn't remember. But she would never forget the reaction of the serene young man. Nonchalantly he walked to the front of her car and gave it a little one-handed push. The huge station wagon dislodged easily from the track grooves, and as the crossing gates came down and warning bells began to clang, it rolled back across the tracks and safely over the little incline, where it again came to a stop.

Almost immediately, the train roared past. Stunned, Carol realized that, without the young man's help, her family would have been hit and killed. But where was he? The train had blocked her view for only a moment. How could he have disappeared in this open area without her seeing him?

By this time, several passersby and commuters were approaching Carol's car. "Need help, lady?" they asked. "Maybe we can push the car across the street to the gas station."

How odd, Carol thought. No one was running or upset in any way. They all acted as if her car had stalled where it *now* was. No one seemed to realize that she and the children had just been rescued. Hadn't they witnessed her close call or the young man?

But her children had. "Who was that guy who pushed us, Mom?" Dave asked from the backseat. "Where did he go?" If the man *had* arrived in a small brown car, it had somehow disappeared, even though traffic was snarled all around them.

"I have no idea, Dave," Carol said. It certainly was a mystery. And it would take several days of musing before she would begin to realize just what had happened.

One commuter stood in the middle of the intersection and directed cars around the scene while another went to alert the gas station. Mechanics and others pushed Carol's car down the rest of the incline to the station. Although the man in the white shirt had dislodged the large vehicle with one hand, it took eight people to move it all the way across the highway.

Carol's husband didn't get his dinner on time that night. He received a far greater gift.

WINGED WARRIORS

An angel is a spiritual being, created by God without a body, for the
service of Christendom and the Church.
—MARTIN LUTHER, *TABLE TALK*

The people of a small village had fervently prayed that they would avoid blood-shed and injury perpetrated by war raging in their country. But one night, an army came to surround the village and capture it. The next morning, the people looked out, saw the gathering soldiers, and were terrified. "We shall all be killed," they told one another in panic.

But one of their number, a young man who often led evening prayers, seemed unconcerned. "We needn't be afraid," he told his friends. "After all, our army is bigger than theirs."

"But we don't have an army!" the villagers protested.

The young man prayed: "Lord, let their eyes be opened."

And suddenly the villagers saw *another* army—soldiers everywhere upon the mountainside, poised for action and glowing with a heavenly light.

The enemy soldiers apparently saw them too. Within minutes, they had broken up and raced to safety. From that point on, the villagers were left in peace. This exciting story is from the Bible. It is related in the second book of Kings (6:15–17). Many incidents like it have occurred in our times too, especially to missionaries.

Corrie ten Boom liked to recount a happening during the Jeunesse rebellion in the Congo, when the rebels advanced on a school where two hundred children of missionaries lived. "They planned to kill both children and teachers," she wrote. "Those people who were in the school knew of the danger and therefore went to prayer. Their only protection was a fence and a couple of soldiers, while the enemy, who came closer and closer, amounted to several hundred."

The rebels were closing in when, without warning, they turned around and ran away. The same thing happened on the second and third day. One of the rebels was wounded and was brought to the missionary hospital. While the doctor dressed the man's wounds, he asked, "Why did you not break into the school as you planned?"

"We could not do it," the soldier said. "We saw hundreds of soldiers in white uniforms, and we became scared."

"In Africa," Corrie explained, "soldiers never wear white uniforms. So it must have been angels. What a wonderful thing that the Lord can open the eyes of the enemy so that they see angels!"[15]

The Reverend John G. Paton was a missionary in the New Hebrides Islands in the southwestern Pacific. One night, members of a hostile tribe surrounded his headquarters, intent on burning out the Patons and killing them. John Paton and his wife, alone and defenseless, prayed all night that God would deliver them. When daylight came, they were amazed to see the attackers leave.

Eventually, the tribe's chief became a Christian, and Reverend Paton asked him what had kept the chief and his men from burning down the Patons' house that night.

The chief explained that he had seen many men standing guard—hundreds, in shining garments with drawn swords in their hands. They seemed to circle the mission station so that his warriors were afraid to attack. Only then did John Paton realize that God had sent angels to protect them.[16]

⋘⋙

Another minister, attempting to reach families living in an obscure valley in Norway, had to descend a dangerous mountain trail. At one slippery and precipitous place, he paused to pray for angelic assistance. Eventually, he reached the bottom safely.

At the first cottage, he met a couple who, he discovered, had been watching his treacherous journey down the mountain trail. "What has become of your companion?" was the couple's first question after greeting the missionary.

"What companion?"

"The man who was with you."

"But no one was with me. I am traveling alone."

"Is that possible?" they exclaimed, surprised. "We were watching you as you came down, and we were positive that there were two of you crossing the mountain together."[17]

⋘⋙

Finally, there is the story told by a pediatric nurse and member of an evangelical sisterhood who was serving in Danzig (today Gdánsk, Poland) in 1945 after Russian troops had overrun many German towns. Local women were being abused, and nights were filled with terror. Nurses gathered as many women and children as they could and found temporary lodging in a small makeshift school. They often worked at night and, because of the lack of electricity, used candle stubs. Because theirs was the only lighted building, they, too, faced the danger of being invaded by the Russians. Yet the people called their building "the island of peace," because nothing bad ever seemed to happen there. Gradually, the stream of those seeking shelter increased. One day a woman brought her children and begged the nurses to take them.

The children had had a completely secular upbringing and had never seen anyone pray. That evening, as the community held a worship service, the new boy, instead of folding his hands with the rest, stared into the distance with wide eyes. The community sang a familiar song, asking God to send angels to "place golden weapons around our beds."

"When we said amen, the boy came up to me and drew me out of the building," the nurse reported. "He kept tapping his breastbone and saying, 'Up to here. It came up to here on them.'"

The nurse asked him what he meant. Pointing to the gutter on the roof of the building, he repeated his statement. "The gutter came up to here on them!"

"What are you talking about?" the nurse asked.

The child told her that while everyone had been singing, he had seen a man ablaze with light at every corner of the building. The men were so tall that they towered above the roof.

"Now it was clear to me," the nurse noted, "why this house could be called 'the island of peace.'"[18]

COMPANION THROUGH THE STORM

❦

Are not all angels ministering spirits sent to serve . . . ?
—HEBREWS 1:14

It was 2 p.m. on a weekday in April 1974, in Louisville, Kentucky. Lynne Coates and her husband, Glynn, were enjoying an unexpected break from work, sitting on the steps of their porch. Their older sons were due home from school. Their youngest child, Collyn, would be at kindergarten at Southern Baptist Theological Seminary until about 5 p.m.

The couple chatted comfortably for a while. Although the early spring day was calm, thin lines of clouds rippled across the sky.

Glynn frowned. "Look at the sky. The last time I saw one like that was when I was twelve, when a tornado hit."

Louisville is part of the Midwest's Tornado Alley, and the weather service routinely issued tornado warnings or watches, especially in spring. "I think we had all gotten a little blasé about tornados," Lynne admitted later. "I certainly didn't expect to see one."

But she did. The sky grew darker, the wind picked up, and Lynne began to feel apprehensive. The two older Coates boys came home, and as the tornado sirens began, Lynne made preparations to go into the basement. Glynn, however, hunted up his camera. "If I climb high enough," he told Lynne as he hoisted himself into the tree in their front yard, "I ought to be able to get some great pictures."

"Are you crazy?" Lynne screamed at him over the rapidly rising wind. "I just heard on the radio that Brandenburg has been leveled. Get into the basement! It's really happening!"

The family huddled together underground, listening first to the roar that sounded like a train bearing down on the house and then to the pounding rain. Everyone's thoughts centered on Collyn. Was he safe? Why hadn't they gone earlier to pick him up? But who could have guessed that this time there would be a real tornado?

In just minutes, the storm had passed, and the family came out of the basement. Their neighborhood seemed relatively untouched, except for occasional debris and some downed power lines. "I'm going over to the seminary to get Collyn," Glynn announced, and then left immediately. They would all feel better once their youngest child was with them.

Lynne gathered the older boys, and they gave thanks to God for bringing them through the storm. Then she found a portable radio and turned it on.

They listened to reports of the damage. That's when they heard that the tornado had passed directly over the seminary. One of the buildings had lost its roof "Oh, dear God—Collyn!" Lynne cried, and she flew to the telephone. She dialed the number of Collyn's kindergarten, but all she heard was the popping and crackling sounds that occur when a line is out of order. She realized that if the tornado had indeed gone in that direction, there must have been a lot of damage. It was possible that telephone lines were down. But she had to know if Collyn was all right! And what was keeping Glynn? An ominous feeling settled upon her heart. The seminary was only a fifteen minute drive. Glynn should have been back before now.

Lynne couldn't have known that Glynn's route took him directly into the midst of the damage. What should have taken fifteen minutes would eventually be a two-hour trip, as he wended his way around uprooted trees, rescue vehicles, fallen wires, houses dumped helter-skelter, and, perhaps worst of all, people wandering the streets in a daze. The storm had virtually destroyed a three-thousand-acre park of old trees next to the seminary, and Glynn had to park many blocks from Collyn's building. There was no way to drive through the devastation.

At home, Lynne tried again and again to phone the seminary kindergarten, but the number wouldn't ring. Instead, she would hear clicks, then the phone would fall silent. She grew more and more distraught, and both children began to cry. *God, I can't stand any more of this*, she prayed. *You're the only one who can help us now. Please watch over Collyn and the other children, and keep them safe.*

Once more, Lynne tried to phone. After a few clicks, the phone suddenly started to ring. A calm, pleasant-sounding woman answered. "Don't worry," she responded to Lynne's frantic questions. "The children are fine. They were all taken to another building before the storm. Their teachers will stay with them as long as it takes the parents to pick them up."

Lynne hung up, and she and the boys shouted for joy. Collyn was safe! They would just have to wait.

More than two hours later, Glynn and Collyn arrived. Glynn told Lynne that he had found a sign posted on Collyn's building door, telling parents where to go to collect their children. He had gone to the building and found Collyn there safe. Collyn had no memory of the tornado at all, except for noticing a bent weather vane on top of one of the buildings.

Lynne accompanied Collyn to his classroom on his first day back to school. She wanted to get the name of the woman who had relieved her fear over the telephone. "I'd like to thank her," she explained to Collyn's teacher.

The teacher looked at Lynne in bewilderment. "But you couldn't have spoken with anyone," she said.

"Oh, but I did," Lynne assured her. "You can ask my older boys. I was frantic until this woman assured me that Collyn was fine."

"Mrs. Coates, that would have been impossible," the teacher insisted. "We put a sign on the door, locked the building, and moved the children before the tornado struck. There wasn't anyone here.

And don't forget—our phone lines were destroyed. No call could have gotten through—or been answered."

Angels have been called our "companions in a storm." The Coates family learned, in a special way, what that lovely promise means.

The Angels and the *Padre*

Make yourself familiar with the angels, and behold them frequently in spirit; for without being seen, they are present with you.
—Saint Francis de Sales

Padre Pio, born in 1887 to simple farm people in Pietrelcina, Italy, was a monk who had the stigmata—the marks of Christ's crucifixion—etched in his hands, feet, and side, as did the founder of his order, Saint Francis of Assisi. Despite his own fragile health, Padre Pio devoted his life to building homes for people who were elderly, ill, or who suffered disability.

Padre Pio had a particularly interesting relationship with angels. It is said that he met his own guardian angel as a youngster and occasionally received counsel from him; later, the two communicated in both prayerful and humorous dialogues. At times, according to witnesses, Padre Pio was able to read and speak languages he didn't know. When asked how he could do it, he said that his guardian angel translated for him. On occasion, a number of his fellow monks heard voices singing in heavenly harmony but couldn't discover the source of the music. Padre Pio explained that the voices were angels, escorting souls into heaven.

Padre Pio frequently sent his angel to someone who needed help. For example, Father Alessio Parente was assigned to assist the fragile monk from the chapel to his monastic cell every day. But Father Parente had a habit of oversleeping. Often he wouldn't hear his alarm clock or, half awake, he would switch it off. "Every time

I overslept," he said, "I heard a voice in my sleep saying, "Alessio, Alessio, come down!" and a knocking at my door. Realizing I was late, I would jump out of bed and run out into the corridor to see who called me, but there was nobody there. I would race down to the church and there I invariably found Padre Pio at the end of Mass giving the last blessing.

"One day I was sitting by Padre Pio's side, feeling ashamed at my lack of punctuality. I was trying to explain to him that I never seemed to hear the alarm, but he interrupted me. 'Yes, I understand you,' he said. 'But do you think I will continue to send my guardian angel every day to wake you? You'd better go and buy yourself a new clock.'

"It was only then that I realized who was knocking at my door and calling me in my sleep."

Padre Pio believed that people could send their angels to others to help or intercede. He encouraged his vast network of friends to send their angels to him if they could not come themselves. "Your angel can take a message from you to me," he would say, "and I will assist you as much as I can." On one occasion, Cecil, an English friend of the padre, was hurt in a car crash. A friend went to the post office to send a telegram to Padre Pio, requesting prayers for the accident victim. When the friend presented the telegram at the desk, the man gave him a telegram from Padre Pio assuring him of his prayers for Cecil.

Later, after Cecil had recovered, he and his friend went to see Padre Pio. "How did you know of the accident?" both asked. "We got your telegram before we had sent ours."

"Do you think angels go as slowly as planes?" the monk responded, smiling.

On another occasion, an Italian girl, hearing of this saintly friar, sent her angel to ask for good health for her uncle Fred. The girl then decided to visit Padre Pio for the first time. When she approached him, he joked with her: "Your angel kept me up all night, asking for a cure for your uncle Fred!"

The mother of a desperately ill infant also sent the baby's angel to ask Padre Pio for prayers. As soon as she did so, she saw her tiny child shiver as if something had touched her. Although the doctors were mystified, the baby quickly improved and was sent home from the intensive care unit.

"When speaking to people about these stories, the comments are often the same: 'Oh, well, Padre Pio was a very holy man, wasn't he?' or 'I'm just a poor sinner—why should an angel do anything to help me?'" said Father Parente. "Yes, Padre Pio was a very holy man, but I believe our angels work well for each one of us, too—if only we have faith."

When Padre Pio died on September 22, 1968, several American tourists in Italy saw angels in the night sky. They quietly disappeared as the sun rose.[19]

HEAVENLY DIRECTIONS

⤴︎⤵︎

Sweet souls around us! watch us still,
Press nearer to our side;
Into our thoughts, into our prayers,
With gentle helping glide.
—HARRIET BEECHER STOWE, "THE OTHER WORLD"

Angels seem to be helpful in giving directions. Consider nineteen-year-old Charlotte, a student some years ago at Pacific Union College in Angwin, a small town about seventy-five miles north of San Francisco. Charlotte had a part-time job as a housekeeper in a town some distance from campus. She traveled back and forth by bus, grateful for the income that made tuition and other expenses easier to meet.

One night, returning to Angwin tired and a bit careless, Charlotte boarded the wrong bus. It was too late to get off once she discovered what had happened. Eventually the big vehicle pulled into a busy terminal in San Francisco.

Charlotte was worried. She was not where she was supposed to be, and to make matters worse, she was surrounded late at night by strangers. Some sailors, recently returned from overseas, were leering at her. A drunk attempted to begin a conversation. She hurriedly walked away.

But where should she go? How would she find a bus to Angwin, that obscure little town, in this big building with its complex of tunnels? Unused to city life, Charlotte looked for someone to help her, but there was not another woman on the platform where the buses were loading. No policeman was in sight. The information booth bore a sign: Closed for the Night. There were only strange men to be seen, derelicts moving about in the shadows.

Then it came to her. The college's dean of women had made sure all the students memorized Psalm 34, which includes: "The angel of the LORD encamps around those who fear him, and he delivers them."

"You never know," the dean said, "when you might need it."

Quickly Charlotte found a ladies' room, went in, locked the door behind her, and fell to her knees. *Dear God*, she prayed, *I'm lost and afraid. Please help me find my way home. According to your Holy Word, deliver me. Amen.*

Charlotte opened the door and stepped into the main area of the terminal again. Just then a young man passed in front of her. She noticed immediately that he was carrying what appeared to be a large black Bible.

A Bible! Charlotte thought. *Maybe he's one of the Pacific Union students returning to school!* In any event, she decided to follow him. Surely a man with a Bible would be trustworthy.

He led her through several long corridors, took an underpass to another part of the terminal, and hurried up a flight of stairs from a dimly lit concourse to a remote loading platform. Never could Charlotte have discovered this circuitous route by herself, she realized. Then all at once, there it was: a bus with big letters on the front that spelled ANGWIN! And it was about to pull out. The last one out of San Francisco that night. How fortunate for her!

Still close behind him, Charlotte followed the young man onto the bus. Only one seat remained, and he turned his back to her, as if to speak to the bus driver, and allowed her to pass him to the seat. Charlotte sank down, her eyes still on the stranger, relieved and grateful, and somewhat amazed, for the driver did not seem to see the young man at all!

In a moment, the young man turned and got off the bus. No one was paying any attention to him. Only Charlotte watched through the window, her eyes following the young man for a few feet when, although he was in clear sight, he simply vanished. *Like a light going out*, Charlotte thought.

As the bus driver closed the door and the big vehicle pulled out of the station, Charlotte shot a heartfelt prayer of thanks to heaven. The Word of God does not fail, she knew. She had been delivered by an angel of the Lord.[20]

"Like Touching God"

*What he did see was light: light from the Heavenly Host as they swept the
sky clean from one end to the other.*
—Frank E. Peretti, *This Present Darkness*

Angels have been a positive and visible presence in my life as long as I can remember; I am unafraid and secure when they are around," Fran Hamilton wrote to me. "I have learned to distinguish their presence by a certain feeling. It is not euphoria or elation or wild heart pounding. It's security, serenity. It's 'all's right with the world.' It's like touching your God."

Fran had several experiences with angels. Once she attended the same morning Mass as her son's school class. It was announced that one of the children would be making his first communion. Mass began, and all seemed normal. Then about midpoint, Fran saw lights coming into the sanctuary area from all directions. "They appeared as small, but extremely bright, little balls," she said. "There were so many and they created a glow so intense that I had to shut my eyes. Apparently no one else in church saw them, but I believed they were holy presences, coming to share and be a part of this child's first-time communion."

The brilliance continued as Fran and the rest of the congregation approached the altar. Then the lights danced and sparkled and gradually merged, creating a radiance so blazing that Fran again had to close her eyes. After receiving communion, she found herself back in her pew—with no memory of how she got there. When she opened her eyes after her communion prayer, the light had gone.

Fran was never able to track down this child after he would have become an adult, but she always suspected that there was something significant about him, and that's why so many angels attended his first communion.

❦

Late one night, Fran and her husband, Bob, were driving south on I-71 to their home in Columbus, Ohio, when they realized they had a flat tire. Too late, they recalled that the spare was also flat.

"My husband decided to drive on the berm to the freeway exit, in hope that an all-night filling station was nearby," Fran explained. "While he inched along, I began praying to my guardian angel. The farther we went, the more evident it became that there was no filling station anywhere. My prayers became more focused, until we reached a parking area of a small grocery store that was closed and stopped under the overhead lights. I became very calm and suspected that I had no more need to pray."

Within moments, a small foreign car pulled up and an attractive woman got out and casually walked up to their car. "She was probably in her late twenties, tall, slim, with long brown hair," Fran recalled.

The young woman seemed unusually serene and calm. "Are you folks in trouble?" she asked through the window. "Can I do anything to help?"

"I need air in my spare tire," Bob explained.

"I can drive you to Grove City, about two miles down the road," the young woman offered. "There's an all-night filling station there."

"That would be wonderful," Bob said.

Fran decided to wait in the car. She wasn't nervous at being left alone, but gradually she began replaying the incident in her mind. Why would a young woman stop on a deserted street at night to help two strangers? And there was that unusual aura of security and peace around her. Fran felt peaceful too, in the familiar way that always graced her when angels were especially near.

Soon Bob and the young woman arrived with the air-filled spare. Bob started to replace the tire, and the woman said good-bye and left. "Did she tell you her name?" Fran asked as she and her husband finally drove toward home. "She told me she was the wife of the manager of the Rax Restaurant in Grove City," Bob said. "Tomorrow, first thing, I'm going to go to the restaurant and thank her again."

"You won't find her there," Fran told him. "She's not married to the manager, or to anyone else, for that matter. She was an angel."

"Oh, for heaven's sake!" Bob scoffed at Fran's prediction.

The next morning, he went to the restaurant. Soon, he was back, amazed.

"The manager has no wife," he told Fran. "When I described her—and insisted that she had helped us—he looked at me like he was questioning my sanity."

Bob and Fran never had the chance to thank their rescuer again. But Fran was sure the lady knew how grateful they were.

The Boy Who Drowned

"See that you do not look down on one of these little ones. For I tell you that their angels in heaven always see the face of my Father in heaven."
—Matthew 18:10

It was April 1981, and the Hardy family of Palestine, Texas, was enjoying a visit with their cousins in Houston. The house had a backyard pool, and three-year-old Jason Hardy had been cautioned by everyone to stay in the front yard, away from the pool.

Soon, however, Sue Hardy realized that her little boy was not where he was supposed to be. She ran immediately to the pool, but its surface was undisturbed. "I thought Jason couldn't have fallen in, because he would be floating on top," Sue said. "I didn't know then that drowning victims sink to the bottom." Sue ran back to the front yard, down the street, then into the house, her concern mounting by the minute.

Finally, following an instinct, she and her niece returned to the pool—and this time Sue saw something on the bottom. Her niece jumped in and brought Jason to the surface. "My world turned upside down when she handed me my dead baby," Sue recounted. "He had no pulse, no heartbeat, and was turning black." Clutching her child's limp body, Sue screamed in anguish. Then she began to pray. The family called the paramedics, and when they arrived, Sue went upstairs.

"I phoned an elder from my church in Palestine," she said, "and I told him we needed a miracle right now. Jason had been without a heartbeat for almost an hour, but I knew God could do anything he decided to do." After the phone call, Sue lay down on the floor of the bedroom and prayed. "Jesus, Jesus," was all she could find the strength to say.

A few minutes later, one of Sue's daughters came to tell her that the paramedics had gotten Jason's heart started again. "Immediately, I was filled with peace," Sue related. "I had Jason when I was forty-one, after my three older children were almost grown up. Somehow I knew that God had not given me this late blessing only to have him taken away."

Hermann Hospital sent its Life Flight helicopter to take Jason to intensive care. By the time Sue drove there, doctors were painting a bleak picture. "They said that when a brain is deprived of oxygen for three to six minutes, damage begins. Jason had been clinically dead when he arrived at the hospital, and doctors felt that if he survived, he would be paralyzed and profoundly brain damaged."

But Sue told them, "No. You watch and see. Jason will walk out of this hospital by himself."

The physicians looked at one another. Obviously this little boy's mother couldn't yet absorb what had happened. They decided not to explain any more of the terrible consequences she faced.

Jason, in a coma and still considered clinically dead, was placed on a life-support system. On the fifth night, he developed pneumonia, and hospital personnel felt the end was near. Clinging to the peace she had experienced in the bedroom, Sue phoned elders from a local church in Houston and asked them to visit her son. They did and anointed him as Sue and her family waited in the hall. "Mrs. Hardy?" One of the elders came to the door. "Your little boy's eyes are fluttering." The three-year-old had just wet the bed. His brain was apparently waking up!

Not only did Jason walk out of the hospital twenty days later, but he soon began to talk. Seven months after his terrible accident, his physician pronounced him healthy. Jason grew into an active boy, completely normal in every way. And Sue continued to give thanks to God, every day, for this awesome miracle. She also continued to pray for extra protection for her son.

Because he was only three when the drowning occurred, Jason was far too young to talk about why he went to the pool and how he happened to fall in. As years passed, Sue assumed that he remembered nothing except what his family had told him about his accident and hospitalization. One night when Jason was about six or seven, however, he was watching a television show when a shot of a swimming pool came into view. "It was dark underneath that pool," Jason suddenly said.

Sue was immediately alert. Was he remembering something about his accident? "Tell me about it," she said.

"It was dark," the little boy repeated, "but the angel stayed with me."

"The angel, Jason?"

"Uh-huh. He was there so I wouldn't be afraid."

That is all Jason ever said about his miraculous rescue. But to his family, it was enough.

WATCHER IN THE WOODS

*The very presence of an angel is a communication. Even when an angel
crosses our path in silence, God has said to us, "I am here.
I am present in your life."*
—TOBIAS PALMER, *AN ANGEL IN MY HOUSE*

Saint John Bosco, as tradition has it, was often bothered by toughs who threatened to mug him as he passed them on his mission to serve the poor. Eventually, a large fierce-looking black dog began to appear alongside John and to accompany him through the danger zones. When John reached a place of safety, the dog would vanish. Perhaps guardian angels are not *always* disguised as people.

Barbara Johnson had completed her general-nursing training at the Royal Adelaide Hospital in Australia. She worked six months in Melbourne, then went to Sydney to train as a midwife at Saint Margaret's Hospital.

Barbara's brother and his wife lived in a suburb of Sydney, so on her first day off, she took the train to their home for a visit. Everyone had a lovely day, and Barbara left at about 9 p.m. for the return journey.

"I was feeling proud," she admitted. "Although I later got to know the underground subway system well, this was my first time traveling beneath the city. Yet I had found my way around and gotten off at the right stop." Confidently, she climbed up to a well-lit street and decided to take a shortcut through a park.

Barbara wasn't apprehensive as she began her walk. "I had walked in cities at night and had learned that you keep your pace brisk but not hurried, so onlookers don't think you're afraid." She moved purposefully down the path, and it was only after a few moments that she realized the park was extremely dark inside, and Oxford Street—and the hospital—was much farther than she had anticipated.

There was no one else in the park, at least no one she could see. But Barbara had the feeling she was being watched. From time to time she saw a glow, like the end of a lit cigarette, in the shadows. Her heart began to pound. Was she in danger? If someone grabbed her and pulled her into the bushes here, there would be little she could do to protect herself. But if she bolted, she could lose her way in the darkness or fall and hurt herself.

There was no choice but to keep going. Barbara quickened her pace and stared straight ahead, fixing her eyes on that distant glow, the streetlights that signaled safety. She was about halfway through the park when she sensed movement to her right. Oh, no! As if everything weren't frightening enough, there was a large white Alsatian dog right next to her.

"This breed was very intimidating, because the police used them as guard dogs," Barbara said. "They were known to be vicious." Frantically, she looked around for the dog's owner, but the park was deserted. What would she do if the dog charged her? Barbara pictured herself lying bleeding on the dirt, vulnerable to attacks from both man and beast. Her heart raced even faster.

Curiously, the dog seemed anything *but* bad-tempered. It simply trotted alongside her as if it belonged. Barbara slackened her pace, hoping the furry monster would pass her, but the dog slowed as well. Then she stopped. "Go away, dog." Timidly she tried to shoo it. "Go away, now!"

But the dog stopped too, as if rooted to the spot, and looked up at her. Its demeanor didn't change, nor was it agitated or responsive. It simply stayed, like an obedient guard assigned to her side.

Barbara saw no other option but to keep moving, and that's just what she did, almost breaking into a run as she reached the welcome lights of Oxford Street. The dog stood beside her as she glanced down the street to check the traffic. Was it going to follow her across?

But just as she stepped off the curb, Barbara looked to her right once more.

The dog was gone.

Relieved, Barbara hurried to the hospital dorm and made herself a cup of tea in the kitchenette. "You look exhausted," one of the nurses said.

"I've had a traumatic experience," Barbara explained. "I took a shortcut just now through the park—"

"You went into the park at night?" another nurse interrupted. "Oh, you're new, you wouldn't have known. But many crimes take place in that park!"

Aghast that she had ventured into such a dangerous and poorly lit area after dark, the two nurses related one horror story after another, and Barbara thought back with consternation to the cigarette glow in the shadows. Oh, what might have happened to her! God must have been watching over her.

"And suddenly I was filled with a sense of guardian angels, and I knew without question that the dog had been mine," Barbara said. "There was just no other explanation for his arrival, his behavior, and his sudden disappearance. I felt grateful that God chose to take such personal care of me, and that he was ready to protect me, even from my own foolishness."

She never saw her angel again, but she named him Giuseppe and felt a bond that endured through the years.

THE QUIET PROTECTORS

The angels keep their ancient places
Turn but a stone and start a wing!
'Tis ye, 'tis your estrangèd faces
That miss the many-splendoured thing.
—FRANCIS THOMPSON, "THE KINGDOM OF GOD"

Impulses. Aren't they just intuition? Sometimes. But the following stories suggest something more specific at work.

As a traveling businessman, Frank was often away from home for the whole week, returning only on Saturday. Many times he sent his guardian angel to watch over his young family in his absence.

One Friday afternoon at about five, Frank had an overpowering feeling that something was wrong at home. *Guardian angel, go to my family and protect them*, he prayed. The apprehension immediately left him.

The next day, Frank arrived home. "How was everything while I was gone?" he asked his wife, still remembering that strange, ominous moment.

"Oh, Frank, we almost had a tragedy!" His wife had taken her eyes off Timmy, their four-year-old, for only a few seconds, and the child had run out into the street. At that very moment, a car was speeding along the lane toward him. Horrified, Frank's wife saw that she could never reach her son in time.

But when the car was about thirty feet away, the driver saw the child and braked with such force that the car turned around in a complete circle twice, then came to rest directly in front of Timmy, who had been frozen to the spot in terror. The driver, instead of giving vent to anger, leaped from the car and shouted, "It's a miracle! A miracle that I was able to stop in time!"

"What time did this happen?" a shaken Frank asked. "Yesterday," his wife answered. "Just at five o'clock."

Sister Martha had a similar experience. She was on night duty in a hospital and had to go to the cellar to get some medicine from the walk-in freezer. As she was searching the shelves, the door closed unexpectedly behind her.

"Oh, no!" Sister Martha murmured in dismay. The freezer had no interior security handle, and she was locked in.

At that late hour, it was useless to call, for no one would hear her. So instead, Sister Martha began to beseech the angels to help her. "I was mainly concerned because the patients in my ward would be unattended all night," she recalled. "My own danger—death by freezing—had not yet registered in my mind."

Just a short time passed, and Sister Martha heard something on the other side of the door. Before she could call out, the handle turned and the door swung open. On the other side was one of the nursing sisters.

The women stared at each other, astonished. Sister Martha was amazed that her prayer had been answered so swiftly. But her companion was even more dumbfounded.

"I had gone to bed," the other nun explained, "but I kept feeling that I was supposed to go down to the cellar and make sure everything was in order." She tried to ignore the prod, but finally, when it would not go away, she gave in. "I just opened the freezer door for a last check," she told Sister Martha. "I had no idea anyone was locked in."

Andrew Smith had been hunting in a wooded, undeveloped pocket of Jefferson County, Missouri, about thirty-five miles southwest of St. Louis, with a friend, Joe (not their real names). It was a dreary, chilly day in late autumn.

Andrew was very much an outdoorsman, thoroughly grounded in safety procedures. He would never carelessly handle a gun or permit anyone else to do so. He had never hunted with Joe before, although the two men sometimes fished together.

"There are several 'givens' in firearms handling," Andrew explained, "A gun is never pointed at anything other than what one wishes to shoot. When two hunters walk side by side, with guns cradled, each points his muzzle in the direction away from the other. When one is walking with a loaded gun, the safety is engaged to prevent accidental discharge. One does not walk with a finger on the gun's trigger. When hunting or otherwise carrying firearms, one must be constantly alert to positions and movements of others in relation to oneself." These rules were second nature to Andrew and, he assumed, to Joe.

The two men had hunted the periphery of a plot of small fields and thick woodland, and they were walking back to the car up a rough road. Joe was on Andrew's right with his gun properly cradled and pointing away from Andrew.

"An ingrained awareness about safety factors was probably what alerted me that Joe had changed position in some subtle way," Andrew recalled. "I glanced to my right and saw that Joe's gun was now cradled on the wrong side, with the muzzle pointing toward my head. I was about to ask him to change the gun back to its proper place. Under normal circumstances, that's what I would have done." But Andrew heard a voice inside his head. It was not a familiar voice, and he knew immediately that it was not audible, because Joe didn't look up or react to the sound. And yet it was as loud and as clear—and as infused into his consciousness—as if the speaker had been standing on Andrew's left side.

And perhaps the speaker was. For he said, "Andrew! Take two quick steps forward."

Andrew does not ordinarily respond to others without question. But he obeyed instantly. He had just taken the second step when Joe's shotgun discharged into the space he had occupied.

The two men stood dazed at the near miss. "What happened?" Andrew, shaken, demanded.

"I don't know." Joe shook his head, appalled.

"Didn't you have the safety engaged?"

"I *thought* so. And my finger certainly wasn't on the trigger."

"It must have been. And why was the gun pointing at me?"

Joe had no answer. He was bewildered and ashamed at what appeared to be three unconscious violations of safety rules. How could such a thing have happened? The men were never able to reach a satisfactory explanation.

"On many occasions I have realized that I was in dangerous situations," Andrew said. "Sometimes I have failed to react quickly enough, resulting in an injury of one sort or another. And I've never had any indication that I'm exempt from the consequences of my own carelessness or lapses of attention."

"But could it be only chance that I had a sudden once-in-a-lifetime compulsion to move away from a gun?" Ordinarily Andrew was able to find natural explanations for unusual happenings. But this event exceeded the limits of coincidence. He concluded that it was direct intervention, on his behalf, by his guardian angel.

In none of the above or similar episodes that people shared with me did participants *see* benevolent beings. "It would be hard—yes, impossible—to 'prove' that anything supernatural was at work," one wrote. "But do I believe that I was touched and protected? Yes, oh, a thousand times, yes!"

SILENT CIRCLE

Around our pillows, golden ladders rise,
And up and down the skies,
With winged sandals shod,
The angels come and go, the messengers of God!
—R. H. STODDARD, "HYMN TO THE BEAUTIFUL"

Viola Rockett had always been a responsible person, graduating from her small high school in Charleston, Mississippi, in three years with a 95 percent grade average. Falling in love and marrying at nineteen was a challenge, but she handled her new responsibilities with her usual maturity and common sense. "I've never been easily scared or suspicious," she explained. "I came to know God when I was thirteen and always had a pretty firm faith after that."

Life with her young husband, A.J., wasn't easy, however. It was tough to find work in their part of Mississippi. Two little daughters were born during those years, straining their budget even more.

When Viola was twenty-five, the couple moved to Mathiston, Mississippi, a small town with just a few stores and a post office. A.J. had been repairing and selling used cars to support his family, so he rented an old repair and body shop, filled with stripped-down autos, tools, and junk—an easy structure to break into, had there been anything worth stealing.

A room that had once been the auto-parts store connected to the body shop. Viola described it: "Two of the walls were made of ceiling-to-floor glass—like show-room windows—with ceiling-to-floor shades. The only lightbulb hung in the kitchen area, with a string to pull it on and off." Here, in this room, the family lived.

Viola had never known such isolation. A.J. was gone several nights a week, buying and selling cars, and she was without a phone, cut off from a support system of family and friends. Viola tried hard to be brave, but at night the room was especially scary. She felt vulnerable with those long windows in front of her, even though the shades were pulled down. It was common knowledge in the town that she was often alone at night. What would she do if anyone tried to break in? How could she protect herself and her daughters?

One night, alone with the girls, Viola awakened in a dreadful, mindless fear. She had not been having a nightmare. In fact, there seemed no reason for the terror that had gripped her so abruptly, but she sensed great danger all around her. "I was so frightened that I believed that someone or something was actually *in* the room with us," she said, "and I knew that I would have to find the courage to get out of bed, make my way across the floor, find the string hanging from the bulb, and turn on the light."

Anyone who has suffered from an anxiety attack will know how difficult it was for Viola to move. Her heart pounding, more terrified than she had ever been in her life, she managed to stumble across the floor and find the string. But when she turned on the light and looked around, nothing seemed to be wrong. The bleak room looked just the same.

And yet, instead of relief, the fear came again, an unbelievable wave, and Viola was convinced that the peril was now actually right outside those covered windows, so close she could almost touch it. If she ran outside to get help, she would plunge right into whatever was there. But if she stayed inside, there was little chance of keeping an intruder out, not with the building's flimsy, run-down construction. Not knowing what else to do, Viola knelt in the middle of the dreary setting. "God, help us," she cried out. "Thank you for your love and care. Please keep us safe now."

She looked up. Suddenly, although the shades had been down, she saw them dissolve from the windows. And on the outside of each of those ten or twelve panes of glass, she saw a huge figure slowly descend and fold his wings to his side. "Nothing seemed like a dream or slow motion. It was all very normal," she said. Except—they were angels!

Facing outward with their backs to her, those wondrous beings were so tall that their heads were above the tops of the windows and she could not see them. But she could see the wings folding behind their bodies as each figure slowly got into position. A phalanx of heavenly guards, sent to protect her in answer to her plea. How much God must love her! It was unbelievable.

The vision lasted only a few minutes. As Viola's stunned eyes traveled from one silent figure to another, the shades suddenly reappeared and once again covered the glass. Viola and her daughters were alone in the room. And yet, she knew that they would never be alone.

Viola never discovered what was threatening her and the children that night. But she was rarely afraid after that night. "God gave me the grace to see what is real, that he never abandons us."

A SMILING CHILD

With silence only as their benediction
God's angels come
Where, in the shadow of a great affliction,
The soul sits dumb.
—JOHN GREENLEAF WHITTIER, "TO MY FRIEND ON THE DEATH
OF HIS SISTER"

Gretchen and her husband, Fred, had had a long and happy marriage, but Fred had died recently. And although Gretchen had a son and four grandchildren who loved her very much, she could not easily recover from such a momentous loss.

During the first few months, Gretchen had been numb with grief and unable to weep. But she had progressed beyond the initial shock stage, and it seemed that all she did was cry. "I was beginning to dread meeting anyone," she recalled, "because I was so afraid that I would burst into tears in the middle of an ordinary conversation." People had been very kind, but Gretchen didn't want anyone pitying her, and she didn't want her sorrow to make others uncomfortable.

On this Sunday, Gretchen went to church by herself and selected an empty pew. She was relieved to see no familiar faces. At least if her anguish threatened to overwhelm her, she could slip out quietly.

As she sat in the pew, she thought again of Fred, and desolation and grief swept in waves across her spirit. "I could hardly keep from crying out," she said. It was hard to endure such continuous mourning. Would it ever end? In another moment, she was going to weep.

Suddenly, a small boy entered the pew and sat next to Gretchen. She eyed him through her tears. He had light-brown hair, was neatly dressed in a brown suit, and appeared to be about six years old. And he was looking up at her in the most familiar way, smiling as if he knew her.

It was peculiar. Children rarely attended church alone in this particular congregation, especially at such an early hour. Where could his family be? Even stranger was the fact that, although the youngster had picked up the church prayer book to read, he kept edging toward Gretchen. "He moved nearer and nearer, very casually. He would read, then look up, catch my eye, and beam. His whole attitude made it clear that he had come to keep me company." What a darling child!

As the little boy snuggled close to Gretchen, something else began to happen. She felt her heart lighten. Somehow, although she hadn't believed such a thing would ever happen again, she began to feel, yes, happy. It was only a fleeting emotion, like a brief kiss, but she felt it.

And she *would* be happy again. She knew it now without question. "A time to mourn and a time to dance . . ." Gretchen was still very much in mourning, but the love and sweetness in the little boy's face had given her a glimpse of a better time yet to come.

But who was this child? Gretchen looked down at him, and again he smiled at her in that intimate and penetrating manner. She *must* know him; why else would he be behaving this way? Of course—he was probably the son of a younger neighbor or friend who, aware of Gretchen's loss and seeing her sitting alone, had sent her little boy up to share the pew. Gretchen would have to thank his parents for their thoughtfulness. She would watch where the child went after the service.

As the service ended, Gretchen and the boy left the pew and headed for the front door. There were people around, but not a huge crowd, and the child was right next to Gretchen. "What is your name?" she asked him. "Do I know your mother?"

But instead of answering, he looked up at her for one last smile. And then, as Gretchen's eyes scanned the crowd to find someone searching for him, the child vanished. He was there—and then he simply wasn't. Gretchen didn't see him go, but when she glanced down, the spot next to her was vacant.

"I kept looking for him among the people until everyone had left, but I never saw him again, nor did I meet anyone who knew him or had sent him."

But after that Sunday, Gretchen never felt quite so alone again. Gradually the truth seemed to come upon her—that an ordinary child, no matter how charming, would not have been able to lift her spirits in that mysterious and welcome way. Instead, the child had been sent by Someone who understood her suffering and was reaching out to comfort and heal her.

THE BOY IN THE BLUE SUIT

Was there no star that could be sent . . . to heal that only child?
—RALPH WALDO EMERSON, "THRENODY"

Michael Sullivan has authored various publications for boys. When he heard about my angel project, he generously offered to let me retell and share with readers the following experience from one of his books.

Michael awakened feverish and queasy on the morning of his confirmation day in 1925. But he couldn't miss this major event! Saint Bartholomew's parish in Elmhurst was part of the Brooklyn diocese, and in those days, the bishop confirmed there once every four years. If Michael had to stay home today, he wouldn't be able to receive the sacrament until he was fourteen.

Reluctantly Michael's father decided he could go, and his older sister, Mary, helped the ten-year-old dress and walked him to the church. She wouldn't be able to stay because there were so many children to be confirmed that the church couldn't accommodate any family or well-wishers.

Michael lined up with the others, slowly marched into church, and took his assigned place in the pew, just as he had practiced. The bishop, wearing gold vestments and a huge gold miter, sat on a special chair at the center of the altar, surrounded by priests. It was an impressive sight.

The organ played. Finally the boys in Michael's pew filed out and walked up the aisle. "I was glad I had only a short distance to go," he said, "because my knees wobbled."

Gently, the bishop touched Michael's cheek and uttered the words of the sacrament. Then Michael returned to his pew to kneel up straight, as he had been instructed. But he ached all over, and there was such a long line of boys still approaching the altar. The candlelight seemed to blur, and the bishop was blurred, too. Michael fainted and fell into the center aisle.

When Michael came to, he was sitting in an oak chair in the sacristy, a small room behind the altar. The pastor, who had been waving smelling salts under his nose, looked relieved. "You'll be all right now," he said. "Just sit here and rest awhile."

A window was open, and a soft April breeze filtered into the sacristy. The pastor returned to the ceremony, leaving Michael with the usher who had carried him out. "Are you feeling better?" the usher asked after some time had passed.

Michael nodded. "I guess so."

"You don't have to wait until the ceremony's over," the usher pointed out. "Do you think you can walk home?"

Michael thought he could. Quietly he slipped out a side door and walked cautiously down an alley and across the street to a path that cut diagonally through an empty lot. He was familiar with this trail—he took it every day to school.

But today the path seemed like a long, winding road. Every step was an effort, and Michael's body started to ache again, just as it had when he had tried to kneel in church. "I recalled Sister's instructions that the Holy Spirit would come upon you in the sacrament of confirmation and give you strength," Michael said. "This thought had a calming effect, and I managed to get halfway before I knew I wasn't going to make it to the end of the path."

He turned and looked back at Saint Bartholomew's, hoping that the ceremony had ended and friends would come out and find him. But there was no one anywhere. He began to feel light-headed and weak, exactly as he had felt just before his faint. In desperation, he looked around for a rock to sit on or a clean patch of grass to lie on.

Just then—although there had been no one in view—a boy in a blue suit appeared beside him. He was older and taller than Michael, but he had a friendly face. Michael was glad to see him. "Were you just confirmed?" he asked.

"No," the boy said with a smile. Strength seemed to emanate from him, and Michael's queasiness passed. The boy started to walk up the path, and automatically Michael took his place beside him. The path didn't seem so long now.

The boy spoke with animation, and they discussed many topics. "My head was still fuzzy, and I couldn't quite place him, but he undoubtedly knew me—all about me," Michael recalled. "He knew that my mother wasn't living. He knew my two sisters, and that my dad was a wonderful man."

As they left the lot and walked up Lamont Avenue, Michael told the boy about the previous highlight of his life. His dad had taken him to the second game of the World Series in 1923. Babe Ruth had hit two home runs, and the Yankees had beaten the Giants, four to two.

The boy listened, and he seemed to know all about it. He knew that John McGraw had taken out his starting pitcher, Hughie McQuillan, and had put in Jack Bentley. He knew that Irish Meusel, Yankee Bob Meusel's brother, had hit a home run for the Giants.

The sun filtered through the maple trees, which were in full bud. There was something about the sun, the spring-green trees, and the warm companionship of this boy that made Michael feel stronger with every step. They reached the corner. "You've only got one more block to go," the boy said, looking toward the white-gabled house in the distance.

"That's right," Michael said, studying his companion's face for the first time. The boy's eyes shone. He walked across the street in the other direction, turned, smiled, and waved at Michael. As he waved, a shimmering light outlined his body. A delivery truck came between the two. Michael waited for the truck to pass so that he could wave back at the boy. The truck passed. The boy in the blue suit was nowhere in sight.

Michael ran the remaining block home and dared not to tell anyone about his companion. During the next few days, he searched the neighborhood, but he never saw the boy in the blue suit again.

He had known he wouldn't. Not in this life anyway.

STRANGERS IN DISTRESS

Do not forget to entertain strangers, for by so doing some people have entertained angels without knowing it.
—HEBREWS 13:2

Michelle Bove, a warm, gracious person, had always been timid. She, her husband, and their three young children lived in a pleasant section of Manhattan Beach in Brooklyn, New York, about a block from the shore. It was an affluent area in which obviously poor or needy people were rarely seen.

One winter night, as Michelle drove home from a meeting, she began praying that she could overcome her fearfulness. But she didn't expect her plea to be answered quite so soon! As she reached home and began to pull into her driveway, she saw two people standing in the middle of the street. Michelle was apprehensive at these strangers blocking her way, but she got out and asked them what they wanted.

The man, older and well dressed, certainly didn't look like a street person. Yet he asked Michelle to help his companion, a woman in her thirties. "What do you need?" Michelle asked the woman.

"A place to sleep," the woman responded quietly. She was dressed shabbily but seemed to be intelligent. And she had the most beautiful blue eyes Michelle had ever seen. Michelle hesitated, then turned back to the man. But he was no longer there!

Michelle hadn't heard him say good-bye or step away, and although she looked up and down the quiet street, there was no sign of anyone there.

Michelle's first response to this extremely peculiar situation was a desire to flee to the safety of her home. But an intuition stopped her. She had prayed for bravery, hadn't she? Instead, she heard herself saying to the blue-eyed woman, "Why don't you come home with me?" The woman accepted the invitation.

First, Michelle phoned local motels, but no rooms were available. She then called a few nearby churches, but none could or would help. Michelle was becoming nervous. Her husband, who had been asleep when she arrived home, had awakened and demanded that she send the woman away. "He thinks I'm an easy mark, far too trusting," Michelle explained. Her husband was also concerned that Michelle had brought a stranger into their home, perhaps putting their children at risk, and he wanted her to do something about it right then. Aggravated, he went back to bed, assuming Michelle would carry out his wishes.

Their house was quite large, so Michelle brought the woman to the basement-level guest room, fixed her some food, and made up a bed for her. The visitor had been almost completely silent up until then, but Michelle's disagreement with her husband triggered a response. "I've had problems with my husband too," she told Michelle.

"Do you have children?" Michelle asked.

"Yes, two."

"Then why are you alone? How did you get into this situation?"

Michelle's guest was evasive. It appeared she was in distress, running from something, and Michelle's concern increased. What had she gotten herself into? But she couldn't bring herself to ask a person in such a precarious position to leave, not in the middle of a cold night.

Instead, while the woman slept, Michelle sat upstairs in her kitchen, worrying. What if the woman intended to harm Michelle's family? What if the man who disappeared was this woman's accomplice, and he would return to rob them? And what would her husband say when he discovered that Michelle had let a stranger sleep in their home all night? Michelle prayed, read the Bible, and kept watch.

As dawn was breaking, Michelle packed some food and warm clothes and wrote down the names of shelters she had been unable to reach earlier. Then she awakened the woman. "You'll have to leave before my husband gets up," she told her. "I can't drive you anywhere because my children will be needing me soon."

"What is your name?" the woman asked. Michelle told her, putting the package into her arms.

"Thank you, Michelle," the woman said, and smiled. She looked much healthier, and her blue eyes shone. "I will never forget your kindness."

"Take care." Michelle opened the back door, closed it behind the visitor, and stood by the window to watch her walk down the driveway, which was the only way the woman could get out of Michelle's enclosed yard and onto the street. Not until the woman passed her would Michelle feel truly safe.

Michelle waited . . . and waited . . . but the stranger never appeared. Like the man who had accompanied her, the woman had simply vanished.

Michelle will never be sure why the man or the young woman stood in front of her house and asked her to respond despite her fear. But she was never quite so timid after that day.

❦

And while we're thinking about Michelle, we might consider a story that is similar but with the opposite resolution.

Michigan resident Helen Griffith and members of her church group were wrapping up a day of the children's summer Bible-school program. Eight or nine women and some youngsters were standing by the room's entrance. "We were all caught up in our activities, collecting money, picking up materials, laughing, eating, busy-busy-busy," Helen recalled.

Suddenly a pale young woman came into the building and hesitantly approached the group standing near the door. "Excuse me," the woman said, speaking barely above a whisper. She looked exhausted. "Could I borrow some money from you ladies? To buy gas?" She had to get to a town about seventy miles away, she explained. Her frailness was evident, and Helen noticed she was expecting a baby.

Someone in the group quickly got the young woman a chair. Then everyone moved away to converse among themselves. Helen had only some change with her, but she suggested that they donate something from the school fund or take up a collection among themselves.

But one of the women objected. "We shouldn't help these kinds of people, Helen," she said firmly. "They go from church to church playing on people's sympathies. Well, this one isn't getting anything from me!"

Several of the others nodded slowly, allowing themselves to be persuaded. "Why don't we send her to one of the other churches instead?" one suggested. "There's a church pantry not too far from here—they might help."

The young woman's face fell when a spokesperson went to her with a negative reply. She got up and walked heavily out the side door. Immediately Helen's conscience began to bother her, so she followed the woman outside, thinking she would give her what she had in her purse.

"But there was no one there," Helen related. "No car, no young woman . . . I was only a few steps behind her, and she certainly wasn't walking quickly, but I saw no car moving through any of the lots or drives. She had disappeared."

To this day, Helen wonders if her church group was visited by an angel and had failed the test of kindness. "She came, asked quietly for assistance—and we who were so busy *talking* about love and kindness failed to *act* on our principles. We were hypocrites, and how I wish we had a chance to undo the mistake we made."

⁓✖⁓

Why would an angel in human form appear in distress? Surely celestial beings have no angry husbands, no children, no worries at all! Maybe they become vulnerable for our sake, to offer us a chance to reach out, to trust, and to grow in the giving.

Angels with Nightsticks

*For he will command his angels concerning you to guard you
in all your ways.*
—Psalm 91:11

Steven Rogers was a rookie officer in the Nutley, New Jersey, police department in 1977 when he was assigned to be partners with Phil. Not only was Phil older and wiser, but he was also an outspoken Christian. For the impulsive and sometimes rebellious Steve, Phil became a role model. Daily, before their shift, the two men would pray or read from the Bible, often reciting the ninety-first psalm, the one that commits us to God's care and summons angels when we are in danger.

Nutley had a growing problem. Recreational areas were being overrun with teenagers drinking, taking drugs, and vandalizing property. Police knew where the kids congregated, but whenever they raided the gatherings, most slipped away and could not be found. Apparently the teens had a hideout—but where? None of the police officers had been able to find it.

One day, Steve and Phil were assigned to plainclothes duty. They were to dress like the kids and, it was hoped, discover their hideout and the source of their drugs. That night, they stationed themselves in a secluded wooded area and watched the young people fighting, cursing, and destroying property.

"What I saw sickened me," Steve related. "I realized we were not dealing with a few kids having fun but with many who were hard-core drug addicts with minds out of control. Many were invoking Charles Manson [the infamous cult leader who orchestrated multiple murders in California] or performing obscene acts. If this behavior spread, it could threaten the whole city."

The main source of the drugs, it appeared, was a young man the officers dubbed Mr. Big because of his apparent emotional hold on the group.

The next day, the officers went to the scene of the gathering, prayed for guidance, and began to check it, inch by inch. They soon came across a well-worn path covered with branches. The path led to a cleverly concealed cave. Inside, the officers found pills, liquor, pornographic material, and marijuana. Here was where so many young people eluded the police. That night, they decided, they would raid the cave.

Before their shift, they requested extra backup, but they were told they were on their own. How could two officers handle a bunch of aggressive kids all alone? Once again, the men prayed Psalm 91. Then they strolled toward the crowd already gathering near a railroad embankment. Mr. Big was there, they noted. "We wanted to apprehend him first, because we felt many of the kids would discontinue their illegal activities if he wasn't around," Steve explained.

But as they approached, a girl recognized them. "Cops!" she screamed. The crowd scattered. Steve and Phil went after the girl, caught her, and called for a backup squad. They knew that some of the others would be hiding in the cave.

They found the hidden path and, despite the fact that they were hopelessly outnumbered, walked boldly into the entrance. "Freeze!" Steve shouted, and not a person in the cave moved. Steve ran his eyes across the group. At least twelve of them. And they had caught Mr. Big!

Phil walked over to Mr. Big and asked for the package he was holding. Meekly the young man handed over a bag of pills. Steve gathered other evidence, read everyone their rights, then stood in bewilderment, staring at the cave floor covered with submissive teens who easily could have overpowered the two officers. Why hadn't they put up a fight?

The van pulled up, and as they led the prisoners out of the cave, Steve turned to Mr. Big. "Why didn't you or any of the others try to attack us when we came in?"

"You think I'm crazy or something?" Mr. Big asked. "There were at least twenty guys in blue uniforms, and it would have been stupid to think of fighting or running."

"Twenty? No, there were just the two of us."

"Yeah?" Mr. Big called to another young prisoner. "Belinda, how many cops came into the cave?"

Belinda shrugged. "At least twenty-five."

It was then that Steve remembered the words he and Phil recited so faithfully: "You will not fear the terror of the night . . . for he will command his angels concerning you."

Within nine months of the time Steve and Phil had been assigned to this special duty, they had made 250 arrests—more than the department's annual total. Former hangouts of drug addicts and vandals were deserted, and Nutley neighborhoods flourished. Whenever anyone complimented the officers on their accomplishments, they gave credit to Jesus for protecting them and helping them solve the crimes.

Jesus, and a very special squad in blue.[21]

HEAVENLY HOUSEKEEPER

❦

A ministering angel shall my sister be.
—WILLIAM SHAKESPEARE, *HAMLET*

Raymond Herzing's mother, Mag, a Bavarian immigrant, settled in Lancaster, Pennsylvania, married, and had three children. The older two died in their twenties. Raymond, the youngest, became a priest in 1938. When Raymond's father died, his mother was alone, with no grandchildren or extended family nearby to take care of her. Because Raymond had become secretary to the bishop of Buffalo, New York, he found it harder and harder to look after his aging mother. He traveled regularly from his Buffalo residence to Lancaster but couldn't keep up with everything Mag needed. And when he wasn't with his mother, he was worrying about her.

Raymond decided to employ a woman to live with Mag. Unfortunately, Mag was growing crotchety, and none of the women her son hired remained with her for long—with the whims of old age, Mag would constantly dismiss them. "This one didn't cook right, that one doesn't keep house the way she should . . . none of them are working out!" a frustrated Raymond once told a relative. He was spending more and more time with his mother and neglecting his growing responsibilities in Buffalo.

Finally Raymond prayed. "God, if you want me to work for you in Buffalo, you've got to help me with my mother here!"

Sometime later, Raymond was at his mother's home when a middle-aged woman knocked on the front door. She was neatly dressed and wore a pleasant expression. "I hear you are looking for someone to take care of your mother," she said.

"You heard right," Raymond told her, opening the door wider. "Won't you come in and talk about it?" He liked the woman instantly. She had a tranquil, kind air about her.

"I'd be willing to stay a year or so," she told him.

A year! Raymond couldn't believe God's benevolence. "That would be wonderful, providing my mother likes you," Raymond explained. "She can be . . . rather difficult."

The woman just smiled.

Briskly Raymond outlined her duties and her salary. "What is your name?" he asked. "How should I make out your checks?"

"Oh . . ." The woman laughed a little. "Just call me Angel. And as far as my salary, why don't we see how your mother feels about me first?"

Yes, that would be the challenge, Raymond agreed. If Angel wanted to test the waters, he certainly didn't blame her. He returned to Buffalo, cautiously optimistic.

Angel proved to be beyond worth. Mag accepted her right away, and the two got along famously. Raymond assumed someone in the neighborhood had sent Angel, but as time passed, he learned that none of the neighbors had ever met her before she came to live with Mag. Angel also seemed reticent about her background, never discussing how she happened to knock on his mother's door. Perhaps Raymond should have asked for references. But Mag liked her so very much.

From time to time, Raymond brought up the subject of Angel's salary, but she always interrupted his concerns and waved them away. "I can't use the money now," she'd say. "We'll settle up when your mother no longer needs me." It seemed almost too good to be true, but by this time, Raymond was director of the Buffalo Family Life Office and steeped in additional duties. As long as his mother was safe and happy, he wasn't about to pressure Angel about anything!

About a year after Angel came, Mag Herzing died. "I don't think I'll go to the funeral," Angel told Raymond that morning. "I'll straighten up here instead." Raymond agreed. But when he returned to his mother's house after the burial, it seemed strangely empty.

"Angel?" he called, looking through the neat but deserted rooms. "Are you here?" But Angel was nowhere to be found, and her possessions were gone. Nor had Raymond ever paid her! And she had lived there, just as she'd predicted, for a year.

Angel went as mysteriously as she had come. But until his death in 1965, Monsignor Raymond Herzing always regarded her as a special answer to prayer.

LEONOR'S CHOICE

Perhaps a book like this would not be complete without including a near-death experience in which the person actually met her angel.

At age eighteen, Leonor Reyes married David, who was only a year older. David received his draft notice a month after the wedding and had already reached Vietnam when Leonor began having health problems. She had developed a goiter in her neck that appeared to be malignant.

In February 1969, David's fifth month in Vietnam, his young bride underwent surgery to remove the growth. But during the operation it seemed the anesthesia was wearing off. "Suddenly I began rising, as if sitting up," Leonor wrote. "I could see the part of the operating room toward my feet; I could see my body lying on the table with my neck still open, and my head tilted way back . . . Then I entered a place where there was total light. Others seemed to be around me, and someone at my left said, 'Do not look around or turn back.'"

Leonor obeyed. Gradually she realized that the beings around her were angels. "You are going to meet someone who is very special to you," the being on her left told her. "Do not be anxious. You will be very happy. He is expecting you." Leonor looked down and saw what looked like white clouds, although she couldn't see her feet.

Could I be on my way to see God? she wondered. She felt ashamed at her own unworthiness, yet excited, too. She grew more and more exultant as her journey continued.

Leonor and her celestial companions halted on the bank of a beautiful river with a green meadow beyond it. The angels began to rejoice, and Leonor saw a figure in white coming from among the trees in the distance. It was Jesus! She wanted to run toward him, but the river was dividing them. Jesus walked across the surface of the water toward her, and she was filled with love and wonder.

"I know you have been tired, sick, and worried," he said in the gentlest voice she had ever heard. "Would you like to come and be with me now?"

"Oh, yes!" She reached for his hand, then stopped. "But . . . what about my husband? My mother? If I died now, it would hurt them so much. My husband might even get wounded when he hears the news." Leonor wanted nothing more than to stay with Jesus forever, but something held her back.

The man in white seemed pleased by her concern. "You can see your husband now if you wish," he told her. "Then you have a choice to make. You can come with me, or both of you can come. Or, if you wish, neither of you will come at this time. It will be up to you."

How could Leonor see David? Wasn't Vietnam half a world away? But she remembered that God could do everything, so she turned away. Two angels traveled with her a very long distance through an atmosphere of pure light.

"And there we were, standing behind a tree. One of the angels looked out. 'You see?' he said to me. 'There he is.'"

Leonor looked around the tree, as the angel had done, and saw David lying on his stomach in a bunker on top of a hill next to a fellow soldier. They were engaged in combat with the Viet Cong.

"Remember," the other angel told her, "you must choose."

Leonor thought of how wonderful it would be for her and David to leave this difficult world behind and be with God forever. But she also thought of both their mothers. If Leonor's death would be hard for them to bear, what of a double loss? Perhaps their parents would even doubt God's goodness if both of their youngsters were taken. Leonor didn't want that to happen.

"Quickly!" the angels told her.

"No!" Leonor cried. "No—we cannot hurt our parents this way!" At that very moment, she saw a hand, almost invisible, reach down and cup over a grenade that had landed right next to David. David was safe.

Now Leonor, in the company of many angels, began hurrying on a journey through bright light. She began to grow weary, and beings on each side supported her. "We must hurry if you still want to return," they told her. At that moment, Leonor felt energy running through her body.

"Leonor, wake up, wake up." Someone was calling her name.

"I'm here," she said. "I'm here." She saw two nurses bending over her, talking to each other, but she could not hear what they were saying. "I'm here," she said more loudly, and both looked at her in surprise.

"We were about to give up on you," one said softly.

Leonor's growth had indeed been malignant. But the doctor had performed a total thyroidectomy, and although Leonor had some health problems after her surgery, no signs of cancer ever recurred.

Even more important to this young bride, her husband returned safe and sound from Vietnam. Years later, Leonor asked him if he was ever in a bunker on a hill with another soldier when a grenade fell next to him during combat.

"Only once," David answered. "But the grenade was a dud. Boy, was I glad!"

THE DAY WE SAW THE ANGELS

[Patriarch Tychon] was seized with a kind of ecstasy and overheard the singing of angels, the beauty of which he was afterwards unable to describe; neither could he at the moment grasp the words of that song, but was aware of it only as the harmony of many voices.
—*A Treasury of Russian Spirituality*, G.P. Fedotov, ed.

Perhaps there would be no better way to conclude these stories than with one from Dr. S. Ralph Harlow, who first shared it with readers of *Guideposts* magazine:[22]

It was not Christmas, it was not even wintertime, when the event occurred that for me threw sudden new light on the ancient angel tale. It was a glorious spring morning and we were walking, my wife and I, through the newly budded birches and maples near Ballardvale, Massachusetts.

Now I realize that this, like any account of personal experience, is only as valid as the good sense and honesty of the person relating it. What can I say about myself? That I am a scholar who shuns guesswork and admires scientific investigation? That I have an AB from Harvard, an MA from Columbia, a PhD from Hartford Theological Seminary? That I have never been subject to hallucinations? That attorneys have solicited my testimony and I have testified in the courts, regarded by judge and jury as a faithful reliable witness? All this is true, and yet I doubt any number of credentials can influence the belief or disbelief of another.

In the long run, each of us must sift what comes to us from others through his own life experience, his view of the universe. And so I will simply tell my story.

The little path on which Marion and I walked that May morning was spongy to our steps, and we held hands with the sheer delight of life as we strolled near a lovely brook. It was May, and because it was the examination reading period at Smith College, where I was a professor, we were able to get away for a few days to visit Marion's parents.

We frequently took walks in the country, and we especially loved the spring after a hard New England winter, for it is then that the fields and the woods are radiant and calm yet show new life bursting from the earth. This day we were especially happy and peaceful; we chatted sporadically, with great gaps of satisfying silence between our sentences.

Then from behind us we heard the murmur of muted voices in the distance, and I said to Marion, "We have company in the woods this morning."

Marion nodded and turned to look. We saw nothing, but the voices were coming nearer—at a faster pace than we were walking—and we knew that the strangers would soon overtake us. Then we perceived that the sounds were not only behind us but also above us, and we looked up.

How can I describe what we felt? Is it possible to tell of the surge of exaltation that ran through us? Is it possible to record this phenomenon in objective accuracy and yet be credible?

For about ten feet above us and slightly to our left was a floating group of glorious, beautiful creatures that glowed with spiritual beauty. We stopped and stared as they passed above us.

There were six of them, young beautiful women dressed in flowing white garments and engaged in earnest conversation. If they were aware of our existence, they gave no indication of it. Their faces were perfectly clear to us, and one woman, slightly older than the rest, was especially beautiful. Her dark hair was pulled back in what today we would call a ponytail, and although I cannot say it was bound at the back of her head, it appeared to be. She was talking intently to a younger spirit whose back was toward us and who looked up into the face of the woman who was talking.

Neither Marion nor I could understand their words, although their voices were clearly heard. The sound was somewhat like hearing but being unable to understand a group of people talking outside a house with all the windows and doors shut.

They seemed to float past us, and their graceful motion seemed natural—as gentle and peaceful as the morning itself. As they passed, their conversation grew fainter and fainter until it faded out entirely, and we stood transfixed on the spot, still holding hands and still with the vision before our eyes. It would be an understatement to say we were astounded. Then we looked at each other, each wondering if the other also had seen.

There was a fallen birch tree just there beside the path. We sat down on it and I said, "Marion, what did you see? Tell me exactly, in precise detail. And tell me what you heard."

She knew my intent—to test my own eyes and ears to see if I had been the victim of hallucination or imagination. And her reply was identical in every way to what my own senses had reported to me.

I have related this story with the same faithfulness and respect for truth and accuracy as I would on the witness stand. But even as I record it, I know how incredible it sounds.

Perhaps I can claim no more for it than that it has had a deep effect on our own lives. . . . Since Marion and I began to be aware of the host of heaven all about us, our lives have been filled with a wonderful hope. Phillips Brooks, the great Episcopal bishop, expressed the cause of this hope more beautifully than I can do:

This is what you are to hold fast to yourself—the *sympathy and companionship of the unseen worlds*. No doubt it is best for us now that they should be unseen. It cultivates that higher perception that we call "faith." But who can say that the time will not come when, even to those who live here upon earth, the unseen worlds shall no longer be unseen?

The experience at Ballardvale, added to the convictions of my Christian faith, gives me not only a feeling of assurance about the future but also a sense of adventure toward it.

ANOTHER BEGINNING

I will not wish thee riches nor the glow of greatness,
but that wherever thou go
some weary heart shall gladden at thy smile,
or shadowed life know sunshine for a while.
And so thy path shall be a track of light,
like angels' footsteps passing through the night.
—WORDS ON A CHURCH WALL IN UPWALTHAM, ENGLAND

People in our culture are uncomfortable with the notion of angels in today's world. When we can explain something, we call it a "natural occurrence." But when we cannot explain it, we shrink from labeling it "supernatural." Yet how many of us, in moments when life has seemed most frightening or painful or bewildering, have heard a whisper, felt an invisible hand on our shoulder, or been helped by a stranger who was just like us, and yet, somehow, *not* like us? At times when we have felt abandoned and alone, how many of us have been touched by a mysterious, unexplainable encounter that has given us the courage and the strength we needed to go on?

Why is it necessary to explain such occurrences? Why *wouldn't* a loving God, intimately concerned with his children, send angels *and* humans to do his work?

For what is it that angels do? They bring us good news. They open our eyes to moments of wonder, to lovely possibilities, to exemplary people, to the idea that God is here in our midst. They lift our hearts and give us wings.

We can do that for one another.

Angels minister to us. They sit silently with us as we mourn. They offer us opportunities to turn our suffering into bridges of healing and hope. They challenge us toward new understanding, fresh perspectives.

We can do that for one another.

Angels offer practical help. As we've seen, they furnish information, provide food, buffer the storms of life. Angels lead everyone in the same direction, although not everyone travels at the same speed. But angels are willing to stand by—and wait.

We can do that for one another.

"There is one trouble with full-time angels: they are completely unpredictable and you cannot send out for one," Lee Ballard, the man who met Pug-Pug, reminds us. "That is why part-time angels are so important. Part-time angels like you and me."

Few of us may identify celestial beings during our lifetimes (although I am sure each of us has been touched by them). But we can all be angels to one another. We can choose to obey the still, small stirring within, the little whisper that says, "Go. Ask. Reach out. Be an answer to someone's plea. You have a part to play. Have faith." We can decide to risk that God is indeed there, watching, caring, cherishing us as we love and accept love.

The world will be a better place for it.

And wherever they are, the angels will dance.

New Stories about Angels

"WHERE THE PICTURES CAME FROM"

Angels are seldom overheard. But try.
Go listen.
They might be remembering.
They might be whispering about the night
They seeded the sky with embers
And it caught.
All over the place, the sky took fire.
Astronomers, on various corners of the earth
Reported a shower of burning embers.
This was the night—angels will tell you—
When they clambered over the poles
And raced each other through the tundra,
And swam a hundred mountain lakes,
Shaking the water off like seals,
And kept on going.
They knew they were wanted.
It had to be night, they'll tell you,
Because night is so simple, so all one thing,
Even when burnt with embers.

And God had poured himself so flawlessly
Into a human heart
That nothing less simple than night
Could venture an explanation.
The angels got there, they will tell you.
They ran up the hill singing a song the color of darkness,
Chanting like sea bells
In places of no horizon.
They stood in a circle on the floor of a cave,
And drew pictures on its walls
To entertain the visitors.
And rocked in their song
An infant of one hour's age
Who was as old as God.
—SISTER MIRIAM POLLARD, OCSO

ANGEL OF VIETNAM

❧

"For I know the plans I have for you," declares the Lord, "plans to prosper
you and not to harm you, plans to give you hope and a future."
—JEREMIAH 29:11

Hello, friends. I am always writing stories about other people, so I thought you might like to read one about our family.

In the late 1960s, as my husband and I were raising four sons, television news was filled with devastating reports of the war in Vietnam. My heart especially reached out to the children in that faraway country. My husband is a Korean War veteran, and we had always felt drawn to cultures from that region of the world known generally as Asia. Now, with little possibility for another child of our own, I dared to hope that a Vietnamese child waited for us. The daughter I'd always wanted! I'd seen a story about a humanitarian group that rescued children from Vietnam, so I phoned the group's office. The woman who answered refused to take my application.

"You couldn't be considered as adoptive parents," she explained. "You have four children. An orphan saved from a war-torn country would go to a couple without any children."

Of course. Wasn't I being selfish, wanting another baby when I had been so blessed already? And yet there was a nagging in my heart. I called other agencies, but the response was the same. Sadly, I hung up after the last lead. God must be saying no. Perhaps he had another plan. After all, the little girl I envisioned was only a product of my imagination. "But just in case," I murmured, "let an angel in Vietnam watch over her."

A few years later, I gave birth to a healthy baby daughter. I was overjoyed. My heart settled. God had given me the girl who'd been missing from our family. He'd had other plans after all. We quickly adapted to life with our new brood of five. Meanwhile, the war in Vietnam raged on.

By April 1975, the Americans were pulling out of the country. Operation Babylift was under way, and military planes were scheduled to rescue and fly several thousand children to the United States. I watched television each night as vast throngs, mostly women and children, flooded the highways in Saigon in an attempt to flee the conquering North Vietnamese. Buses, tanks, and broken-down trucks carried hundreds of people, all hoping to reach a US helicopter that would fly them to safety. Thousands more fled on foot, without possessions, water, or food, dodging bullets as they went. Desperate mothers passed their babies over barbed wire to strangers at the American embassy—would they ever find their children again? By month's end, the fall of Saigon was complete. It seemed as if even the angels had left.

I couldn't get those desperate pictures out of my mind, and that familiar nagging feeling returned. If America had airlifted so many children here to the United States, wouldn't they need homes?

"Dear God," I asked one morning, "was my timing off all those years ago? Is there a little girl out there who needs us now?"

"Our first job is to find foster homes for these children while we try to locate their relatives," a social worker explained. Then she paused. I knew what was coming. "However," she said, "your family is far too large to be considered for placement."

Her rejection stung. Still, it was time to concentrate on the treasures I already had, time to give up the dream. "Good-bye, little girl," I said in my heart. "May your angel keep you safe."

Years passed, and our children grew, left home, and became independent. Our third son, who had learned martial arts at an early age, spent a year teaching in Japan as well as visiting China and Korea. I was not surprised when he announced that he was bringing a girl from an Asian family home to meet us.

Anh was lovely, and we liked her right away. But it wasn't until our second or third evening together that I had the chance to ask about her life. "My father is from Korea," she explained. "When he was on a business trip to Vietnam, he met my mother. They eventually got married there, and my two older brothers and I were born there."

A funny tingling started at the back of my neck as I quickly calculated the years. "That must have been during the war," I said.

"Oh yes," Anh said. "I was only two when we escaped. My father was stranded in another country and couldn't help us. It was during the fall of Saigon."

Shivers ran up my spine. Those televised news reports from all those years ago—could I have seen Anh's mother, one of those struggling to save her children? "How did you escape?" I asked.

"It was amazing," Anh explained. "My mother saw a man in the shadows, watching as people tried to cross the one narrow gangplank to board a boat. It was impossible for her to carry me and my two brothers. She asked this stranger if he would take the boys and somehow get them on the boat. Mother prayed she had done the right thing."

"And then?"

"She was afraid of heights, and the gangplank was little more than a heavy rope. It swayed back and forth as she took one small step after another. The people on the boat were watching, expecting us to fall into the water. My mother was terrified. But when she stumbled into the boat, my brothers were already there!"

"But . . ." I was confused. "How could the stranger have gotten across the gang-plank without being seen?"

"We never knew," Anh said. "No one remembers him."

Tears stung my eyes. The angels had not left Vietnam. They had worked their quiet miracles in the midst of devastation, just as they do in every disaster. And there was at least one angel on special assignment, the one I had sent so long ago to watch over a little girl. This girl. God had known how good it would be for Anh and her family to be "adopted" by a welcoming community in Texas. It was there that she grew to be the confident and charming young woman who would become a won-derful wife to our son. My Vietnamese daughter hadn't been a dream after all, and God hadn't said no. It had simply taken twenty-eight years for me to understand how he'd answered my prayer.

I didn't mind. Some things are worth waiting for.

SUSAN'S STORY

❧

How great are his signs, and how mighty are his wonders!
—DANIEL 4:3

Susan comes from a rural town in southeastern Alabama. All her life she has gone to church, but it's been more of a habit than anything else. "I would see my parents praying about things and trusting God, but I never got that close to him," she says. "I believed in him and that Jesus came to Earth and died for me, but I wasn't ready to give my whole heart to him."

Susan had suffered for years from anorexia. It started when she was fourteen, and by the time she was twenty-five, she weighed only eighty-four pounds. She was in and out of therapy and even force-fed, but nothing helped. Going out in public, when she was able, was a nightmare. "People would yell out, 'Hey, AIDS girl' and things like that," she says. "I couldn't believe the cruelty. Eventually I became housebound, mostly due to my health, and when I got the news that my kidneys were failing, I refused all further treatment and prayed that God would help me. I told him that if he would help me, then I would live for him. I didn't really think I would die because I always pulled through before."

That night Susan woke up trying to breathe. She couldn't. Shaking violently and so sick that she could barely move, she still assumed that she wouldn't die. The doctors were about to put her on dialysis, and perhaps the treatments would help. But Susan realized then that she was leaving her body.

"I didn't go through a tunnel—just kind of floated around," Susan says. "Before I knew it, I was in heaven. I knew it was heaven because I had never smelled flowers like that before and had never seen so much beauty."

Then Susan saw her grandmother. She had been seventy-five when she died, but now she looked to be about thirty. And there was Susan's grandpa. He had died when he was ninety-two, and she had never had a real relationship with him due to their age difference. But it was definitely her grandpa. "He kept saying to me, 'Look what I can do!'" Susan says. "He was walking on his hands, but I didn't understand this or why he was showing me that he could do it."

Then her grandmother asked Susan if she wanted to see Jesus. Susan literally screamed, "Yes!"

"The second I saw him, I started to cry," she says. "I could feel his compassion for me. He comforted me as I told him how I had been wronged by people on Earth because of my condition and how I had suffered with anorexia." He was so kind, she says. He told her that he knew about all her difficulties and that everything was going to be all right.

"Do you promise?" Susan asked. Jesus agreed.

"Then I told him something that maybe I shouldn't have," she admits. "He was about five feet nine and probably weighed about 150 pounds. He was slim, with dark brown hair and brown eyes. I said to him, 'You are a very handsome man.' He just laughed. Then I laughed. It was such a great time!"

Many people and angels were around Jesus, but Susan was able to go right to him and talk to him. "It's not like it would be here," she explains. "You can't just go up to someone that important and talk to them. But with Jesus you can."

Along with the people, Susan saw all the pets she had had as a child: dogs and even her favorite parakeets. "They had a caretaker, a man who took care of all the animals. So if anyone ever asks me if animals survive death, I'll have to say yes!"

Susan was told to go back to the earth and tell everyone what she had seen. She said she would, and Jesus hugged her. It felt like a million volts of electricity going through her body. Nor could she stand up because of the intense power she felt coming from him. Then she began to fall, so fast that she was literally slammed back into her body on the bed, so hard that she sat up, shocked. *Out of his presence, back where everyone is so cruel.* She could still feel the electricity coursing through her body. Once again, she was very sick.

The next morning when Susan awakened, however, she realized that something monumental had taken place. For the first time in eleven years she ate a full meal, not having any of the anorexic impulses she'd always had before. Later she went to her doctor's appointment. He was stunned at Susan's news. He examined her, took some tests, and phoned a few days later.

"You have healthy kidneys," he told her. "No sign of failure or disease, and no medical reason for your kidneys to be normal." He couldn't explain it, because anorexia rarely heals on its own. But Susan knew why.

"Jesus touched me, my soul and body, and healed me," she says. "The next time the doctor saw me, I had gained about fifteen pounds. Now, nine years later, I weigh about 135 pounds. I have never had any kidney problems or any other kind of health problems that anorexia can cause. I am fine. I am healthy. And I will *never* forget seeing Jesus. I can't even think of him today without crying. I feel so special to have been touched by him and being able to talk to him."

Susan was so shaken by her out-of-body meeting with Jesus that she found it impossible to tell others about it, at least for a few years. And when she did attempt to explain it to her mother, her mother did not believe it.

Susan was frustrated. Did her mother think she would lie, especially about something so important? Again she insisted that she had met her grandfather, and he had demonstrated his talent for walking on his hands. "My mother's face went white. I asked her what was wrong."

"When your grandfather was a teenager, he used to do that to impress people," Susan's mother said. "He was very good at it and enjoyed showing off. You must have heard about that from someone in the family."

"No, I never heard about that from anyone," Susan said. "Grandpa was very old when I was born, and I knew nothing about him when he was a child. So how would I know that he could walk on his hands?"

Susan's life continues to be one of good health, service, and commitment to Jesus. "I live in such a way that if I were to die, heaven would be my home," she says. It's a wonderful goal, for anyone.

O HOLY NIGHT

*We will discover on reaching heaven that God's angels are not strangers
but old friends who have known all about us from the day of our birth
to the hour of our death.*
—NORMAN MACLEOD, POET

Where there once was an extended family ready and able to care for them, many older relatives today live alone, vulnerable and lonely. It's a perfect situation for an angel's reassuring touch.

"It was a bizarre version of the Christmas story," observes eighty-seven-year-old Albert Leo of Ontario, California. "We were visited, not by the three wise men bearing gifts, but by three robbers bent on financing their own holiday sprees." On that twenty-third of December, Albert and his wife, Georgie, age eighty-three, went to bed, as always, asking angels to watch over them. (Albert, a retired scientist, sometimes doubts their existence or purpose but has no real reason to object.) A few hours later, Albert awoke abruptly. He was sleeping with his "good ear" in the pillow and should have been difficult to rouse, but tonight he came awake quickly and with a sense that something in the house needed his attention.

At about the same time, Georgie's chairlift started to beep. As the couple would later discover, the would-be robbers had discovered the house's main electrical box and turned off all the power, hoping to disable any alarms in the house. Unfortunately for the burglars, the exact opposite had been arranged; whenever the power failed, Georgie's chair (on its own battery) was programmed to beep. And so it did, loud and insistent.

By now, two of the robbers were disconnecting the couple's plasma television while the third wondered why the break-in had seemed like such a good idea. They could hear Albert's footsteps as he checked out the upstairs den and, finding nothing, made his way to the top of the stairs. "Let's go!" The men ran for the front door, which had been left open, and Albert heard a car revving up in the driveway. Seconds later, it sped out of the drive and down the street.

It took a little while for Albert's heart to stop racing, but when his next-door neighbor stopped by to reassure him, Albert started to see an angel's fine hand (wing?) in the entire episode. For wasn't the timing of the break-in perfect? Albert's angel had awakened him at the very last minute, without enough time to go downstairs and get involved in something dangerous. What would have happened if he did confront the burglars? How could he have protected Georgie or called 911 if events had escalated?

In another "coincidence," their neighbor happened to be up late that night. He witnessed the fleeing suspects and helped the police quickly apprehend two of them and even retrieve the plasma television.

Albert and Georgie had much to be thankful for as they hosted their extended family. Occasionally they had worried about being protected, but now they saw there was no need. "We have learned to accept the frailties that accompany a long life," says Albert, "but we have not given in to them." And perhaps, with angels surrounding them, they never will.

WHERE ARE THE CHILDREN?

See that you never despise one of these little ones. I assure you, their
angels in heaven constantly behold my heavenly father's face.
—MATTHEW 18:10

It's not as sensational as some stories," Kathy Cruise says, "but there are so many feelings wrapped up in it." She is talking about an experience that her family had while visiting Kathy's grandmother in Buffalo, Wyoming, one summer. "My mother grew up in Buffalo," Kathy says, "and Kevin and I wanted our three sons to experience some of the same things I had known as a child." So the family planned a fun adventure, driving from their home in Nebraska to Wyoming. The boys, Kolby, Kaleb, and Kasten, ages ten, eight, and three, respectively, could hardly wait.

There was another reason the Cruise family needed a vacation. "Kevin had a very stressful matter going on at work," Kathy says. "And both of us had been tense over buying a house and other family projects. We really needed to get away for a while, but as we had discovered, driving a thousand miles in a van with three children does not relieve stress."

By the time they reached Kathy's grandmother's house, everyone was exhausted. And although the next day dawned bright and inviting, Kathy and Kevin would have preferred to stay home and nap. But they had promised the boys some sightseeing, and Kathy remembered a lake area where they could picnic. "I was sure that the lake was quite close," she says, "but after driving thirty miles, we were all hungry and crabby and still had not found it."

The stress had finally caught up with them. "Kevin and I had a terrible argument after driving so long and not reaching our destination," Kathy says. "I am pretty stubborn and refused to speak to him while we turned around and headed back down the mountain."

They pulled into the first picnic area they found so they could eat. It was a camping area in the Bighorn Mountains, heavily wooded with a creek running through it. Kolby and Kaleb leaped out of the van and ran toward a nearby hill. "We're not coming down until you start talking to each other," Kolby shouted.

Kathy ignored them, still miffed. In her anger, she did not think to caution them about their unfamiliar surroundings or the safety measures hikers recommend. Instead, she fed Kasten and sat in silence, waiting for Kolby and Kaleb to come back and have lunch. She knew she should apologize to her husband, but her pride just wouldn't let her.

Then, out of the blue, she heard a stern voice. "Aren't you going to look for your kids?" She looked around. Nothing, and no one, anywhere.

At the same time, Kevin spoke. "We should call the kids." Kathy ignored him, too. The stern voice spoke again. "Your children are lost."

What was the matter with her? Kathy's anger abruptly stopped. Her children were missing, and she had no idea about where to find them!

Kevin started to call them, then climbed up the hill where the boys had gone. Kathy followed him, but she was carrying her three-year-old, and as they climbed higher, they reached boulders and brush that threw them off course. "I couldn't go any farther with Kasten," Kathy says, "but I continued to call." But when Kevin reached the top of the hill, he was shocked. There were trees as far as they could see, in all directions. And nothing else.

They needed help, immediately. Kathy stumbled down the hill. There was no phone service, she realized belatedly, and they hadn't seen any people either. It was as if they were the only ones on earth. Heartsick at her own carelessness, Kathy prayed as she had never done before. "I begged Jesus, Mary, and Joseph to help us. And then I called on Saint Anthony, patron of lost things."

It had been nearly two hours since the boys had vanished—and Kathy and Kevin had seen no one during this time—when suddenly two small figures appeared about half a mile away from the camping area. One was waving his arms, and both seemed to be crying. It had to be . . . Yes! Kathy and Kevin shouted with joy.

"I'll never forget the looks on their faces," Kathy says. "Kaleb ran to us, crying, and Kolby was as white as a sheet. They hadn't had anything to drink since that morning at breakfast, and their lips were parched. But they were alive!"

The boys described the near tragedy in specific terms. They had climbed to the top of the hill and walked for a while. But they had soon lost their bearings because everything looked the same. Kaleb thought that Kolby might be leading him in the wrong direction, and Kolby cried because he was so hungry. Both boys thought they would probably die there on the mountaintop, so they knelt in the leaves and prayed. Then, as they finished, Kaleb looked up. There, just a few yards away from them, stood a deer. "Kolby, look!" Kaleb whispered.

Kolby was entranced. The deer's soft brown eyes seemed to be telling him that everything would be all right. For a moment, they all stood motionless, and then the deer turned quietly, eyes still upon Kolby, and set off on what appeared to be a path. The boys followed as closely as they could manage without frightening the deer away. Soon they heard the soft ripple of water. The creek! They had not been very far from it earlier. Was it nearby?

The deer had increased its speed, and it then ran gracefully into the forest and disappeared. But before the boys again began to cry, Kolby heard the faint sound they most needed to hear: their names being called. They had followed the creek around the mountain, which led them back to their parents. They were safe.

"There is no doubt in my mind that the deer was an angel, sent to lead them to safety," says Kathy. Perhaps the stern voice was also connected in some way. The family might never know. "But the experience made us realize how we sometimes take our children for granted," says Kathy. "It makes us shudder to think of how this might have turned out."

The family spent the rest of the day playing miniature golf, eating ice cream, and hugging one another. That evening when they went to Mass. Father's homily was about being lost and then being found. Kathy cried all the way through it. Tears of joy.

ANGELS UNAWARE

Do not forget to entertain strangers, for by so doing, some people have entertained angels without knowing it.
—HEBREWS 13:2

James Raffan, a miner in a small town in southern Alberta, Canada, experienced a Christmas event he'll never forget. "At the time I was dating a girl from a nearby town, and I was at her house on Christmas Eve, goofing around and opening presents with her family," James says. "About midnight, it was time for me to drive the twenty miles back home." James warmed up his mother's car, which he had borrowed for the occasion, and got on the road quickly.

The night was cold, the road deserted. James was looking forward to getting home and into bed. About seven miles into his journey, he came through a covered bridge and passed a hitchhiker.

"He didn't have much on, just a jean jacket and blue jeans," James reports, "and it was so cold that I had to stop." The man approached James's car. He looked to be in his midthirties, had dark, curly hair, and was in need of a shave. "When he got in the car, I caught a whiff of booze but not really overpowering," says James. "He kind of struck me as a guy just down on his luck."

The two introduced themselves, and James headed for the next major town, where he lived. Silence descended for a few minutes; then James couldn't resist asking the obvious question: "How come you're out hitchhiking on Christmas Eve?"

"Well, I had a big fight with my wife, and I took off," the man explained. "We just got married here two weeks ago, and I guess it was a little much for me, and I ran out on her. But now all I want to do is be with her on Christmas. I called her and told her I was sorry and was coming home to be with her. I got no money, so I have to hitchhike."

"Where is she?" James asked.

"She's in Winnipeg. I ain't gonna be there by tomorrow at this rate."

Winnipeg—it was almost a thousand miles away. It could easily take the man a week to hitchhike that distance. James thought hard. "If I could get you a bus ticket to Winnipeg, would you use it to get home?" he finally asked.

"Really, man?" The hitchhiker turned to him. "Could you do that? I mean, that would be the greatest. Of course I would go home; it would be the best Christmas. Her parents are supposed to be coming into town to be with her. I could see them again and, you know, make up for leaving like I did."

He seemed pretty excited, James noticed. And, coincidentally, James's father owned a small truck stop in town, which was the Greyhound bus depot for the area. Further, James often worked late at the truck stop and had a set of keys. "We talked a little bit more and eventually pulled into the station. I unlocked the door, and we both went in. It didn't take more than ten minutes to fill out the ticket. We grabbed some goodies for him to eat while he waited for the bus and headed back outside."

It was snowing now. James took the hitchhiker over to the old pickup that he kept at the store. "You can run the pickup to keep warm," James told him. "The express bus should be here at 3:30 a.m. It will be heading straight through to Regina, then Winnipeg, and you should be there by about 6:30 p.m."

The stranger smiled. "Thank you," he said simply.

"Do you need anything else before I leave?"

"No, thanks. Merry Christmas."

"You too." The men shook hands, and James walked back to the store to lock it. When he turned around, just a few seconds later, he noticed that the pickup wasn't running. Maybe the hitchhiker was having difficulty starting it. James walked back and looked inside. There was no one there.

"Initially I was worried," James says. "I thought that maybe he'd had more to drink than I suspected, and he could die in weather this cold." But as James looked around the wide-open expanse of driveway and buildings, the newly fallen snow covering everything, he realized that no one could have disappeared that quickly. And where were the stranger's footprints? The snow was still undisturbed except for James's own footprints.

A few days later, James spoke with the bus driver on the Winnipeg route. "He told me that he hadn't picked anyone up at our stop on Christmas Eve," James says. "And the ticket was never used."

James has no reasonable explanation for this experience. "There were no heavenly hosts openly proclaiming an unfathomable truth," he says, "but instead, a kind of encouragement to continue. Maybe these experiences are God's way of supporting us in our choice to believe."

WILLOW'S MYSTERY

Suddenly an angel of the Lord appeared and a light shone in the cell. He struck Peter on the side and woke him up. "Quick, get up!" he said, and the chains fell off Peter's wrists.

—ACTS 12:7

Willow Hale is a professional actress and songwriter. She's very versatile. She loves what she does, even though she occasionally suffers small temporary strokes, called transient ischemic attacks. These can be frightening but usually end within a few hours. Willow copes and depends upon the angels to watch over her.

Two years ago, she was hired to work a home show at the Los Angeles Convention Center. At the same time, auditions were being held nearby for Shakespeare's *Twelfth Night* production, and Willow wished she had time to try out for a part in that.

Instead, that morning at the convention center she suffered a small stroke and had to leave her booth to stay in her car and rest. "People working around the booth watched my things," she says, "and of course I gave up all thoughts of trying to get to the audition—I just let it go in prayer." Gradually she recovered and was able to finish out the day at the center.

About a month later, Willow received an email inviting her to read for a Shakespeare play. Willow assumed it was another production from another company, not *Twelfth Night*. But when she arrived, the director smiled in recognition and greeted her by name. "When we sat and introduced ourselves and read," Willow says, "it was clear that I had been at this audition—everyone had seen me—and I had done a good enough job to be asked to be part of the company!" When Willow mentioned that she had been ill and not able to make it that day, everyone looked at her as if she was confused. "The director had my résumé and photo, too," Willow says. "How could that have happened?"

Perhaps Willow's medical condition was severe enough for her to be unaware of what she did for that entire day! Or did Willow's guardian angel assume her own appearance, go in her place to an audition, even read Shakespeare well enough for Willow to get a part?

Such a thing seems utterly impossible—until we look at an encounter Saint Peter had with an angel after Christ's death and resurrection. Peter had been arrested, but an angel came one evening, undid his chains, and led him out of the prison. When Peter entered the house where Christ's supporters were staying, more than one assumed that the newcomer was Peter's angel, not Peter himself. In the early days, it was often thought that one's angel resembled the person. That could be the explanation for Willow's mysterious experience.

Perhaps. Either way, angels are near.

10 Percent Solution

Each of you should give what you have decided in your heart to give,
not reluctantly or under compulsion, for God loves a cheerful giver.
—2 Corinthians 9:7

Harriet Cimock grew up in a small Iowa town, working alongside her husband and raising five children. Harriet had many interests, but she loved collecting (especially butterflies) and shopping garage sales. She spent a lot of time making rosaries and baby blankets to give to those who needed them. Hers was a rich and full life until she was diagnosed with inflammatory breast cancer, an especially quick-spreading type. Chemotherapy was started immediately.

Back in Illinois, as Harriet's daughter Jo Pabon and her sisters struggled to handle their fear, a strange situation developed. Jo began to find dimes. "Not quarters, nickels, or pennies, but dimes. Dimes in unusual places: peeking out from under a baseboard, in the back of a dusty broom closet, in the shower! It became almost comical." Jo told her good friend Vicki about it, and Vicki started finding dimes too. "We joked about where we had found them, and somehow the dime would turn the day into a good one."

In October, Jo went to Iowa to be with her mother. Harriet was not doing well. No amount of chemo seemed to stem the rapidly spreading cancer, but she kept her hopeful attitude. One day, Jo accompanied Harriet to chemotherapy, and after Harriet stood up from the chair, they both saw it where she had been sitting: a dime.

When Jo returned home, the dime discoveries continued: in a forgotten coat pocket, a taxi, a store parking lot. Surely the law of averages would have intruded by now. How could all these "found" coins be dimes? But they were.

Jo couldn't help wondering what the purpose of it was. She longed to turn it all into a sign, something to reassure her that her mother would have many healthy years ahead. But Harriet's decline continued. She died just five months after her diagnosis.

"Her service at their country church was beautiful," Jo says. "She had planned everything in advance, from the music to her obituary, and her memorial was filled with butterflies. Afterward, we were taking funeral flowers back to the house, and I lifted up a big vase. Under it was a dime."

Back at the house, the family received another surprise. The siblings began to sort through Harriet's treasure trove of garage-sale finds, and Jo discovered a clear plastic piggy bank. It was stuffed to the top—with dimes. "My brother mentioned that he had given my mom a bank several years earlier, and he went to the bedroom to find it," Jo says. "He returned and turned it over on the tabletop. We could not believe our eyes as the dimes started pouring out!"

Jo returned to Illinois, trying to accept the suddenness of this great loss. Her mother had lived a healthy life—why her? Strangely, the only consolation the family could muster was the fact that they were now *all* finding dimes. "The kids found them in their school classrooms, at baseball games, on planes," says Jo. "I have found them while digging in the garden and even under the dog when he got up." Once, at the grocery store, one dime was left on the conveyer belt as Jo began unloading her cart. "And of course, the lifesaving dime from my nephew, from when he was waiting at a busy intersection to cross the street," Jo recalls. "The light changed, and he started to go. Just then, he spotted a dime. Knowing Grandma's story, he bent over and picked it up. Right then a car ran a red light and came flying through the intersection. Had my nephew not stopped to pick up that dime, it could have been a very bad outcome."

Surprisingly, many people report finding dimes in this way, and they do seem to appear more frequently during times of sorrow or stress. But there is no scientific explanation. "They remind me of little bread crumbs along life's journey," Jo says. Perhaps the best reaction is simply to enjoy them.

One day, Jo was searching for breast-cancer awareness items on the Internet. She came across a picture of a pink breast-cancer pin. Next to it in the photo was a dime! The ad said that the dime was in the picture to show the size of the pin. "That was a lightbulb moment for me," Jo says. "It was not right that we would save our dimes and sit around and look at the pile. We were to pass them on for a good cause, and what better cause than breast-cancer research and awareness?"

Today Jo and her family have a special jar in the kitchen, and her family knows just where to put the dimes they continue to find. (Her nine-year-old son even cashed in his $25 savings account, in dimes, and added them to the jar.) Their friends and neighbors contribute too. When the jar is filled, they change the dimes into a check and send it to the Inflammatory Breast Cancer Research Foundation, in memory of Harriet.

"I have two beautiful reminders of my mom," Jo says, "every time I see a butterfly and every time I find a dime. Or should I say, a dime finds me?" She knows there will be more coming their way.

If you would like to learn more about the IBCRF, visit *http://www.ibcresearch.org*.

More about dimes

From Dee: My family finds dimes from heaven at times of transition and difficult choices. We believe they come from Nanny, my maternal grandmother. We find them under things, on things, in things. We call them "Nanny dimes" and know that she (and perhaps others who are with her on the Other Side) sends them to let us know that we are never alone.

From Annette: My boyfriend kept telling me he was finding dimes in the strangest places. At first, I really thought nothing of it, until one day he was putting his shoes on for work and there was a dime in his shoe. After that, I, too, started noticing dimes in the weirdest places. I would vacuum the living room, then turn around to find a dime right in the middle of the floor, face up.

From Monica: When my eight-year-old autistic son had an AVM (a brain bleed), I didn't think he was going to make it. He was flown to the hospital, and with the grace of God and the wonderful staff, he pulled through. As I was sitting with my son in his room, I was telling my husband about a story I had read earlier that day about dimes from heaven. My son was lying in his bed with a feeding tube in, and he made a sound, so I got up and walked over to his bed, and lo and behold, there was a dime on the floor. I took comfort at that moment that I was not alone in this journey with my son. God was right beside me. For the next year, during my son's recovery, I would find dimes and smile, and know God was with me the whole time.

MIRACLE IN MISSOURI

❦

I can feel the brush of angels' wings, there is glory on each face.
—LANNY WOLFE, COMPOSER

Lord, we pray that angels surround Katie as she travels today." It was a simple prayer recited whenever a member of the Lentz family was on the road. On Sunday, August 4, 2013, everything seemed routine. Nineteen-year-old Katie Lentz prayed with her parents, then pulled out of the driveway in her ancient Mercedes convertible. She was driving from her parents' home in Quincy, Illinois, to Jefferson City, Missouri, where she had just finished a summer internship and was planning a few days with friends before returning to classes at Tulane University in New Orleans.

Shortly before 9 a.m. deputy sheriff Richard Adair received a call reporting a head-on collision on Highway 19. He sped to the scene and discovered that a drunk driver had crossed the center line and totaled a big Mercedes, flipping it onto the driver's side. The Mercedes was registered to Katie Lentz, and the sheriff originally had little hope that the young woman had survived the crash. As first responders began to arrive, they too realized the gravity of the situation. All anyone could see was the top of Katie's head and her right hand. She was stuck inside the wreckage, almost upside down, her cheek on the pavement and the steering column pushed into her stomach. Sheriff Adair leaned over.

"We're going to get you out," he promised, hoping he wasn't giving her false hope.

No. She had something else on her mind.

"Officer," he heard her say, "will you please call my mother?"

Father Patrick Dowling, a Catholic priest originally from Ireland, was on his way home from saying Sunday Mass for a congregation whose priest was ill. Up ahead on Highway 19 he saw the commotion, the rescue vehicles, and the worst sign of all: a wrecked carcass of a convertible lying on its side. How could anyone inside still be alive? Father works in a prison ministry and is deeply spiritual and normally quite reserved, but he felt compelled to help. Authorities were blocking the highway, telling drivers to turn around and find another way out. Father waited until all the cars were gone, then parked and headed for Sheriff Adair.

Despite the arrival of rescue vehicles and trained personnel, no one could get Katie out of the car. The Mercedes's frame was so sturdy that the equipment used in most accidents couldn't tear it apart. First responders had kept Katie conscious and talking, but her blood pressure and heart rate were starting to sink. They had to get her out soon! But to do that, they would have to lift the Mercedes and turn it right side up so they could reach her—a very dangerous maneuver. They needed better equipment.

Father Dowling had reached the sheriff. "Would it be all right if I anoint that young woman?" he asked.

Sheriff Adair hesitated. Wouldn't Katie assume people were giving up on her if she thought that a priest had been called? And yet, she seemed surprisingly calm.

"If I had not been clinging to my faith during those most desperate moments, I do not believe I would have survived," Katie says today. She had been praying alone, but her strength was ebbing and she needed others to support her. She then asked the men to pray too. "Out loud!" she added. Father went quietly to the mangled vehicle, reached down to anoint Katie and give her absolution. (The fact that Katie belonged to an Assemblies of God congregation was of no consequence: prayer is prayer.) He then started to move away. But Katie called him back. "Father, can you pray that my leg stops hurting?" she asked. What an amazing girl, still holding on. Father looked around, concerned that he might be in the way, but it was obvious that the men nearby were discouraged and worried.

"So I prayed again," he says, and then he stepped away to say a silent rosary.

Suddenly one of the rescuers experienced an unusual peacefulness that seemed to cover the area like a mantle. He caught the eye of another firefighter. Both men "very plainly heard that we should remain calm, that our tools would work now and that we would get her out of that vehicle." Was this a real voice or an emotional response to the scene? The men could only describe later what both of them heard.

Almost immediately, the local fire department arrived, bringing heavier equipment, and lost no time turning the Mercedes right side up. One of the workers was finally able to crawl inside and brace Katie. Soon a helicopter arrived to airlift her. Everyone watched as the plane soared over miles of cornfields on its way to Blessing Hospital in Quincy. Thank God this ordeal was finished. Sheriff Adair turned around to thank Father Dowling and realized that the priest had disappeared. Not unusual, he thought. And yet there had been something odd about today's events:

- A priest just happens along at a critical moment, on a route he rarely travels. Why didn't anyone see where he came from? Why didn't anyone see him leave? Over sixty photographs were taken at the scene. Why did he not appear in any of them?

- This is a close-knit community, and yet no one who saw the priest knew him.

- The two rescue workers heard a human voice promising that all would now be well. No one came forward to affirm that message. What ordinary mortal would know the outcome? And yet, the voice had been correct.

The men looked at one another, the same question on every face. Could the priest have been an angel in disguise?

Twenty-five years ago, such a possibility would be laughed off; angels didn't appear to ordinary people, did they? But since 1992, when the first contemporary popular books on angels appeared, information about the heavenly hosts has been growing. Today the veil between heaven and earth seems thinner than ever before, and anything seems possible. As word of these unusual happenings spread, people everywhere were caught up in the story. Where was the priest?

Some four days later, Father Dowling surfaced. He hadn't expected to be noticed; in fact, it was only after he mentioned the event to a colleague that he learned of the public's interest in finding him. He wrote a letter to the local paper explaining his role, hoping that would put an end to requests for interviews. He had done nothing out of the ordinary, he felt. Nor could he explain the occasional mystery in the story—the "voice" and its predictions, for example. But questions continued. Obviously God was working his will in the world, so Father Dowling accepted his role.

Katie had arrived at the hospital with fifteen broken bones, a lacerated liver, bruised lungs, and a ruptured spleen. According to her doctors, she should have been brain-dead. Instead, she spent five weeks in the hospital and fourteen months in rehab. "People were praying for me," she says, "so I needed to keep going." Despite the difficulties, she and her family remained surprisingly happy. "We all believe that God gave us divine joy during that time," she says. "I was alive and would recover—why wouldn't we celebrate? What the enemy had planned for evil, God intended for good."

Life has settled since that turbulent time. Katie made a complete recovery and has no physical limitations. She graduated from Tulane University in spring 2016, with a BS in public health. Father Dowling continues his quiet ministry in Jefferson City, and heroic rescue teams still answer emergency calls. If anything has changed among the people here, it may be a new awareness of angelic presence, a deepening of faith. For, despite our attempts, not every angel question has an answer. People are sometimes left with doubts as well as wonder, questions of logistics and timing that require a suspension of ordinary beliefs. But from the very beginning of her journey, Katie's family had placed her under the protection of angels—perhaps an extra layer of protection. And those who played a role in her rescue came to realize that by their shared prayers, they made a miracle. The details can wait until eternity.

As one of the rescuers put it, "Whether it was an angel that was sent to us in the form of a priest, or a priest that became our angel, either way I'm good with it." So are we all.

MY TWENTY-FIVE YEARS
WITH THE ANGELS

In 1973, I began a freelance writing career on our kitchen table, surrounded by my young family, orthodontia bills, and an idea for a newspaper article. Amazingly, the article sold for the princely sum of twenty-five dollars, which allowed the kids and me to purchase paint to upgrade our "handyman's special" house. A second sale provided some patio chairs (in case we ever got a patio), along with the realization that I had found my niche! (Although I collected twelve rejection slips before selling a third piece, the die was definitely cast.) For the next several years, I juggled family, home, and the lecture circuit along with columns, magazine assignments, and an occasional humor or how-to book. My husband wore a path from our house to the airport, doing chauffeur duty and learning to iron clothes. The kids gradually left home. (See books about our family listed in the front of this book.) By 1990 I was ready for a new career path, but one final project loomed: *Where Angels Walk*.

Where Angels Walk was like nothing I had ever contemplated: a collection of true stories about people who believed that they had been blessed by an angel, that for a moment heaven and earth had connected in a miraculous way. My own son's mysterious rescue one memorable Christmas Eve had been the catalyst. But I had a massive case of writer's block. Angels seemed to have been on hiatus since the 1940s, and entire generations had missed hearing about them. Why devote at least a year of my life to research if there was no interest in this topic? Would the book be taken seriously by an increasingly secular society? And what did God (my agent) think about it all? Since I rarely took a risk without knowing the outcome, these were important considerations.

The next time I checked the mailbox, there was a little package there, sent from a fellow writer in Canada. This was odd. She and I had never exchanged gifts. I opened the box and gasped: there was an angel statue, chin in hands, looking somewhat puzzled, just the way I felt. "Don't ask me why," read my friend's brief note. "I saw her at a yard sale and knew you had to have her." I stared at the angel while the hairs on the back of my neck stood up. My Canadian friend had not known I was thinking about writing a book about angels. She and I had never discussed angels . . .

Well, I had needed a sign, and she had stepped out in faith to deliver it. During the next year, I followed every lead and stumbled across a willing publisher; a national organization devoted to the collection of angels (who knew?); and, most important, nice ordinary people who had experienced what they considered encounters with angels. Some were hesitant to let me use their names, for fear of ridicule. But I insisted on full disclosure for the book to be taken seriously, and eventually they agreed. I also wondered how I could be sure that these events actually happened. There was no need to prove angelic intervention—only God could do that. But the facts themselves had to be verified. I prayed, asking the Holy Spirit for the gift of discernment so that every word would be true. And still I fretted. Was this emerging manuscript good enough? Would the angels be pleased?

One evening at my prayer group, we hosted some out-of-town teens who had a healing ministry. We were invited to approach one or two of them and be prayed over. It was a bit different—teenagers praying over adults—but my pair started in the usual way, and then both paused almost immediately. Was I working on a spiritual project? one asked. Something that was causing me anxiety? Unexpected tears filled my eyes.

"God is asking you to get out of his way," the second young man added kindly. "Everything is taken care of. Be at peace."

A reassuring message. But what could be "taken care of" without my control? Soon I came across a *Wall Street Journal* review of a unique book. On angels. I was stunned. "But God," I protested, "if there is already a book coming out about angels, why would I write another one?"

And then God whispered to me, in the most loving and compassionate way. "I have plenty of angels for everyone," he said. And I saw. It was not necessary to comprehend his plan in order to support it. I put the angel figurine on its shelf and got back to work.

Where Angels Walk became a reality in July 1992. Then came the real work: promoting it. With thousands of titles published every year, this was a formidable task, especially since my small publisher had limited financial resources for ads or travel.

My first clue that this book promotion would be somewhat unorthodox occurred during an outdoor festival in downtown Chicago, where I was booked for my first radio interview about angels. A few minutes before airtime, a tornado rolled through the festival, knocking out power lines and downing all booths but ours. (Did I mention it was a Christian radio station?)

I dropped a book off at our local newspaper, hoping for a modest mention. Their feature writer phoned. She had seen the *Journal*'s story and wanted to write a follow-up featuring local people. But where to find them? I shared my notes, and a week later, her front-page article appeared. Our local bookstore promptly sold out of copies, and it took many weeks to get more. This situation happens frequently and usually causes a slowdown in sales. In our case, it created a demand.

I also became a fixture at our reference library, looking up phone numbers of small radio stations that might want guests. Producers would usually say, "Well, it sounds interesting, but we're not a religious station."

Me: "Well, this isn't a religious book. The topic was just covered in the *Wall Street Journal*. Want me to fax it to you?"

Producer: "The *Journal?* Maybe we could fit you in after the soybean report."

My long-distance phone bill was scary (and it took a while to master the fax machine), but from time to time I would remember God's promise. He did have plenty of angels, and the more I was able to give up control, the more they could lead.

We were still having trouble keeping up with orders, but as Christmas 1992 neared, I was invited to be a guest on a network TV talk show. Eagerly I went to New York and arrived on the set, only to be overlooked as each time segment passed. Belatedly, the hostess realized that I was pacing in the wings, and with about four minutes remaining, she called me on stage, held up the book, and said to her audience, "This is a beautiful book. You should buy this as a Christmas gift." By the time my flight landed back in Chicago, *Where Angels Walk* was sold out everywhere, and there would be no more copies available in time for Christmas. Was this what the angels meant by "taking care of"? I wondered. *Remain faithful*, came the quiet instructions.

A few days later, my publisher called. "Have you ever heard of an auction?"

"You mean selling things like antiques and tractors?"

"Like books. Three companies want to buy your paperback rights." Each could guarantee good distribution and adequate publicity. Was I interested? Are you serious? An even greater surprise ran parallel to this one: *Guideposts*, a popular inspirational magazine, decided to run its own printing for its subscription list—and ultimately sold hundreds of thousands of copies.

By then, the publishing world recognized a trend, and every company had a few angel books in the works. I was thrilled to do a short hop to Birmingham, Alabama. The signing was in the afternoon instead of at night, so my marketing escort expected just a few people. When we turned into the bookstore parking lot, however, it was full. "Wonder what's happening here," I commented. Puzzled, my marketer looked at her notes: yes, this was the place. Then the store manager came running out. "*Please* come inside," she said. "People have been waiting since we opened!"

It was true. The line stretched around the inside of the store, and everyone cheered when we came in. "But why?" I asked.

Turns out I'd done the morning radio show with the city's most popular DJ, and lots of his fans had come. Because of the crowd, people had passed the time getting acquainted and sharing stories about their own angels and their prayer needs. Even my marketer got in line: Selling books, yes. Missing my flight home, yes. Comforting a stranger, priceless.

After Birmingham, my novice status was even more apparent. At a publishing lunch, I spent some time with a young woman who, I assumed, was new in the PR department. New because she asked a lot of questions. I explained that I thought it was wasteful for the company to send me to New York and California because most of my readers would come from places like Nebraska, Iowa, and Wisconsin. "Just put me in Midwestern Motel 6s and I'll be fine," I promised.

The following day, my tour had been rearranged to include smaller cities. "Joan," the note read, "I have never met anyone who wanted to go to Omaha. Enjoy!" The signature was familiar. It belonged to my companion from the day before—the president of the company.

Because I was a professional speaker, I worked my dates around the tour schedule my new publisher was developing. One of the earliest and most unique requests came from a parish in Wichita. "We are having a festival of angels," the chairwoman explained, "and we would like you to do two speeches for us." What was an angel festival? I asked.

They hadn't planned that far yet. But they were certain the angels would handle things. They sounded like my kind of people.

The festival consisted of booths displaying angel arts, jewelry, and crafts, choirs, angel food cake, and tours of the church for non-Catholic neighbors. Anything vaguely resembling wings and halos had a role. (Did I mention that we sold nine hundred copies of *Where Angels Walk* during an eight-hour period?) While few events garnered audiences of this size, it was obvious that interest in the celestial reign was rising.

By now I had read the *Wall Street Journal*-reviewed book (our books were not alike, but they fit together well) and was also meeting authors who had written the books now being published. Each one seemed unique; some were quite biblical, while others delved into New Age philosophies and psychic phenomena. Not every reader approved of our topic or its slant, either. One author, despite audience eye rolling, claimed that she could sometimes see a person's guardian angel. She told me mine's name was Dominic and he was a large warrior angel because I needed protection and courage. I don't know if this was true, but I would never question her sincerity. Another manifestation involved auras, which people occasionally saw around me, or little signs the books themselves provided: *Where Angels Walk* falling off the shelf in front of someone at a library, being used at eulogies, remaining intact in a fire. I began getting stacks of mail addressed to "Angel Lady" from people describing how the book was changing their lives. Many had a new understanding of God's love for them, and of course, this was wonderful to hear. But I felt a huge responsibility too, especially to those who felt angels were overlooking them during a time of sorrow. For them I wrote a sequel titled *Where Miracles Happen*, which explores the other ways God connects with his people.

Some of our books (including mine) began to appear on *Publishers Weekly's* religion best-seller list, which was a major thrill for all of us. As Christmas 1993 approached, word spread that *Time* and *Newsweek* magazines were preparing cover stories on angels. How exciting! I organized a list of things to discuss. The *Time* story appeared. I was not mentioned.

Forgetting that the angels were still in charge, I cried.

On January 9, 1994, *Where Angels Walk* (paperback edition) appeared at the No. 13 position on the *New York Times* best-seller list. My astonished editors sent me flowers and pointed out that I could forever refer to myself as a *New York Times* best-selling author now, even if the book never appeared on the list again. (Were they trying to tell me something?)

On January 16, 1994, *Where Angels Walk* (paperback edition) was not on the list. The editor sent consolation flowers. I came back down to Earth. *Let not your heart be troubled . . .*

On January 23, 1994, *Where Angels Walk* appeared at the No. 10 position. For the next fifty-four weeks, I received a copy of the list from my professional organization. No other angel book came close. (The highest ranking I received that year was several No. 3s, thanks to Maya Angelou and M. Scott Peck, who just wouldn't get out of my way!)

Then there was Mother Angelica, a true angel believer. She made me feel welcome and affirmed, and EWTN reran our episodes frequently. (Mother Angelica was not always saintly. On one bad day, her doorbell rang, and a sister came to announce that someone wanted to pray over her. Mother threw up her hands. "Just what I need—another mystic!" she barked to no one in particular. We couldn't help laughing, but that "mystic's" prayer led to a healing, and there wasn't a dry eye anywhere.)

The people who had shared their stories for my book were fascinated by all this activity. Some got very involved, helping with publicity or joining me on shows; if they turned up at a signing, I asked them to autograph books too, and they were delighted. I had decided to let attendees share their stories after my speeches, even though that meant giving up temporary custody of the microphone. One evening, when I asked for questions, an eight-year-old boy in the first row raised his hand. "I live in Geneva," he began. "Geneva is a very small town. Smaller even than Saint Charles." *Uh-oh*. One of those moments speakers dread. The child would appear foolish, people would start to leave. *Angels, how can I fix this situation?*

The boy went on. "There's a girl in my school who has a rosary. I've seen it. All the links are turning gold."

"Oh, I see," I said, relieved. "And you believe the golden links are a miracle?"

"Maybe," he said. "But I think the real miracle is that it's happening in Geneva." Who could have said it better?

By now, angels were "in." Wearing an angel pin was a sign of solidarity, and I saw them wherever I traveled. Flight crews, not allowed to wear anything extra on their uniforms, fastened pins on the inside of their lapels. At least two hundred angel and craft stores were launched, providing jobs for artists of all types. TV hosts devoted entire shows to guests who had stories to tell. (Media people used to consider "miracles" as anything odd—a weeping statue or a saint's face on a tree trunk—but today they are far more sensitive to what these things might mean.) My favorite radio venue usually ran two hours, with a hostess I loved. Something wonderful was happening—even if we couldn't quite identify it—and her job was to play devil's advocate. Mine was to keep the switchboard lit up and to open doors for listeners who might have something spiritual to share.

Film producers also jumped into the mix; most popular was the one-hour TV special similar to *Unsolved Mysteries*, with dramatizations, talking heads, and interviews. I was usually on these because I could talk easily without a script. Crews would come to our house, move furniture around, and set up outside lighting. (Our neighbors worried about the black bunting occasionally hanging from the gutters.) I don't remember most of these shows, because they usually came on about 2 a.m.

By then I had six angel and miracle books in print.

Like every author, I hoped to guest on Oprah Winfrey's show. It was said that she could put sales through the roof. On the night before Good Friday, the call finally came: be there for makeup at 7:30 a.m. tomorrow. The show was live; the theme, miracles.

One of my sons worked in the media, so I knew he would understand as I gripped the phone and slid down the wall. "Bill, what should I wear? Business or dressy? I don't know who else is on the stage with me. I can't imagine. I'm already nervous . . ."

Bill offered his usual casual but forthright response. "Mom, I think you're forgetting something."

"I am? What?"

"Mom, this isn't about you. It has nothing to do with you. You have a chance to sow some seed—whether that's a minute or the full hour makes no difference—so just let go."

Where had I heard that before?

The show was lovely, with Oprah at her very best. A pleasant and knowledgeable priest and I were the two official guests, along with the owner of a tortilla with Jesus' face on it and some good stories from the audience. Interestingly, as the months passed, I never saw any surge in our sales figures. I did do an interview with Tom

Brokaw, which played constantly on an airline's inflight TV and attracted attention from fellow fliers who would look at their screen, then at me, then back at their screen. I could usually sell any remaining books before we landed.

I also worked for a production company during this time, finding and adapting stories for film. This required an occasional trip to Hollywood, but crews also continued to visit us. One couple phoned and asked for a full day of shooting on angels. They lived in California and were coming cross-country on another assignment, and they wanted some extra footage for a possible series. We had a very pleasant day—they were a little older, with less hair than our usual crews—and as they packed up, one mentioned how much "Mom" would enjoy *Where Angels Walk*, which I had given to her. "Would she like it signed?" I asked, grabbing a pen.

"Oh, yes."

"What's her name?"

The couple looked at each other and started to laugh. "I guess neither of us mentioned it," the man said. "My mother is Loretta Young."

Loretta Young, movie star, floating through the door on her television show. Six months later, she had read my entire angel series and asked me to write her biography. "Hollywood is bursting with biographers," I told her. "Why me?"

"I want a book about my faith journey, not just my movies," she explained. "You know, walking the walk."

"But I've never done anything like this."

"Neither have I, dear," she said. "Can't we learn together?"

We did. I spent a few weeks with this lovely lady, wrote her book for her, and again saw that if you say okay to the angels, they will give you the tools you need to complete your assignment (maybe not on your timetable but definitely as part of God's plan).

I was still speaking and traveling, mainly in California and Texas by now, but my pace was slowing. "Look at this: four flights in one day!" I exclaimed to our West Coast PR person. "Would you make your mother do that?"

West Coast (puzzled): "My mother? My mother could never—"

"Well, think of me as your mother!"

That was the only time I threw a tantrum on the job (and West Coast sent me flowers), but as Dominic pointed out, "Be careful what you pray for because you just might get it." I had certainly received many answers to prayer, although few were the answers I had anticipated. For example:

- The wife of a United States senator invited me to speak at the White House to the spouses of senators and congressmen. We had a full house.

- I, a Catholic, gave an address at a Southern Baptist college and probably spoke in hundreds of Christian churches of varying denominations. Amish, Mormons, even a Native American group came to hear about angels and add their own rich experiences.

- The books? Several stayed on one or another best-seller list for years, but eventually society's interest in angels waned. I was not concerned about this, for I now know that the books (and everything else in my life) are under the care of God.

Before I started this journey, I depended on myself for almost everything. Now I ask Dominic and the other angels to take care of it all. I know they will because they serve God, and God wants me to accomplish what he put me on Earth to do. He wants the same for you.

Did I mention how grateful I am for the presence of these holy beings during the past quarter century? For the love and guidance they freely gave simply because I asked? Do I look forward to whatever they have in mind for my next assignment?

I think you know the answer.

BONUS STORIES ABOUT ANGELS

SPECIAL NOTE FROM THE AUTHOR

❦

No one was more surprised than I when, in 1992, my book *Where Angels Walk* became a *New York Times* best seller. I hadn't thought about what would happen next. Fortunately, my editor was the "plan ahead" type. "You'd better write another book," she told me. "It looks like angels will be popular for a while."

Another book? It did make sense. I was hearing from many readers wanting to share their own awesome experiences. But some were going through troubled times without much consolation. "Where's *my* angel?" they asked.

I responded with my own question: "Have you ever received a sign or experienced a moment that seemed unusually blessed?" Sure, they all had. "That was probably God," I told them. "Sometimes He sends angels, but there are lots of other ways to communicate." *Where Miracles Happen* became a collection of those "other ways" and also a best seller.

Soon a book just for children would follow. *An Angel to Watch Over Me* was a welcome addition to what was rapidly becoming a popular series.

During the following years, I added four books to the original three, relying on readers' suggestions. But I had questioned book seven. Was it time to stop writing about the heavenly host?

"I hope not," a friend remarked. "I wanted to suggest that your next book be about dogs."

"Dogs?"

"Many think some dogs are angels in disguise," she went on.

I had never owned one, primarily due to allergies. Also, my parents considered dogs to be a nuisance. I continued this attitude when I grew up, despite my children's pleas to have pets. Honestly, by the time I reached adulthood, dogs terrified me. Yes, puppies were adorable, but they also made messes. What was the point?

Yet I discovered my friend was right: a dog loves unconditionally. It doesn't carry grudges and listens as patiently as a friend. Despite my fear, I could see the appeal of a book about dogs. I started researching *Angelic Tails*.

One day my daughter phoned. "Hope you're sitting down," she began. (This is never a good sign.) She and her husband had just returned from a kennel where they had rescued a young dog. His name was Major. He was a mixed breed and he was theirs.

Angelic Tails was almost finished when I dropped in on my daughter one day. We were chatting away when I felt something near my leg. Major sat in front of me, one of his paws resting on my knee. Our eyes met, and he wagged his tail—slightly at first and then in a wide arc. I felt a little quiver in my soul.

He loves me! I realized. Major was not the one who had put distance between us. How ironic that I was writing awesome stories about other people's angel dogs, while overlooking the one in our midst.

Angelic Tails has taken its place in the angel series, and as part of this Guideposts exclusive edition of *Where Angels Walk*, I've selected my most beloved dog stories. And I'm sure you'll enjoy a few of my angel stories from *Guideposts* magazine too.

May you continue to love and enjoy your dogs and welcome new experiences with angels.

Joan Wester Anderson

To Sir, with Love

※

Behold, I send my angel before you to guard you along the way and to bring you to the place I have prepared. Give him reverence and listen to him; and if you heed his voice, I will be an enemy to your enemy and a foe to your foes.

—Exodus 23:20–22

Bill and Marcia Holton and their three children lived on a wheat ranch in Oregon; Marcia's parents, Verne and Kay, lived next door. The two family homes were at the bottom of Juniper Canyon, with some of the wheat fields on top of the hill behind the houses. "Our neighbors out here are spread apart, and the nearest small town is Helix, ten miles from our ranch," Marcia explains. Sometimes it seemed as if they were the only people on earth. Occasionally Marcia got a little lonely, but she was a woman of faith who prayed regularly that God would watch over her family. So far God had not disappointed her.

It was a beautiful Sunday afternoon in early spring, and Marcia had flung open the kitchen door, put boots on the kids so they could run wherever they wanted, and gone outside with them. The sun and promise of warmth were all around them, and planting had begun. Marcia loved this time of year.

"Mommy, look!" Her six-year-old was pointing to the top of the hill behind the house.

Marcia gasped. There was an animal the size of a minivan up there, sitting calmly and looking down at them. It was huge, at least two hundred pounds. A bear? Marcia thought not—its fur was yellow and fluffy. A mountain lion? "Walk real slowly toward the house," she whispered to the children. "Wait there, and don't come back until I tell you."

Then Marcia took a careful step toward the animal. She knew she would have to investigate it before she'd feel safe letting the children play outside again.

As she got closer, Marcia could hardly believe her eyes. It was a dog! The biggest dog she had ever seen, probably part mastiff, part Saint Bernard. Where had he come from? She knew all the dogs in the Helix area, and no one owned one like this. Was he friendly? "Here, boy . . ." She put out a tentative hand.

As if he had been given permission, the dog got up and trotted down the hill, directly to Marcia, tail sweeping the driveway. He allowed himself to be petted, his ears to be scratched and—once she had called the children over to him—hugged and ridden on. "Isn't he nice?" Marcia said. "What shall we name him?"

"I think we should call him 'Sir'," one of the children suggested. "Because he deserves respect."

He did seem regal. Now all that was needed was Bill's permission to keep him. The family could hardly wait until he got home from plowing.

"Oh, come on—he won't eat much," Marcia teased that night. "Look at him—isn't he cute?"

"'Cute' isn't quite the word I'd use," Bill responded. Sir reminded him more of the lions he had seen in zoos.

"But he seems to know us, Daddy," the five-year-old pointed out. "As if he's always lived here." Everyone stared at Sir, who seemed to be following the conversation, his massive head moving from one person to another.

"Well . . ." Bill was definitely weakening. Although his in-laws had two blue heeler dogs to help with the cattle they raised, Bill's family didn't own one. Yet what better place for such a big dog than a ranch? "But we'll have to advertise in the 'Lost and Found' in case he belongs to anyone else," Bill said. "And if we have to give him back, I don't want you all to be sad." Everyone cheered and agreed.

This cabbie probably didn't know it was his final Sunday on earth, Paul Smith* mused, as he lounged in the backseat, his pistol pointed at the hijacked driver's head. But he wasn't going to leave any witnesses to this last robbery. The clerk in the Walla Walla convenience store hadn't seen his face—he'd locked her in the storage closet before he emptied the cash register. But it wasn't much cash, and he was going to have to pull another job soon.

Most important, however, was finding a spot where he could hide for a while. He was an escaped convict on the run, and out here in Oregon the little homesteads were so few and far between that he could easily dispose of the residents, then portray himself as a visiting relative or friend if any nosy neighbor happened by. Eventually he'd commandeer another car and driver, just like this one, and set out again, working his way east. The police would never find him if he stayed out of sight for a while.

The cab driver's hands were shaking. "I-I know you told me not to talk," he said, "but we've gone sixty miles and my gas gauge is on E. I was already low when you pulled the gun on me . . ."

_____

*not his real name

Paul Smith looked out the window. They were passing a wheat field, which looked down into a canyon. At the bottom were two houses. He could see no other dwellings around for miles in any direction. Perfect. He could wait up here until dark. "Turn into this field," he told the driver, who obeyed just as the engine began to sputter. If anyone in those houses did hear the shot, Smith reflected, they would probably assume it was just a hunter bringing down a rabbit. He looked at the terrified cabbie and reached for his gun.

It was a perfect setup; later, from his perch on top of the hill, he watched the families move about the two houses. At times, it looked as if the two women and the little kids were alone. He considered strategies. He could go down now, surprise and overpower the women and children, or he could wait until dark when the men would probably be back, break into one of the houses, and take command of everyone at the same time. But he couldn't afford to make a mistake in judgment, because he had very few bullets left. Ultimately, he had to get far away from here, before the authorities in Washington figured out where he had gone.

It would have to be tonight, when they were asleep and unprepared.

Meanwhile, the Holtons were debating on whether Sir should sleep in the house or the barn. But the massive canine settled down easily on the porch across the back door threshold, as if he'd always done so. There was no point in trying to move him, and quiet eventually descended on the Holton household. Until a little after midnight. Then Sir started to bark. At first it was just a few short yaps, followed by growling, then howling.

"Sir, stop it!" Bill called through the open screened window.

Sir obeyed, but a few minutes later the whole process started again.

"What is the matter with that dog?" Bill asked irritably. He got up again and looked out the windows of the porch door. There was no sign of a wild animal. It wasn't that unusual for a coyote or badger to run through the yard and set off a brief chorus of barking from the dogs next door. But tonight their in-laws' dogs were absolutely quiet.

"Maybe he's homesick," Marcia suggested.

"Wouldn't he be whining?" Bill asked. "This sounds more like aggressiveness. Sir, be quiet!"

Again, Sir obeyed, but only for a moment. He refused to leave the back door, to go in search of what was bothering him. But he also barked and growled continuously, as if he was keeping something at bay. It was almost dawn before the adults in the two households all fell asleep. "None of us were very happy with Sir or me that morning," Marcia recalls. "But we all agreed to try him one more night."

That day Marcia and the children played with Sir continuously. Wherever they went on the ranch—into the barn, across the road—he accompanied them. "When we were in the house, Sir would lie in front of the door. Nothing could get him to move, until we came out of the house again."

That night, Sir barked only a few times. Marcia relaxed. He was settling into his new home, and she was delighted about it. She loved him and depended on him already in a way she had never thought she could.

⚜

A few days later, Marcia's dad, Verne, was on his way to town when he passed one of the wheat fields and saw something shining, looking like a car windshield.

There shouldn't be any cars there. Verne drove closer until he spotted a taxi with Washington state license plates on it. Something was definitely wrong, but he wasn't about to investigate by himself. He turned around, drove home, and called the state police. "Get your family, your rifle, and lock yourselves in one of the houses. And don't open the door for anyone," he was told. The police were on their way.

Slowly, over the next several hours as the authorities investigated, Marcia, Bill, and their folks absorbed the shocking story. On Sunday an escaped convict who had just robbed a convenience store had forced a cab driver to take him just past Helix, to their own wheat farm, where he then murdered the cab driver.

The sheriff took Marcia and Bill up the hill, about 100 feet from their back porch, and pointed to footprints, several cigarette butts, and a discarded cigarette package. Marcia was shocked. The killer had obviously stood here in the dark, waiting for a chance to come down and . . . she didn't want to think about it.

But why hadn't he done so? "I think the only thing that saved all of you was that dog sticking to you like glue," said the sheriff. "If Smith was running low on bullets and had to get past Sir's attack before he could get to you . . ."

"He'd also lose the element of surprise," Bill commented. He had complained about Sir's noisiness. But what would have happened to all of them if Sir had not warned the criminal away? What would have happened if they had not adopted Sir?

No one knew where Paul Smith had gone. Later, it was discovered that he had flagged down another farmer, taken him hostage, and repeated the scenario across the country. He killed one more person before he was caught in Pittsburgh about a week after he had left the Holton farm. Immediately he was sent back to prison in Washington. Sir stayed with the Holtons for about a year before everyone sensed that it was time for him to move on. Ultimately, he went to live at the fire station in town.

Why was the Holton family spared, and not the unfortunate hostages? Another mystery, for we know that God loved them all. But "In the Bible, it tells us that if we pray, God provides angels for our protection," Marcia says. Perhaps Sir was not really an angel. But that he was sent from heaven, Marcia has no doubts.[2]

GUARDIAN IN THEIR MIDST

❧

I was a guest on KLIF radio in Dallas. A caller told us that he had been part of a recent search for a lost teenager. "The only reason we found her," he said, "was that we kept following the sound of a dog constantly barking."

"Her dog?" I asked.

"She didn't have one," he answered. "The barking stopped just as we came upon her, but no one ever saw a dog."

Guardian angel in disguise? Or maybe a real dog acting like an earth angel? It happens.

❧

Rusty was the first puppy Diana and Ernest Bensch owned, a sweet little Queensland heeler with a laid-back attitude. Diana had not been all that enthused about adopting a dog, but when their daughter was born in 2007, she realized that having pets would be a real advantage for Victoria. The Bensches, along with various family members, live outside the small town of Cordes Lake, Arizona, about thirty miles east of Prescott. The terrain is mostly desert, with a lot of brush, cactus, and smaller trees surrounding their sprawling eighty-acre ranch. There are no other children around, so from the first, Rusty became little Victoria's companion. (Not to mention the two horses, Trooper and Chex, ten or fifteen head of cattle, and various other species.) Rusty was also in charge of chasing off the occasional coyote or wild pig that invaded the area, and she worked at it faithfully. Eventually a friend unexpectedly presented the family with another Queensland heeler named Blue. "Rusty needs a partner," the friend observed, and the Bensches okayed the plan.

However, if Rusty was mellow, Blue was anything but. Active and feisty, older than a puppy but not quite an adult, Blue didn't seem to know where he fit. He did learn to play fetch, and soon toddler Victoria was throwing the ball for him, squealing in delight when he brought it back to her. However, things were done on Blue's timetable, and if he had another plan, nothing got in his way, not even Victoria. Often he'd spy a rabbit and take off after it in the middle of a game, leaving her and Rusty behind. Queensland heelers, intelligent and aware, are usually very loyal to their owners. Willful Blue didn't seem to fit the pattern.

The Bensches' ranch is completely fenced, with two outbuildings, some unused trailers, and several vehicles. It abuts open government land. Victoria has a fenced play area, including a swing set, near the house. During this past Christmas season, Santa had brought her a trampoline to use in that area. The little girl had figured out how to entice Blue onto the trampoline, and so the two of them now spent many hours bouncing off their energy. The trampoline also encouraged Victoria to play near the house. She and her parents often walked the acreage, but she had been cautioned many times never to explore by herself. Her dad acknowledges that Victoria "is headstrong and adventuresome." But she is usually obedient too (her aunt Kimberly calls her the family's "little angel"). And that's why, when three-year-old Victoria vanished on Thursday, February 22, 2010, her parents didn't initially believe that she would have gone into the remote and rocky woods alone.

"It was an ordinary day," Diana recalls. "We had purchased a bunk bed for Victoria, which had been delivered and set up that morning, and she was very excited about having a bed with stairs." Diana had made up the bed, and she didn't want Victoria to play on it yet. Time for some outdoor exercise, she decided. Mom, daughter, and the two dogs went outside, and Victoria started to jump on the trampoline. It was about 4:30 on a warm and sunny afternoon, and Diana started thinking about planting the garden. What seeds should they start? At this point, she realized she needed to make a quick trip inside. "I'll be right back," she told Victoria, who was still bouncing, and hurried in. In a moment or two, she was back, talking on her cell phone to Ernest, who had called to let her know he was on his way home from work. Diana scanned the backyard and immediately noticed that her daughter was gone. "Ernest," she cried out, "Victoria's not here!"

"What?"

"She's not in the yard!"

"I'll be home in about five minutes," Ernest reassured her. Diana started to run, calling her daughter's name. It was then that she noticed Blue was missing too. "I was freaking out," Diana says. "I had just seen her. How could she be gone?"

She kept calling, and when Ernest sped into the driveway, he joined her. "As we searched, I thought of every possibility," she says. Had the three-year-old tumbled down a ravine? Was she injured somewhere and unable to respond? Worse, had someone snatched her? Given the fence around their property, that was highly unlikely, but still . . . They searched the outbuildings, and even the horse corral. Victoria had already sat on a horse but was not yet ready to ride—would she have attempted something like that by herself? The area was so vast. At about 6 p.m. Diana, now in a state of terror, phoned the Yavapai County Sheriff's Office. The family's nightmare had begun.

Law personnel take a missing child very seriously. Many of them, of course, are parents, and can identify with a distraught mother or father. But they must also remain as detached as possible while investigating. The first officer to arrive at the ranch declared the house a possible crime scene and told Ernest and Diana that, not only could they not enter their home, but they also could not leave the property to search for their child. (In case of a kidnapping, one of them would have to be there to receive a call.) A police officer was stationed in the yard, where he would remain until the next day. As the word spread, despite the setting sun, searchers assembled at the sheriff's office, along with their all-terrain vehicles, high-powered lights, and tracking dogs. Some came on horseback. The sheriff deputies set up roadblocks where they grimly flagged down cars and popped trunks. "She's wearing a brown T-shirt and pink pants . . . only three years old . . ." The details were circulated, but there were no answers. As darkness set in and many searchers temporarily suspended their efforts, deputies visited every registered sex offender in the area. All were cooperative, and nothing suspicious was found.

Diana had called her sister in Florida "to keep me from losing it," and the police were sensitive as they continued to ask questions of her. Relatives were arriving, and around midnight, the house ban was lifted. Someone called the media so Diana could plead for her daughter's return, should the police allow her to do so.

"There was a report of a child in a Family Dollar Store in Phoenix who looked like Victoria, but it didn't pan out," Diana says. By now she was pacing the floor, watching the TV for any news, and praying. Nighttime temperatures in February usually sank to thirty degrees or below, and Victoria had not been wearing a coat. How could she stay warm? There were predators in those mountains too, including bobcats and wolves. A little child would be no match for them.

And where was Blue? He had disappeared at the same time, but was he with Victoria? "Would he stay with your daughter and try to protect her?" a police officer asked. Given his lack of loyalty, Diana had to say no. If Blue saw something more interesting than Victoria, he would have been off like a shot. What if Victoria had been abducted and Blue had been killed? Kim and her husband stayed with Diana but tried not to speak of what was on everyone's mind.

By the time the sun rose, at least sixty search-and-rescue volunteers had gathered, but their fervor was flagging. The little girl had been missing for fifteen hours by then, and if she had spent that time in the freezing cold, the outcome was probably not going to be a good one. It had been a tough night for Ernest too, but now his search ban was lifted. "I'm going!" he told Diana and sped to join the others.

Now, with the dawn, they could use helicopters. One of the paramedics climbed into a Department of Public Safety plane. He felt strongly that Victoria was nearby. She was small, and darkness had come quickly after she was reported missing. She would not have had time to travel very far from her home. Not fifteen minutes into the air, the paramedic squinted down at a dry ravine about three-quarters of a mile from the ranch—and thought he saw movement. Yes! He alerted his partner. Wasn't that a dog?

It was a blue-gray dog, the color of Blue! He had been moving around but peered upward as the helicopter approached. The men looked for a place to land on the rough vegetation, and it was then that they spotted Victoria. She was lying facedown in the ravine, motionless. If it wasn't for Blue's activity, they might not have seen her.

Quickly the plane landed, and the men approached the little bundle on the ground. Then suddenly, she moved! Relief washed over the men, as Victoria turned over and saw them. She was dirty, with tangled hair and scratches on her face. Her cheeks were smudged with tears, and she was barefoot. But she was alive! The paramedic started toward her, but Blue was not happy about it. He trotted back and forth in front of Victoria, growling and agitated, not at all sure whether anyone should get close.

Slowly, the paramedic walked toward Victoria, hoping to avoid getting attacked by Blue. He knelt down next to her. "I'm going to take you to your mommy." Her face lit up in a smile, and she lifted her arms. At that point, Blue's entire demeanor changed. His body relaxed, his tail began to wag, and he scampered around almost playfully as the men attended to Victoria. When it was time to go, he jumped eagerly into the helicopter after her.

It seemed as if the entire town had turned out to welcome Victoria. People were hugging one another, cheering, and waving as the chopper landed at the command post to pick up Diana. The joy had not set in as yet, for she was still stunned. Despite all odds, her daughter was alive! Blue leaped out of the helicopter to greet her but ran back to Victoria once he realized she was still on the plane. He seemed a bit confused, and a bystander took charge of him so mother and daughter could reunite with tearful hugs.

The doctors at Phoenix Children's Hospital told Diana that Victoria was extremely lucky to have survived the frigid night with only swollen feet and possible frostbite, especially since she had taken off her shoes, which kept slipping on the rough terrain. The damage could have been much worse. As the story unfolded, it was obvious that Blue had saved Victoria's life. Instead of running off on his own pursuits, he apparently recognized the danger she was facing, and he had lain next to her the entire night, shielding her from predators and cold, just as he would have done for any member of the pack. Blue had grown up at last.

But why had Victoria left home in the first place? As she tried to explain at the hospital, she'd simply been looking for Rusty (who had actually been on the porch the entire time). But when Blue saw Victoria wandering off, he followed her. "I don't think she thought she had done anything wrong," says her aunt Kimberly. "She probably just got turned around. It's easy to do." But darkness fell quickly, and the toddler was hopelessly lost. "I looked at the moon all night," she told her family. So far it's the only thing she remembers.

Her parents, of course, lived a lifetime in those terrible fifteen hours. "The things I thought were important before—not important," says Diana. "She's the most important thing to me." Diana is still sleeping in Victoria's room, and she isn't sure when she'll stop. Ernest chokes up each time he praises the rescue teams. Neither can find words to express their gratitude to the hundreds of people, mostly strangers, who put someone else's emergency ahead of their own convenience and made a miracle. Even a dog food company has expressed its pleasure in the outcome by giving Blue free dog food for the rest of his life. Its name? Blue Buffalo Pet Food Company.

But on the night of the rescue, Blue had his very own steak. It was a small enough gift for the guardian in their midst.

OLD DOG, NEW TRICK

❧

Deafness: This is a malady that affects dogs when their person wants them in and they want to stay out. Symptoms include staring blankly at the person, then running in the opposite direction, or lying down.

—ANONYMOUS

The little ball of dirty white fluff was apparently frolicking on the railroad tracks in Kerns, Utah, that night when Fred Krause's freight train approached. It's the situation engineers dread most, and Fred and his conductor both froze. The two engines were pulling ten cars on a local run, and there wasn't enough time to stop. "I saw the dog on the rails ahead," says Fred, "but it was too late to do anything about it." As he passed over the furry pup, he knew it would have had no defense against the huge mass of steel, and the result was inevitable. "There's nothing you can do," he says. "It breaks your heart." Would someone be looking for this cuddly little mutt? Would they ever discover what had happened? Best to just put it out of his mind.

Fred made his delivery at Kennecott Copper Mine, the only stop on this sixteen-mile route, and started his return trip. "Normally on a Sunday night we would have picked up cars from other trains, and then proceeded on to Provo. We almost never do a Kennecott flip (a run up to Kennecott and back) without a trip to Provo." Fred remembered where the accident had occurred. As he approached the spot, he slowed down. A mile, another mile, and then . . . Wait! Fred leaned forward. What was that, trotting toward him down the tracks?

Fred could hardly believe his eyes. By the flare of the engine light, he saw the white dog, alive and unscathed! He must have scooted between the rails, and the train had probably passed right over him without doing any harm. However, like a bad dream, it was all happening again! "Come on, buddy, get off the tracks!" Fred flashed the lights, blew the whistle, and tried to slow down, but the dog scampered *toward* the engine. Right before it hit him, Fred got a clear look at the dog. "Oh, no!" he shouted. "It's a Shih Tzu!"

Fred and his wife had a Shih Tzu, seven-year-old Milo.

Everything was happening so fast, and then the train ran over the dog. Fred heard an unmistakable sound, the thud of something hitting the snowplow mounted on the front of the engine. If he hadn't been crushed, the stray would have been struck by the plow. Either way, it was definitely over.

The train sped on, but Fred couldn't stop thinking about the dog. It was 11 p.m. when his shift ended, and as he was pulling out of the parking lot, he made a decision. "I had convinced myself that no dog could survive an impact with the train, but this was going to be my only chance to know for sure. That's when I decided to go back." He drove his car to a site that he judged to be close to where the dog had been hit. Taking along his flashlight, he walked down the rails, calling and whistling in the darkness. He felt himself being prodded to go just a little farther, and then a little more. Then he saw a forlorn ball of matted fur lying between the tracks. Fred shone the light on the little pile. The pile quivered, got up on all fours, turned around, and looked at Fred as if to say, *What took you so long?*

Fred was stunned. "The last thing I expected was to find him alive," he says. But it was another chance, and Fred couldn't abandon him now, not after all that had happened. Instead, the two went to the vet emergency room.

The "little guy," as Fred had already named him, was about ten years old, and in a somewhat dazed condition. His encounter with the train's snowplow had left him with only a concussion, no broken bones or any other damage. However, he had probably been homeless for some time, since his fur was matted, and he had infections in his eyes and feet. (The eye problems may have accounted for him running toward the train instead of away from it.) But it seemed obvious that some-one had loved him up until the recent past. He was also hungry, so after the amazed vet had released him, Fred brought him home for breakfast. His wife, Lori, was astonished at the story.

Later that day, the area experienced a major snowstorm, and Fred realized that if he hadn't rescued the dog when he did, given his injuries, the freezing weather, and the fox population, the little guy would not have lived much longer. "I have hit a few dogs in the past," Fred says, "but I've never gone back to check on any of them. It's too difficult. Why I did this time, I just don't know." And was it mere coincidence that his run that night kept him in the vicinity of the little guy, rather than miles away in Provo? Once again, the timing had been perfect.

An owner never showed up, so Fred and Lori decided to adopt their invalid, after convincing Milo that it might be fun to have a pal. And Little Guy is delighted with his new digs.

"I must admit that I am not a spiritual person," says Fred, "but Lori and I both agree that there almost seems to have been some sort of 'divine intervention' in this particular situation, so many details that never or very seldom occur, that happened that day. It's enough to make someone like myself go, 'Hmmmm, I wonder . . .'"

MORE THAN MAN'S BEST FRIEND

Oh! I have slipped the surly bonds of earth
And danced the skies on laughter-silvered wings . . .

—JOHN GILLESPIE MAGEE, "HIGH FLIGHT"

B y the time Gary Lorenz graduated from the Air Force Academy in 1967, he had become not only a full-fledged pilot, but, more important to him, also a good leader. He seemed to have a natural set of values that attracted others, and though somewhat quiet, his look was worth a thousand words. One of the many who were drawn to him was Sandra Clark, and soon they were married. The two began their military life in the Philippines, at the first of fourteen different addresses.

Gary rose through the ranks to become an F-4 pilot and served in Vietnam. Eventually, as a colonel, he became the commanding officer of the strategically important airbase at Incurlik, Turkey. Again, his leadership qualities were evident. At one point, with Desert Storm moving in, Gary wanted to evacuate the American families, but no one in Washington seemed to be listening. One morning, he intercepted the visiting secretary of state on his morning run. Wearing his dress blues, Gary fell in stride with the secretary and presented his case. The evacuation was on. "When he was right," said a fellow officer, "Gary would go all out to get things done."

Sandee adjusted to military life, raising their two children and offering fellowship and comfort to the Air Force wives, many of whom were lonely for their families and activities back home. She understood their yearnings because she was a true animal lover and missed riding her own horse, left back in the States. At Incurlik, however, there was a riding stable, and Sandee happily took over temporary guardianship of a horse whose hind legs needed medicating. She and Gary were working on the horse one day when it kicked Gary in the face. He recovered, but the injury would have significance later.

Gary retired with full military honors in 1991, and the couple built their retirement home on 180 acres in the small town of Cotopaxi, Colorado, between Salida and Canon City. The natural beauty and slower pace suited them both, and they enjoyed having animals around again. Gary decided to raise some cattle at first and soon became the neighborhood Pied Piper, leading the herd around the large property by offering them cow treats. Sandee learned to drive an ATV, and she shoveled snow off their long driveway. Probably the best additions to their lives were two golden retrievers that they adopted as puppies from a friend. The goldens were brother and sister, and Gary named them Merry and Pippin, after the two hobbits from the Lord of the Rings series. The dogs were friendly to everyone, and they had been unusually docile as puppies, but from the start, Gary was their favorite. "They never left his side," says Deanna Lorenz, Gary's daughter. "They were homebodies too; when they were about six months old, they had gotten lost for a few days, and they never wandered again." Whether Gary went into the house or trod around the trails, the dogs were at his side, not wanting to miss a single minute of whatever was going on.

The family felt that Gary was in good hands. And that was important because he was beginning to show some signs of distress. Deanna noticed that her father fumbled for a word now and then, but she brushed it aside—didn't everyone forget things here and there as they aged? Sandee saw a more specific progression, slow but steady, involving Gary's lack of memory. There was that long-ago kick from the horse—could it have left some lingering damage? Yet when other members of the family came to visit, they saw little or no symptoms.

The women were hesitant to push their observances too firmly. What if they were wrong? But in 2003, Gary's doctor diagnosed him with aphasia, damage to the left frontal lobe where words are formed. He continued to decline, and by 2005 he was an Alzheimer's patient. As the days passed, Gary became more silent. It seemed that only Merry and Pippin were able to understand him.

On Sunday, September 23, 2007, Deanna celebrated her birthday at her grandmother's house in Denver, along with other family members. The following day, she and her mother had an appointment with Gary's doctor to decide if Gary needed to surrender his driver's license. The women knew that he was still capable of driving, but they were worried about him getting involved in an accident with others. Needless to say, they were not looking forward to the appointment.

When the birthday gathering broke up, "I drove home alone with my dad," Deanna recalls, "and I was happy that we were able to share this time together, even though we couldn't communicate in words. I didn't know it would be the last time."

The following day's appointment was unexpectedly cancelled, because both Deanna and Sandee came down with the flu. Gary, attempting to help, apparently remembered that the horses needed to be fed. But when he went out to drop the hay, the horses had not yet gathered. This was of no real consequence, but Gary took Sandee's four-wheeler to look for them anyway. Merry and Pippin, of course, were following him as they went over a ridge above the house.

Some hours later, when Gary and the dogs had not returned, a worried Sandee called Deanna. "I'm on my way," she reassured her mother and suggested that Sandee phone Debbie, to start getting the word around. Debbie was a friend who knew everyone in town, but the women had forgotten that she was away on a cruise. No matter. When she got the news, Debbie stood on the ship deck and phoned everyone in her cell phone address book to get the search started. It was so effective that by the time Sandee had climbed the hill to start looking around, she encountered a neighbor already walking the paths, checking.

As night fell and volunteers assembled, the Lorenz family fought panic. It was terrifying, knowing that their disoriented father was lost somewhere on the rugged mountain terrain, where there are numerous drop-offs, caves, and canyons. He was wearing light clothes and a sweatshirt too, not enough warmth for the cold nighttime temperatures. There was one hopeful factor: the dogs were probably with Gary. "Merry would never leave Pippin, and Pippin would never leave Gary," Sandee says. It was not too much to hope that, even in his confused state, Gary would show up somewhere, or a searcher would come across a clue and be led to all three of them.

Almost a hundred people turned out on the first few days, and they soon found Gary's ATV at the bottom of a ravine. But where were Gary and the dogs? Despite the diligence of the searchers, along with helicopters sent by the Air Force base, horseback riders, and infrared lights, nothing more turned up. Some volunteers would later say that they had occasionally heard dogs barking but thought they belonged to a nearby house, and perhaps they did. But too much time had passed. Sandee had to face the fact that her beloved husband was not coming home.

Days dragged by. As hunting season began, Deanna was featured several times on the local radio station. "Don't forget to look for my dad and the dogs," she reminded listeners. But no responses came. Should the family have a memorial service now or wait in this strange kind of limbo until everything was over? But would it end? Mysteries were not always solved. And what about the dogs? As time passed, and no golden made his weary way out of the woods to their home, their grief deepened. Weeks of searching had turned up nothing. On October 9, the search was officially discontinued.

In the end, it was a hunter who found Gary's body. He and his buddies went to this same location each year, and on the first day, the hunter set out alone against a stiff wind. "Before I lost complete cell contact, I phoned my wife, and we talked for a few moments about the beauty of the surrounding area," Pat says. In a later letter to Sandee, he traced the route he'd taken, following deer up the mountainside. Was he hearing some faint barking?

Pat continued to work his way around a high ridge, and suddenly a thin but beautiful golden retriever bounded up to him in friendly fashion. Then Pat remembered something, and using his walkie-talkie, he radioed his buddies. "That fellow they told us about, the one that's been lost, did he own a golden retriever?"

"Two retrievers," came the answer.

By now, Merry was barking at Pat, her tail wagging furiously. It was as if she was begging him to follow her. Pat did, and she scrambled down the ridge about thirty yards. Pippin then came into view, barking loudly. Next to Pippin, Pat could see what everyone had been searching for during the last several weeks. He hit the switch again. "I think I found all of them."

For the next three hours, Pat stayed on his cell phone (which, remarkably, still had power) as he directed the sheriff and 911 dispatchers to his location. "During that time I attempted to feed the dogs with a half a sandwich I had in my pocket," Pat told Sandee, "but neither of them would leave Gary's side. Finally Merry came over and took a piece of bread, and later, I brought her some water." Pippin, however, refused to move away from Gary, and when searchers finally arrived, he snarled and continued to bark until he recognized one of the neighbors.

"I was touched by the love and loyalty the dogs showed for Colonel Lorenz," Pat says. "At one point, Merry came over and buried her head in my lap, as if to express her sorrow. I could see the sadness in her eyes."

Neighbors brought the stunning news to Sandee and Deanna. "Gary's been found. And the dogs—the dogs are alive!" The women could not believe it. The dogs must have been with Gary when he died. Had Merry and Pippin kept their lonely vigil for another three weeks, guarding his body, never leaving his side?

As details emerged, the family learned that Gary was discovered almost four miles (by a bird's flight) from his home. Helicopters had flown over that area several times, but he was lying under a tree, partially hidden by a rock. The dogs were probably leaning up against him, attempting to keep him warm. The coroner later confirmed that Gary had died of hypothermia and dehydration on September 29, five days after he disappeared.

Five days! It was heartbreaking to imagine how Gary had probably struggled to find his way back. And yet as Sandee opened her arms to receive the dogs, she could not help but be grateful that they had survived. In many ways, they were a part of her husband.

But *how* had they survived? No food, no water for almost a month. The dogs were emaciated and ravenous when they were returned to Sandee, and each had lost nine pounds. She fed them a small amount every few hours at first, so they wouldn't overeat. Merry had a slight limp, and Pippin—at one time a clown—was more aggressive than usual. But their vet pronounced both dogs amazingly fit.

Gary Lorenz's funeral mass attracted hundreds of mourners and was held at the Air Force Academy's Cadet Chapel on October 29, 2007. He received full military honors at the graveside service. The American flag was folded and presented to Sandee.

Deanna spoke of the remarkable life her father had lived. "If you want to know what kind of person a man is," she told the crowd, "ask his dog."

Lying quietly on either side of the casket, wearing black scarves around their necks, Merry and Pippin gave testimony to Deanna's words. They were calm, gazing serenely at the crowd, yet at the end of the ceremony, both dogs seemed bewildered and had to be gently urged away. It was finally time to let go.

Sandee believes that had the hunter not found them, the dogs would have stayed with Gary until they took their own last breaths. "To know that Merry and Pippin were with him when he passed from this world to the next, that he wasn't alone, means everything to me," she says.

And Deanna has observed something wondrous as well. "When Merry was returned to us, I realized that her face was no longer golden," Deanna says. "It had turned completely white."

The touch of an angel? Someday we'll know.

Views from the Bridge

❦

You think dogs will not be in heaven? I tell you, they will be there long before any of us.

—Robert Louis Stevenson

Do dogs go to heaven? There's an Internet legend among dog lovers about the Rainbow Bridge, a mythical place between heaven and earth, where dogs wait for their masters to join them for all eternity. In more theological discussions, the point is frequently raised that dogs may indeed have souls, although lower in the ranking than humans'. Animals, as part of God's creation, were declared "good" (Genesis 1:25) and by their mere existence they bless God and give God glory. Author Ptolemy Tompkins, writing in *The Divine Life of Animals*, points out that "nothing of what we love down here on earth is ever truly lost. . . . Though this world is imperfect and fallen, there exists a place where the pain of that imperfection will be healed. Not just for humans, but for every creature, great and small."

What do we conclude? Perhaps we simply listen to the stories.

Dr. Candace Williamson Murdock of Rome, Georgia, had just had a miscarriage. The night after she returned from the hospital, she stayed awake, restless and upset. This baby had not been her first, but like all children, it was irreplaceable, and she grieved deeply at the loss. "Suddenly a scene appeared—as if it was on a movie screen—right in front of me," Candace recounts. She blinked, but the vision remained.

It was a sunny green meadow. In its midst were dogs playing and chasing each other, crossing her vision toward the right side. "The dogs seemed somehow familiar," she says. "I suddenly realized that they were our family pets, dogs from my childhood!" Watching intently, Candace saw her father running into the center of the scene, the dogs leaping joyfully about him. Her father had been killed in a plane crash seven years ago. He had raised and loved many dogs in his lifetime.

Then Candace realized that her father was not alone. He was gripping the hand of a small blond child. They were looking toward the right. Candace's father seemed to be pointing at something, as if he were explaining it—and both were smiling. Instantly Candace knew this child was the baby she'd just lost. Obviously her father was welcoming the child into heaven, and God had allowed her to witness it so she would be consoled.

"I cannot explain how much comfort this vision gave me," Candace says. "I had never experienced anything like it, nor would I have pictured heaven in this way, but I was *not* hallucinating. To know that my child, my father, and his beloved dogs were all together was the best answer to prayer that I could have asked for. God does care."[3]

⚬⟨✦⟩⟩

Mary Ellen Hansburg, of Columbus, Ohio, was pleased and proud when her daughters, Eliza and Lilly, went off to different colleges, each wearing an unmistakable badge of confidence and anticipation. Wasn't this what she had hoped for? Yet Mc (it's what everyone calls her) missed the girls terribly. She was sure that Waddles, the family dog, did too.

Waddles, a brown and white terrier-sheltie mix, was small in size, but he had a huge and loving heart. He had been the girls' joy and comfort since their childhood and was very sensitive to the moods and nuances of their lives. He seemed to know if anything was amiss, and he could raise a ruckus if he felt one of the girls was distressed or needed defending.

Me was a teacher, and the same autumn her daughters went to college, Me returned to the classroom. She was pleased that the fall quarter was unfolding with its pleasures and challenges. One early morning as Me drove to school, she cast a sideways glance out the passenger window. There was Waddles, running along the shoulder of the highway! "He was running hard and panting, so I slowed down and watched as he slowed down too." What was he doing out here on the road?

Finally able to pull over, Me looked to see where Waddles was. That dog was always full of surprises. But Waddles was gone—vanished. This left Me a bit apprehensive and edgy. She wondered about her daughters. Was Waddles bringing her a message? Was everything all right with them?

Arriving at school, she sent off a quick email to each of them, asking in a general way if all was okay. Later that day, each girl called her and left a message:

"Mom, good to hear from you. Keep me in your prayers—lots of challenges," relayed Eliza, a senior.

"Hey, thanks. I do want to talk and will call back today," said freshman Lilly.

Indeed, as Me later learned, each of the girls was facing demanding situations in their classes, and a reassuring conversation with Mom was just what they had needed. Relieved, Me was so glad she had contacted each one.

She reflected on all of this while pulling into the driveway at the end of the day. The vague fears she sometimes had about letting her daughters go had disappeared. Instead she felt confident and ready to get on with her life. Thank goodness for

Waddles and the signal he sent. Me knew that their special little dog had not been on the highway today, because he had died almost a year ago. But he had sent her the message she needed most. "Waddles had always been the girls' playmate and protector. He still is, just this time from the other side of the Rainbow Bridge."[3]

Snow Angel

They say that every dog lover has one dog in their life that is their soul mate, the one with whom they share a wondrous and unexplainable connection.

—Linda Baxter

Looks like a major snowstorm is heading our way, folks," announced the radio weatherman. Linda Baxter paused momentarily while buttoning her coat and peered out the window of her Marion, Indiana, home. Yes, she could see a few flakes already swirling in what appeared to be a rising wind. How fortunate that her seven-year-old son, Michael, had already boarded his school bus, and kindergartner Lesley's school was only a block and a half away, if they left by the back gate. Fleetingly, Linda wondered why classes hadn't been cancelled already—Indiana storms could get quite heavy in a brief amount of time. But she pushed the worry out of her mind as she reached for her keys and directed Lesley onto the back porch. "Wait for Mommy, honey," she called over her shoulder, as she locked the door and caught up to Lesley.

Linda enjoyed walking her daughter to and from school each day. It was an easy route, great exercise for Linda's degenerative arthritis, and a chance for them to talk quietly one-on-one. Lesley enjoyed their routine, too, because it meant that she could stop to pat her best friend, Punkie, the handsome German shepherd who lived next door. Punkie's owners, the Roths, were an older couple who had moved in about a year ago. Punkie was Erv Roth's constant companion ("joined at the hip" was the way Jane Roth put it), and because Erv liked to tinker in his garage, it was just a matter of time before Michael and Lesley had met him and fallen in love with Punkie too.

"Somehow our families blended," says Linda. "One of the kids' favorite things to do was to swing with Jane, Erv, and Punkie on the front porch. Michael's favorite game was to shovel Erv's walk and not get caught. One Mother's Day we snuck over during the night and planted flowers in Jane's flower barrel."

Each day since the beginning of school, Lesley had been telling Punkie all about kindergarten, as well as her special secrets. The large black and tan dog would listen patiently, then give Lesley a sloppy kiss to show she understood. However, as the days grew colder, the Roths were keeping Punkie inside most of the time. "I miss Punkie, Mom," Lesley said as they passed the empty yard.

"I do too," Linda agreed. "But you want Punkie to be safe and warm inside, don't you?"

Lesley nodded. It was almost too cold to talk. Flakes were coming down in full force, and the wind had picked up. Quickly Linda took Lesley to her classroom, gave her a good-bye hug, and hurried home. The snow was already a few inches deep.

By midmorning, the announcements of school closings were all over the TV news. "Blizzard conditions are predicted," warned the forecasters. There was the chance of whiteouts, those situations in which the falling snow became so dense that a person could lose perspective and a sense of direction. *At least I don't have to drive,* Linda thought as she bundled up again. That would certainly be dangerous. Lesley's school was letting out early, and with any luck, they'd be safely home in a matter of minutes. Hopefully, Michael's bus would be a little late. Linda left the front door open, but she knew Michael would worry if she was not at home when he arrived. This day was becoming so complicated!

When Linda stepped out the back door for the noon hike to school, the snow was already up to her knees. None of the neighbors had shoveled yet, knowing that the wind would simply whip the drifts back onto their sidewalks. This made walking almost impossible. For the first time, Linda was afraid. How was her small daughter going to cope with the deepening snow? How she envied Punkie, as she passed the Roths' house and pictured the dog lying on a warm rug near Erv's chair. And there was no one she could call on for help—their street was populated mostly by retired couples such as the Roths. It was up to her to protect her children.

Staggering into the school, her back aching from the effort, Linda went to the kindergarten room and helped the teacher bundle the last few children into their coats. Then she took Lesley's hand and started out again, pushing the outer door hard to get it open. The school was nearly deserted.

"When we stepped outside, the wind stole Lesley's breath and nearly lifted her off her feet," Linda says. "She clung to my hand, and I tried my best to shield her, but the snow had drifted so high she could hardly walk." Each step was a battle, and within minutes Lesley was wet, exhausted, and in tears. "Come on, honey, just a little bit farther." Linda tried to encourage her, but it was almost hopeless. Lesley was too short to make headway through the mounting drifts and too heavy for Linda to carry.

The snow swirled around them, hitting their faces with needlelike flakes. "Our fingers and feet were numb, our chests ached, and our cheeks were wind-burned," Linda says. The harsh wind bit at their noses, and the wetter they were, the more painful each breath became. Linda dragged Lesley on, a few inches at a time, but finally Lesley collapsed into a snowbank and Linda fell alongside her, her back burning with pain. They lay for a moment, exhausted and spent, then Linda struggled to her feet again. She knew it was dangerous to lie down in the snow; people fell asleep and froze to death that way. They had to keep going. Reaching for her daughter, Linda looked up at the sky, and suddenly she was terrified.

In the few moments they had taken to rest, the storm had intensified. The snow was so thick now that it was blotting out the items around them, even the trees and houses, and Linda was completely disoriented. The dreaded whiteout. "I couldn't tell which direction we were facing or where we were. I was afraid to move because if I went the wrong way we could be in the street, and any oncoming traffic would never see us." People died under those conditions too. What should they do? What *could* they do?

They could pray. They could ask the God who made the snow to deliver them out of it. Linda gathered Lesley into her arms and, still lying in the drift, they prayed. "Dear Lord, help us to find our way home." Then Linda pulled her exhausted daughter to her feet. With the last of their strength, they had to try again.

Just then, Linda spotted a dark shape just ahead—a large bush, a trash can? No, this shape was moving. "Out of the blinding snow came an angel sent by God to help us," Linda says. It was Punkie! The dog ran straight to Lesley and gave her a wet kiss.

"Punkie!" Lesley cried in delight. "Take us home!" She grabbed hold of Punkie's collar with one hand and tightened her grasp on Linda with the other. As if she understood everything, Punkie began to lead them in a specific direction, fighting her way through huge drifts.

But Linda wondered how Punkie would know the right path. Even a dog with a fine sense of smell was at a disadvantage in this terrible weather. But Punkie seemed to know exactly what she was doing. She leaped forward again and again, scrambling over the snowbanks, dragging Lesley with her. Each step was a struggle, but Punkie wouldn't let them stop. When Lesley occasionally lost her hold on the dog, Punkie would stop and bark to get them going again. "She seemed to realize how dangerous it was for us to be out in the storm, and she kept urging us on." The journey seemed endless, and Linda had lost all track of time and location when suddenly a familiar shape loomed ahead. Her backyard gate! Punkie had brought them safely home.

"Oh, Punkie, thank you! Thank you!" Lesley gasped. She gave the dog a final hug, and then Punkie turned away. As quickly and mysteriously as she had appeared, the dog was gone.

Linda and Lesley struggled through their backyard. With frozen fingers, Linda managed to turn the key in the lock and, exhausted, the two fell into the kitchen. Linda looked at the clock. It had taken them over an hour to travel two blocks. They were soaked and freezing, aching in every bone, but safe. Lesley would have a warm bath, and they would share cocoa with marshmallows—everything would taste better now, for the rest of their lives. But before another minute passed, Linda had to call Jane Roth and thank her for Punkie's extraordinary help.

"How did you know we were in trouble?" she asked Jane. "Why would you send Punkie out in that storm?"

"I didn't," Jane explained. "Punkie had been sleeping peacefully next to Erv's chair when, suddenly, she leaped up and started to bark. She seemed very agitated and kept jumping around the back door. Erv finally let her out."

Punkie had disappeared into the blizzard as Erv watched, puzzled. What would possess a dog to go out on such a freezing day? And when Punkie didn't return right away, Erv became worried. It was too dangerous to go out and search for her, so he had begun to call her. His voice was becoming strained when, almost an hour later, an exhausted Punkie dragged herself into the yard, walked wearily into the house, and collapsed beside Erv's chair. "She's sleeping soundly," Jane reported. "And now we know why." Punkie would definitely get a special supper that night.

Tears stung Linda's eyes as she hung up the phone—tears of relief and gratitude, but mostly of love. Punkie's love had saved their lives. She would never know how, but that wasn't important.

The Indiana blizzard turned into a state of emergency, with factories, offices, and schools closed for several days. The temperature dipped below zero, and wind gusts caused many cases of frostbite. However, the mood in the Baxter household was definitely upbeat. "How often we come to a place in life when we are unable to see a way 'home' and every turn seems impossible," Linda says. "It is in those moments that we must trust that the Father is in control, that he knows the way, and he will not let us surrender to the 'blizzard' that surrounds us."

Instead he sent a furry, four-legged angel to guide them home at last.

DOGGONE DARLING

✦

Dachshunds are ideal dogs for small children, as they are already stretched and pulled to such a length that the child cannot do much harm one way or the other.

—ROBERT BENCHLEY

When Colt Urquhart of Kennewick, Washington, set out with his friend Josh for a day of fishing, he had no inkling what he would catch. The men were up to their knees offshore on a lake when one of them spotted something small, brown, and wiggly struggling toward them underwater. It was a puppy! Quickly Colt scooped it up. It was a little dachshund, obviously running out of strength to keep paddling. If the men hadn't come along, it wouldn't have lived much longer.

The puppy was shivering, so Colt tucked him inside his shirt. "We've got to find his owner," he told Josh, who agreed. Someone among the hikers and picnickers must be awfully concerned right now. But oddly, as they walked from family to family holding up the dog, no one seemed to be missing one. An older couple admitted that they had shooed it away because it had gotten into their belongings, and they had seen the pup scamper into the water. With its stubby legs, the pup had run out of solid ground very quickly. Colt had to get it warm and fed. Both men lived in trailers, but Josh had more room, so he took the dachshund home.

As it happened, Josh couldn't keep the dog. His park owner had a rule against having any pets. "Ours didn't," Colt's wife, Diane, says, "and over the years we have taken in lost dogs and kept them until their owners came." But this dachshund was very small, and might not have anyone looking for him. Perhaps they would end up keeping him. "We had a family meeting, and the vote was yes," says Diane. Sure, they had heard all the jokes about "wiener dogs." But this one seemed especially sweet-natured, and it loved to cuddle—just the kind of dog children need.

They named him JoJo, and he settled in without much trouble. The kids soon noticed that his ears usually expressed his feelings. "When happy, he does a perky droop, when hungry, his ears are gathered at the top of his head," says Diane. "When in trouble or embarrassed, they are out and fanned—we call them elephant ears." Jojo was simple to read, which made his care even easier. In fact, as the months went on, he developed a bit of an attitude, as if he were in charge of the family. He was fiercely protective of the children, and chose then-eight-year-old Kalen as his bunkmate. They soon slipped into a routine: JoJo would sleep with Kalen but would come out every hour or so to check on Colt and Diane as they watched television. "If we were up too late for his liking, he would wait patiently at our feet, until we went to bed," Diane says. If the couple stayed up later than JoJo thought acceptable, he would sigh dramatically and return to Kalen's room in defeat. In an hour or so, he would be back to prod Colt and Diane again.

But the pattern changed one evening in February of 2010. It was past midnight, the trailer was quiet, and Diane and Colt were watching the end of a movie. JoJo came out of Kalen's room, somewhat agitated. The adults were surprised. "JoJo had been fed and had already gone outside," Diane says. "It wasn't like him to be busy and up so late." Diane told him to go back to bed and, being the obliging pooch that he was, he obeyed.

But only for a few moments. Then he appeared again, almost pacing. "If a dog can look worried, he did," Diane says. JoJo went back and forth four times, each time returning to Kalen's room. It was then that Diane noticed his ears. They were straight down, which in some breeds denotes danger.

By now, the drowsy couple realized that something was wrong. JoJo had returned to Kalen's room, and when they entered, the dog was on her bed, shoving his nose against her and trying to wake her up. "We didn't see anything out of the ordinary," says Diane, "but then I smelled an odor of burning rubber." And when she touched the wall at the head of Kalen's bed, it felt hot. Colt yanked the alarm clock and lamp out of the wall, and a puff of smoke followed. "Get out!" he yelled. Quickly he awakened the children while Diane phoned 911. Grabbing their two cats and JoJo, the family fled.

Firefighters arrived quickly. Diane, the children, and the animals waited in their car while Colt took the firemen into the trailer to show them where the smell was coming from and where the electricity could be shut off. "When they came out, they told us that Kalen's outlet was minutes away from catching fire," Diane says. Holding their children and pets closely, the couple looked at each other. There had been no smoke or flames, no injuries or even deaths, because of JoJo. The bossy little dog with the short, stubby legs had saved his entire family.

JoJo continues to be an absolute treat of a dog, says Diane. "I am forever grateful that he floated by my husband and Josh, so we could share his precious life."

A ROSE FOR MARGARET

〜❧〜

Margaret was beaming as we walked home from school on that early spring day in the mid-1950s. "Doesn't it seem like the whole world is smiling?" she asked.

I certainly wasn't smiling. Sister Bonaventure, our eighth-grade nun, had just announced the names of the six girls who would comprise the honor guard for the parish May Crowning. Despite my yearlong effort to raise my grades (which I had) and grow in personal holiness (which I had not), I was not among the six. Even more astonishing, *Margaret* had been chosen. It was she who would wear a long blue dress ("No bows, sequins, or flashy decorations, girls"), she who would carry flowers up the center aisle of the packed church, every eye upon her, while the rest of the school sang, "Oh Mary, we crown thee . . ." It wasn't fair.

"Life isn't always fair," my mother pointed out that evening at home. "Besides, you've had several successes this year—winning the spelling bee, being elected class treasurer. . . . Margaret hasn't had many chances to feel special."

That was true. Margaret, shy and plump, the youngest of a raucous family, was overlooked even in her own busy household. Why she had been selected for this honor was anyone's guess, but my Christian duty was clear: I was supposed to feel happy for my friend. I was again failing in personal holiness.

"I do hope," Mother said, frowning, "that Margaret can find a blue dress that fits."

My mother was tactful but I saw her point. What if Margaret had trouble finding a gown to fit her ample proportions, something blue and without elaborate decorations?

If that happened, my skinniness would be a decided last-minute advantage. I went to bed with visions of a blue dress dancing in my head.

The next day I met Margaret at the corner as usual, and noted that her customary slouch had been replaced with a brisk, shoulders-back stance. Her eyes sparkled. "You look different," I told her.

"I do?" She grinned broadly. "I guess I'm excited. Mom is taking me shopping for my May Crowning dress tomorrow. No hand-me-downs this time!"

"What if you can't find one?" I asked, somewhat boldly.

"Oh, I will. I've asked Saint Therese to take care of it for me," Margaret said.

My spirit plummeted. If Saint Therese was on the job, the dress was as good as hanging in Margaret's closet.

Margaret and I had been nine or ten when the nuns introduced us to Saint Therese. The nuns liked all saints, of course, considering them and the angels as the aunts and uncles of the church community. (And wouldn't we ask advice or help from senior members of the clan?) But God had given Therese, the Little Flower, special abilities. According to tradition, if one sought a favor from heaven, Saint Therese would send that person a rose if the favor was to be granted.

Margaret and I had tried it out right away. We requested a rose if I was going to win the essay contest. A rose appeared one week later, lying in our path on the way to school. Margaret's brothers had teased us, pointing out that earlier, a florist truck had parked in that exact place to make a delivery. But Margaret and I weren't fussy about *how* we got our rose from Saint Therese—and I won the essay contest the very next day.

"You'll pray for me, won't you?" Margaret asked now as we reached school. I saw a hint of the old uncertainty on her face.

"Well, sure," I answered. It was only a little lie. Besides, Margaret wasn't going to need my prayers. Saint Therese was a special friend of Jesus's mother, Mary, and Margaret wanted a blue dress so she could look beautiful for Mary. Saint Therese and the angels were probably arranging the whole thing at this very moment.

Margaret called me late Saturday afternoon. She and her mother had spent all day downtown looking at dresses and came home empty-handed. "They're all either too old for me or too small," Margaret explained, dejected.

"Don't worry," I said, mustering a loyal tone, "you've got three Saturdays left." Secretly, of course, I was delighted.

Two more fruitless weekends passed, and Margaret, who had started to look so confident, so alive, was slowly slipping back into her shell. "Weren't there any blue dresses?" I asked.

"None that were right for the occasion." Margaret sighed. "Are you sure you're praying for me?"

"Of course I'm sure!" I squirmed uncomfortably. "Your rose will come."

But walking home in the early dusk, I faced the situation honestly. There was so little time remaining before the May Crowning, so few stores left to visit. Saint Therese was obviously saying "no" to Margaret—and that probably meant a "yes" for me. (I had recently noticed Sister Bonaventure glancing at my easy-to-fit frame). It was simply a matter of time.

Only . . . why did the knowledge bring pain instead of the joy I had anticipated? Margaret was so unhappy, and I felt like the worst friend in the world. . . . How would she feel if she knew I was actively working against her? As if a dam had burst inside, I heard myself begging Saint Therese for a rose and a blue dress, this time for *Margaret.* "Just a plain one," I reminded the sweet saint, "something appropriate for the occasion."

A few days later as we walked home from school, Margaret shifted her books and looked at me. "I'm giving up," she said quietly. "I'm going to tell Sister Bonaventure tomorrow."

My mouth dropped. "No, you can't!"

"I have to! There's only one Saturday left before the rehearsal. There's no place else to look. I guess I'm just too . . ." Margaret's voice broke.

"Don't!" I dropped my books and hugged her hard, feeling my throat constrict, the tears spilling down my cheeks. I had cried for myself many times. But now I knew that nothing hurt more than not being able to help a friend. "Try just this one last Saturday," I pleaded. "What do you have to lose?"

She wiped her eyes. "I'll ask Mom."

I bombarded Saint Therese for the rest of the week, avoiding Sister Bonaventure and pressing my family into prayer duty. My parents, amazed at my sudden growth in personal holiness, obligingly mentioned the matter each day during their morning prayers; my sister and I took the evening shift. The days dragged. Saturday arrived, and no rose had appeared. I resisted the impulse to buy one and put it in Margaret's mailbox. Saint Therese could not be manipulated. If it were to be a "no," we would simply have to accept it.

At six o'clock that evening, the phone rang. Margaret's jubilant voice was on the other end. "We found one!"

"Oh, Margaret!" My heart soared. A quick vision of myself in a beautiful blue dress shimmered in front of me, then vanished in a wisp. I was glad to see it go. This was so much better, so right in every way. "Is it blue?"

"Blue and modest and unadorned," she assured me. "I won't take it out of the box until you get here."

I dashed for the door. Strange that Saint Therese had granted the favor without sending a rose first. Well, that was something I'd ask God about later. I bounded up Margaret's front porch steps and into the living room, filled with Margaret's beaming family. For the first time, she was the center of attention. "Open the box!" I demanded.

And as she did so, the soft tissue falling away, everyone gasped. The dress was indeed blue, but we all saw the delicate pink rosebuds scattered like tiny kisses along the neckline.

Margaret's mother was shocked. "There weren't any rosebuds on this dress in the store, not when Margaret tried it on. How on earth . . . ?"

Margaret's eyes met mine. We knew how. The Little Flower had sent this dress and something even more precious, the gift of love. Margaret, learning to love herself, would make an exquisite honor guard for Mary's May Crowning. And I, learning to love others, would be the proudest person there.

AN ANGEL TO CATCH HER

❧

"I have talked to my guardian angel for over fifty years," says Patricia Rousseau. "I feel so safe, knowing that she is always right by my side."

One New Year's Eve, Pat was more than glad that her guardian angel was so close. Her daughter was catering a holiday dinner for senior citizens at their residence, and Pat had volunteered to help.

"We were serving individual salads to the guests, when I caught my foot on the leg of a chair and fell on my back," says Pat. Three plates of salad flew up in the air, and fell on some of the guests. Several residents cried out in shock, but quickly their concern was more for Pat than the scattered lettuce. Pat immediately got up from the floor. She had no pain at all.

"I cleaned up the mess, continued serving the entire meal, and never once felt an ache or pain," she recalls.

As she continued serving and smiling away the residents' worry, Pat kept thinking about the fall. How was it that she had landed on a hard floor, but it felt so soft? Like a cloud or a pillow, or perhaps a pair of wings. Suddenly Pat knew how she had escaped injury.

"It was my guardian angel who cushioned my fall that night," she says. "I feel very blessed that she made an appearance to me on New Year's Eve."

A MOTORCYCLE MIRACLE

❧❦❧

John was a teenager in the '70s, raised in a very religious family. But he was more interested in hot cars and pretty girls. "My faith was very superficial," he says, "consisting mostly of a strict adherence to the rules except when my parents weren't looking."

Shortly after getting his driver's license, John landed a well-paying job at a local grocery store chain. Soon he talked his dad into letting him buy a motorcycle. "Now my independence was complete," John explains. "I earned my own money. I was buying my own vehicle. I felt like an adult." (And at six feet tall and 250 pounds, he certainly looked like one!)

So one day when John's mother forbade him from visiting his girlfriend after school, he was immediately rebellious. "I'm going, and nothing you can say or do will change my mind!" he shouted. His mother, stunned, began to cry. John had never defied her before. But now her son was storming out the back door. "I'll be home by ten!" he shouted over his shoulder.

After school, John went to his girlfriend's house in a nearby town about thirty minutes away. The teens spent the evening together watching television. "I was so wrapped up in her that I paid no attention to the time," John says. Finally at 9:45, he headed home.

But getting home normally took a half hour. To shave time off his drive, John decided to take a shortcut across a highway closed for construction. Veering around the yellow-and-black-striped barricades, John sped up to about 70 miles per hour. A few moments later, he lost control and the motorcycle began to flip.

"Time seemed to slow to a crawl," John says. "I hit the pavement, headfirst, and tumbled down the highway, head over heels. I remember seeing the moon pass my knees! And as I rolled to a stop, I remember the extreme silence of the night." Clothes torn, John was bleeding from head to toe and could barely move. He was also in the middle of nowhere, on a detoured highway, with no hope of traffic coming by. Would he die, he wondered hazily, before the road crews discovered him the next morning?

"As I lay there drifting in and out of consciousness, I saw two very bright lights approaching," John says. "It was a car, and I knew I needed to stop it." Shakily, John stumbled to his feet, stood swaying in the middle of the road, and waved his arms for a moment, then fell again onto the pavement. But the driver had apparently seen him, for the car slowed, then stopped. It was a recreational vehicle.

A man stepped out of the RV and quickly assessed the situation. He lifted John's huge motorcycle to the side of the road, then easily picked John up in his arms and carried him to the back of his RV. *How did he have so much strength?* John couldn't concentrate. Everything seemed to be happening a million miles away.

He passed out until they reached his girlfriend's house. "Her surprised mother opened the door, and the man carried me inside and laid me down on their couch," John says. He faded again.

Later at the hospital, John and his mother heard an amazing story. His girlfriend's mother explained that with hardly a word of explanation, the stranger had deposited John on their couch, and while the women were caring for John, he disappeared.

The incident was a turning point for John. He became far more serious about his behavior, his respect for his mother, and especially his faith in God. Today, John is still a major skeptic when it comes to miracles, except for that night. "I have thought about that accident over the years," he admits, "and have found several things that I cannot explain."

For example, how did John escape a high-speed crash with only minor cuts and abrasions? Why was the stranger driving on a barricaded road? How could he be strong enough to move the motorcycle, and to easily carry John in his arms? How did he know where John's girlfriend lived? How did he leave without the women noticing?

Finally, why didn't the man stick around to see how John was doing? Perhaps he already knew John would be fine. "I believe in angelic beings, although I am skeptical about the popular view of their interventions," John says. "But I can't help but wonder if my rescuer that night wasn't an angel."

Who else?

A Small Gift Becomes an Angelic Sign

One of my favorite episodes in Scripture has Jesus telling his followers that the more they give, the more they will receive. It cannot be otherwise, he explains, because God will never be outdone in generosity. The concept of tithing is explained in a different part of Scripture. It's the idea that the first fruits—perhaps 10 percent of one's earnings—should be given to God as an act of faith. (The actual money can be given to charity or to church.)

It sounds simple, but putting it into practice is very difficult. We all have reasons for not giving money away, especially now, with so many people jobless or earning reduced wages. But a principle is a principle, and it works all the time, not just when it seems easier to accept.

Colleen W. knows it firsthand. Her story is typical of how most of us take the first step. Finances had been somewhat tight for Colleen. One day she received a letter from a woman for whom she had done a favor. Inside was a gift card for $25, along with a brief "thank you" note from the woman.

Colleen hadn't expected to be paid, and she was thrilled. She couldn't remember the last time she had received money that had no specific destination. The possibilities were exciting. A new, pretty spring outfit, perhaps? She headed out to one of her favorite stores.

While wandering up and down the aisles, she passed a display of Easter bunnies and angels. She immediately thought of her dear friend Grace who was mourning the death of her son. He had died around Easter of last year. With the anniversary approaching, she wondered how Grace would handle it.

Grace had started a collection of angels and another of bunnies shortly after the funeral. "They just make me feel better," she once explained to Colleen. Now Colleen was looking at a display of the same items, and . . . she moved closer. There was a statue of an angel holding a bunny. Just perfect for Grace. The price? A little under $25.

No, Colleen thought. *I can't spend my gift card on something for someone else* . . . But she could and she knew it. *You will be repaid*, said a voice in her head, but what did that mean? Quickly, before she could change her mind, she bought the statue, went home, wrapped it, and left it on Grace's porch.

When Grace phoned, Colleen could hardly hear her through the tears. "It's the nicest thing that's happened to me in a long time," her friend told her. "How could you possibly know that I was asking God for a sign that my son is in His arms?"

Colleen cried too, then. She had definitely been repaid, as the words in her head had promised. What could be more enjoyable than making someone else happy?

God probably feels that way too, which is why Colleen received an unexpected check in the mail a few days later, from a utility bill overcharge. The amount? $25.

A modest sum, indeed. But being a part of God's answer to prayer is priceless.

COMFORT, WHEN SHE WAS SICK

⚜

Diana T. was a happily married mother of two daughters, working at a grocery store, when she slowly slid into a depression. Like many in this situation, she did not know why, so she eventually changed jobs, hoping her spirits would brighten.

But they didn't. And one day on her new job, she was hit in the head with a heavy box. While in the hospital emergency room, Diana's doctor told her that she had a buildup of fluid in her skull. This could lead to swelling in the brain, he explained, and she should consult a neurologist if she developed any symptoms.

"Though I didn't notice any significant changes in my health or behavior, I was still depressed," Diana remembers. Medication didn't seem to help, and her crying and outbursts continued, compounded by a feeling of guilt that she couldn't "snap out of it." One day she lost her balance outside and was unable to get up. "I made an appointment with a neurologist," she says, "but he couldn't see me for several months."

Dizziness, nausea, loss of muscle control and mental acuity all followed quickly. Although she was now bedridden, Diana's husband, Rick, refused to let her give up. Eventually he found a clinic to run some tests, and after four days, a surprising diagnosis occurred. There was a blockage in her brain that was causing hydrocephalus. If the blockage was removed, the problem could likely be fixed! Diana's family was overjoyed. Her surgery would be at the UCLA Medical Clinic in Los Angeles, in just two days.

Diana was understandably nervous. She had already suffered greatly, and now worried that she would not be the same person after the surgery. But she had no choice. "I told my daughters to stay home with the therapy puppy we had purchased recently," Diana says. It would be easier for her not to have visitors aside from her husband, in case anything went wrong.

But nothing did. Her surgeon unblocked the ventricle, draining the pressure that had caused the extreme emotions, nausea, and lack of balance. A few hours later, Diana was completely coherent, and called to reassure her daughters. "My oldest said it made her cry to have a real conversation with me," Diana said. "It had been such a miserable year."

Yet Diana remained tormented. She felt angry, even bewildered, and refused to have visitors except Rick. Why? Had she traded her depression for another uncontrollable problem?

On her third day of recovery, Diana looked out to the hallway and thought she saw her daughters walk by her room. "Rick, the girls are here!" she told her husband. "Impossible," Rick said. "They're at home with the puppy, remember?"

"But . . ." She had been so sure. Had she been hallucinating?

A few hours later, Rick had gone for the evening, and Diana saw the girls again, coming down the hallway. This time they turned and came into her room. "They sat down in the chairs next to me," she recalls. "I could see them clearly but their faces were blurred, like on TV when they hide a person's identity." The figures didn't speak or move. They were simply a still, calm presence, waiting, encouraging her to rest.

"I know I was on medication from the surgery," Diana says, "but I wasn't afraid of these beings at all; in fact, the comfort they gave me completely changed my disposition. I was filled with gratitude and joy." She does not know how long the visitors stayed, but her sense of relief remained.

In a week, Diana walked out of the medical center and has been in good health ever since. The women? "I believe they were angels, a vision God sent to help me get through a difficult time," Diana says. "Miracles do happen."

Her Spirit Was in the Pink

⌒◦∞◦⌒

Rose was getting ready for bed one evening, and had just turned off all the bedroom lamps and said her prayers.

As she finished, she saw a radiant light, just ahead of her, a pinkish-gold color. Was she dreaming? Rose thought of her mother, who was very ill, and decided to call her to make sure she was alright.

"I have a radio alarm clock right next to my bed," she says. "And when I saw the time, I remember saying to myself that it was too late to call my mother and disturb her. I decided to call her first thing in the morning."

Rose turned back to where she had seen that beautiful light, and when she saw that it was still there, she was flooded with a feeling of calm and peace. The light was so comforting, Rose let herself relax. Life had been difficult lately, especially the constant worry over her mother's health. But now she felt herself dozing off, while the warm bright light continued to watch over her.

The next morning Rose was awakened by a phone call from her sister. "Mom was taken to the hospital by ambulance last night," Rose's sister said. "You'd better come."

Because Rose lived a few hours away, she did not make it to the hospital to say good-bye to her mother. "But it comforts me to know that this radiant light that visited me could have been my mom or my angel assuring me that everything would be alright," Rose says. "I learned that pink-gold radiant light or auras represent love. I know it definitely was something very beautiful."

Rose has not seen the light again, but she is at peace. "I know my mother, and my angels, are always with me."

THE MYSTERIOUS DIVER THAT
SAVED HER

⸌❧⸍

Dave and Joyce Keel were stationed overseas in Naples, Italy.
One weekend another couple joined them to camp on a Mediterranean
beach farther north than where they usually went. Al and Sonnie were into snorkeling and had brought their gear along. "Joyce, you have to try it," Sonnie urged her.
"You'll love it."

Joyce warned Sonnie she was not a proficient swimmer, but her friend persuaded
her to try. Al and Sonnie gave Joyce a snorkeling crash course, and despite her mis-
givings, she decided to give it a try. "Stay real close to us," Sonnie told her. "If you
do run into trouble, we'll be right there to help."

"Well . . ." Joyce already had her gear on, and it seemed relatively simple. Al had
forgotten something in the car, but urged Joyce to go ahead anyway.

"At the beginning, it was so fascinating," Joyce says. "I couldn't believe everything
I was seeing. The sun was out, so I could see a long way off, and we were moving
along the beach instead of going out in the sea. I was so enthralled that I forgot about
staying with Sonnie and Dave. Then I began to notice that the waves were getting
stronger, and the tide was coming in."

When Joyce looked up, she could barely see Sonnie and Dave. They were far
ahead of her. The waves swamped her, filling the breathing tube in her mouth.
"They had told me to blow the water out, but I couldn't get it out fast enough to take

a breath in," Joyce recalls. "So like any novice, I pulled the tube off so I could get my head up, and breathe." But the waves were higher now, and the fins on her feet seemed to be pulling her down. Joyce gulped for air. "Help!" she screamed. Water pushed over her head and she went under.

"They say you go down three times before you drown," Joyce says. "But I think I popped up four or five times." At one point she felt the bottom and she pushed off as hard as she could. But it was no use. She bounced help-lessly along, tossed by the sea's power, each wave pulling her under again and again. Where was Dave? Their friends? She screamed again, but her strength was fading.

Suddenly, an arm came around her. *It must be Al*, she thought, though she couldn't see, flailing to get her head above the water. "Stop fighting me! I'm trying to help you!" the man shouted, and began to swim, pulling her along. His grip was strong and Joyce noticed he was wearing a wet suit. Had Al brought one along? She could hardly think . . .

In a moment or two, she was lying, exhausted, on the beach, and her hus-band and Sonnie were running toward her. "We saw you thrashing around and we knew you were in trouble," Dave told her, grasping her hand, "but we were so far ahead . . ."

"It took us a while to get to you," Sonnie explained, tears gathering. "How did you make it to shore?"

Joyce looked at her, puzzled. "Why, Al saved me."

"Al?" They turned as Al came running up, completely dry. "I saw you struggling, but it was too late for me to go in," he explained. "Dave and Sonnie were closer to you than I was . . ."

"You didn't grab me?" Joyce asked him, bewildered. "But . . ." She looked around. The man in the wet suit had disappeared. And one other odd thing: her rescuer had spoken perfect English, not Italian.

An angel? "I have always wondered," Joyce says today, glad that on her first day of snorkeling, a mysterious diver had come to her rescue.

A Vehicle of God's Love

꧁❧

We don't always sense angels working around us. But sometimes life's coincidences are so compelling only a heavenly being could be involved.

Jim would agree. It was one of those tragic situations in life that everyone eventually goes through, even those who are very close to God. It was 1993, and Jim and his wife were divorcing. Jim's wife had been awarded primary custody of their ten-year-old son.

"She also was given the good car, although I was still making payments on it," says Jim. "With the other financial settlements, I was left pretty much broke."

To make matters worse, one day Jim's wife left town, taking their son with her. They settled in a town about 130 miles away, but it might as well have been 13,000 miles since Jim's old car was rusted and extremely unreliable.

"I was terrified that my son might feel abandoned," Jim says, "and I knew I needed to see him regularly. So I started praying extremely hard."

Jim told God all about his need for more reliable transportation, and at the same time began researching cars. He thought a 1989 Omni might be economical, but when he looked up the price, it was about $4,000—much too high for his budget. One morning, however, as Jim drove past a bait shop he saw a 1989 Omni parked in front, with a For Sale sign on it. He pulled into the parking lot for a look.

"How much are you asking for your Omni?" he asked the store clerk. "$850," the man replied. *Impossible*, Jim thought. *The engine or transmission must be bad.* "Can I try it?" he asked. "Sure," the clerk agreed.

The Omni was a wonderful car. The only flaw that Jim could find was a bad wheel bearing, but he could get that fixed. He came back to the shop with his heart pounding. This *had* to be his car. "How about $750?" he asked.

"$800," the clerk countered. And that was that.

Jim's job was a hundred miles round trip every day, and with trips to see his son, he put 56,000 miles on the Omni during his first year of ownership. Though he was able to get a transfer much closer to his home, by the third year, the car had 200,000 miles on it and was starting to act up.

"One day as I started out to visit my son, the car began to die at every corner," Jim says. Somehow, he knew that this was the end of the partnership. But he had recovered somewhat financially and could afford modest payments on a better used car now.

He turned the Omni toward home, and said a prayer of thanks. God had found him a car just when he desperately needed one—and kept it going so he could build a deeper relationship with his son. He would always be grateful for that.

At that moment, he wasn't sure he imagined it, but he heard a voice say, "I can do better than that!"

Suddenly a deer ran out and struck the side of his car. No one was hurt, but the insurance company sent a check to Jim for $850, enough for a down payment on another car.

Today Jim's son is a college graduate and a husband, and has a good relationship with his father, honed during those difficult days. Turns out God's love takes many forms—even that of an old Omni.

Help for Nuns in Angel White

❦

Nuns usually enjoy telling people of the miracles that graced their order's founders, and the Sisters of the Third Order of St. Francis are no exception.

The primary objective of this order is to care for the sick and the poor, and through the years they have had some interesting experiences. One of their favorites occurred around 1885, several years after they had come to America and settled in the Peoria, Illinois, area.

A contagious disease had broken out, and many ill people were being brought to Mother Krasse and her sisters. Most of the sick were delirious with high fever.

The sisters took in everyone who was brought to them. Patients lay on the floor in the narrow hallways after the nuns had given up their beds. The sisters worked night and day caring for the sick.

At one point, a doctor stopped by and noticed how exhausted the nuns were. They obviously needed relief and rest, but he knew they would never abandon the patients. "I'll send some women from town to help you so you can all get some sleep tonight," he told Sister Krasse. She was thrilled.

Sure enough, later that day three women arrived, dressed in white. "We came to help you care for the patients," one said. Needless to say, they were greeted with joy by the sisters.

That night, the three helpers insisted that the sisters find places where they could rest, no matter where. The sisters, exhausted, needed no encouragement and slept soundly.

The next morning, the patients were all resting quietly, and many of them no longer had a fever. Several remarked that the three women had been wonderful nurses and very kind throughout the night. But where were they? Sister Krasse and the other nuns looked for the women to thank them, but they had apparently left.

The following day, the doctor returned to check patients, and Sister Krasse told him how helpful the visitors had been. "Thank you so much for the extra help," she said. "I don't know what we would have done without them."

"Sister"—the doctor shook his head—"I never sent anyone to help you. There were so many ill people in town that I never found anyone."

But helpers did come! Everyone saw them. We know *who* they were, don't we?

An Earth Angel on the Trail

Angels don't always announce their arrival. And they don't always have wings. But however angels come, they change our lives. Tammy Kline would agree.

Tammy, her husband, Rich, and several others had embarked on the Grand Canyon climb. An experienced hiker (and married to one), Tammy had never had a serious problem climbing hills in Colorado. But now as the group approached Phantom Ranch at the bottom of the Grand Canyon, the huge, uneven steps going down the trail were about 18 inches apart. Each time Tammy landed on one, she jarred her knee and gradually the pain began.

At first, as she soaked her leg in the cold creek, she thought she would be fine. "We reached Phantom Ranch around lunchtime, and I would be able to rest until our early morning departure the next day," she says. "I kept my leg iced, elevated, and wrapped. My husband, Rich, went to the general store and bought an Ace bandage because the wrap that was in our first-aid kit wasn't supportive enough."

The bandage didn't seem to help either. As the time passed, Tammy began to worry. *What if her leg didn't respond to rest? If she needed a mule to ride, would one be available? What if she got partway up the mountain, and couldn't go any farther?* "I prayed all night that God would help me find a way out," Tammy says. "This trip had been Rich's dream since I could remember and I didn't want to let him down."

The next morning, the hikers were on the trail by dawn. Rich set a slow pace up the canyon and the group stopped frequently. But the rest had done little to relieve

Tammy's pain. By the time they stopped for a break at Indian Garden, she wasn't sure if she could take another step.

A climber named Tom was there finishing his break. He had already passed their group earlier that morning, and now noticed Tammy's limping. "Trouble with your knee?" he asked her.

"The wrap I'm using isn't supportive enough," she told him, "and every time my foot hits a rock, the pain shoots through my leg." She sighed, looking around. There were rocks everywhere.

"I have an extra compression knee brace in my pack," Tom remarked. "Let me find it."

An extra compression brace? As unlikely as an extra pot of gold, Tammy thought. Even so, it probably wouldn't fit. Tammy was very small, and Tom was large. She held her breath as Tom pulled out the brace and handed it to her. It fit her perfectly.

Tom did not vanish, as angels sometimes do. He simply waved away her thanks, and continued down the path he was following. The trip was still very trying for Tammy. "But the brace, unlike the wrap, held my knee rigid and it didn't twist every time I stepped on a rock," she says. "We made it to the top in about eight hours, which is within the average time span. But I couldn't have made it without Tom. He saved our vacation." And if that's not what angels do, what is?

For many days after this experience, Tammy could think of little else. It was such an obvious answer to her prayers. "I know in the depth of my heart that God answers prayers," she says. "And he truly listens when we talk to Him. We just need to open our hearts so we can see and understand His answers."

The Angel on the Beat-up Bike

꧁❧꧂

Paula Steinke was enjoying Prospect High School immensely.

She was now a sophomore, but her parents were still hesitant about giving her more freedom. "I especially worry when you stay late after school and walk home alone," Paula's dad explained to her. "Promise you'll phone me to come and get you."

Paula promised. But she felt a little guilty. The Steinkes had six children, and her father was busy enough without adding yet another run to his personal taxi service. But she obeyed.

One afternoon, Paula stayed after school to attend a sports match. The game went overtime, and the sun had long set by the time she left the gym. Though she knew she should phone her dad to pick her up, she decided to walk home alone. It wasn't that far and she'd save him an extra errand.

However, Paula hadn't realized how absolutely dark her route was, now that winter was approaching. The streetlights threw little brightness on the sidewalks, enclosed as they were by bushes and overhanging trees—which rustled ominously as she passed. No one was outside, and few cars passed her. Paula became increasingly nervous. *Why hadn't she called her dad?*

Suddenly Paula heard a sound behind her. She half-turned, preparing to run . . . and saw a boy about her own age, riding a bike slowly behind her. "Hi, Paula!" he said and smiled.

Paula stared at him: he was skinny, with short blond hair and a casual air. His long legs were touching the ground, rolling the beat-up bike from side to side. She must know him, she thought. Only he didn't seem at all familiar. "Hi. Have we met?" she asked.

"I've seen you at Prospect High," he answered.

Paula still couldn't remember ever meeting him. But the boy began to ask her about the game she'd just attended, and the two fell into easy conversation. As the blocks passed, Paula relaxed. Her escort had come along at the perfect moment.

Just two houses before Paula's, as if he had known her destination, the boy abruptly pushed down on the pedals. "See ya!" he called over his shoulder and rode away, shirt flapping as he disappeared into the dark.

Paula went into the house, feeling oddly contented. She waved to her mother in the kitchen, then went upstairs, still bemused. Her father was right, she knew. She shouldn't be out in the dark alone, and she wouldn't do it again. But how lucky she had been, to run into that boy . . .

She realized now that he had known her name, but she didn't know his. She grabbed her yearbook to look him up.

But there was no photograph of the blond boy, not in homeroom or activity photos. And although Paula attended high school for two more years, she never saw him again.

"He said he saw me at Prospect High," she says today, "and I have no doubt that he did. Guardian angels don't always have wings."

No Batteries Required

⌒◈⌒

Debe's mother-in-law passed away in Wisconsin during freezing January, so the family decided to hold a memorial service at the funeral home chapel instead of at a gravesite.

With so many friends and family members traveling to say their last good-byes, "We put all her photos and favorite memories out for all to see," Debe says. "One item I wanted to have on display was an angel that had fiber optics in her outstretched wings." Debe and her husband had given the angel to his mother the previous Christmas, and she loved looking at it and watching the colors changing on the wings.

"On the morning of the service, I had some new batteries, just purchased, and I put them into the angel to be sure it would light up," Debe says. "But nothing happened." Maybe she hadn't put them in correctly. Debe asked her husband to see if something was wrong with the batteries. While she finished dressing, he checked them out again. "You put them in right, but I did it again," he told her. "They still won't light."

By now it was 9 a.m. and the family was to meet at the funeral home chapel at 9:30. Maybe something had broken inside the angel? But everything looked fine. "We have to go," Debe's husband told her. He had taken out the batteries again (although she didn't know it). "Let's just have the angel sitting by her photo," he suggested as he went to start the car.

Debe was terribly disappointed. The lighted angel would have made the display so beautiful. She buttoned her coat and picked up the angel. *Just one more try*, she thought, flipping the switch. The angel lit up. Shocked, Debe turned the angel over to check the batteries, but there were none.

Heart pounding, Debe looked around, and saw the four AA batteries on the table. She snapped them in and got in the car. "Oh, you found some other batteries," her husband remarked, looking at the angel's beautiful glow. "Uh-huh," Debe murmured, her shock preventing her from telling him the rest of the story. If they had ever wondered where their mother was, they knew now that she was close as could be.

A few days later, Debe told her husband what had happened. He had no trouble believing it. "Well," he said, "that's Mom. She wanted to have that angel at her service. And she did."

"You see?" Debe points out. "You never know when angels are around!"

THE NEST EGG

Liz had separated from her husband. She was emotionally devastated, and the reality of keeping her two preschool daughters fed and cared for had all but shattered her spirit.

She believed in God, but where was He? She felt so alone. Reluctantly, she applied to get financial aid until she could find a job.

A few days later, Liz realized that she had no money and no food in the cupboards. She checked her purse and pockets just in case, but there was no money anywhere, no way to buy even a small bag of groceries.

"I sent the girls next door because I knew my nice neighbor would feed them," she recalls. "Then I sat on the couch and cried." She prayed for just enough money to buy some groceries for the next week.

As Liz wept, her five year-old, Crystal, came back into the apartment. "Mommy, what's the matter?" she asked. Not wanting her daughter to see her upset, she answered, "Nothing, honey. Why don't you go outside and do something?"

"Like what?" Crystal persisted.

Liz wiped her eyes, thinking. "Why don't you take out the garbage? That would be a big help."

"Okay!" Crystal took the garbage bag and headed out to the apartment complex Dumpsters. A moment later, she was back. "Mommy, can I keep this plastic egg that I found in the trash? I can put my Barbie doll clothes in it."

"No, honey," Liz murmured absently. "You're not supposed to bring things in from the garbage. It might be dirty."

"It's not, Mommy. Please?" Crystal insisted. "I'll keep the egg and you can keep the money in it."

Liz's heart seemed to stop. "What money?"

"Here," Crystal said, and she pulled four twenty-dollar bills out of the egg. Liz stared at the bills. The Dumpsters were huge—there was no possible way she could find the owner of those bills. Did God mean them for her? Hadn't she asked? "I will never leave you nor forsake you. . . ." The comforting words from the Bible washed over her, and she understood.

"The money bought us groceries until my aid came through," Liz says. "I found a job, and things are much better today, but I've never forgotten that moment, and the reassurance it brought me." It wasn't so much the money itself, she says, but the certainty that God was near and caring for her, answering her prayer in His own way, in His own time.

WHEN ANGELS HAVE NO NAMES

 ❧

As a journalist and author, I've reported on countless stories of angels. It's important to me that each of these stories is checked out as thoroughly as possible. I like to talk to the witness directly, and if there's corroboration, such as newspaper clips or onlookers or medical reports, I'll use them as well.

But there are moments when I'm unprepared: Someone approaches me at a book signing when I have neither notepad nor tape recorder, or phones in on a radio show where I am a guest, or speaks up at a lecture, to tell a story of her own. Invariably during the hubbub these people get away before I am able to jot down their full names and addresses. But their stories are too good to go untold. Here are some of my favorites. I may not have gotten all their names right, but the facts are exactly as they were related to me.

When I was a guest on CFRB Radio in Toronto, John phoned in. Two years earlier as a college exchange student he had been touring Germany and had lost his way. By the time he found the bus station it was dark and he had missed the last bus back to the hostel where he'd planned to stay. Now what? He barely spoke German, and as he walked away from the deserted depot he noticed three unsavory-looking men following him, like hungry foxes closing in on a chicken. John clenched his fists, ready to defend himself.

Just then a car pulled up. "Jump in!" a woman called from the passenger seat.

John did. His rescuers, a friendly middle-aged couple, spoke English fluently, and agreed that it was fortunate they had happened to be passing the station at that moment. But when John told them where he was staying, the woman looked doubt-ful. "That's way on the other side of the city," she said.

"Oh, drop me anywhere," John said quickly. "I don't want to take you out of your way."

"Why don't you just come home with us?" the man suggested. "We've got plenty of room, and we can bring you back to the bus station tomorrow morning on our way to work."

John protested, but the couple assured him he would be no bother at all. Weren't Europeans noted for being hospitable, perhaps more casual and trusting than North Americans? John decided that this was part of his adventure abroad. He would relax and enjoy it.

Their route became increasingly deserted until they wound up in a forest on the outskirts of town. The stretch they traveled was dark, surrounded on both sides by tall trees and dense vegetation. But this serene and attractive couple—Frieda and Hans—chatted with him like longtime friends, dispelling any doubts.

Eventually they stopped in front of a charming house. "It's a bit on the quiet side," Frieda told John, "but we love it here." The couple escorted John to the kitchen. Hans whipped up a quick meal while Frieda arranged the guest room. The three of them ate together, talking late into the night. John had never felt so warmly welcomed. He slept blissfully, enjoyed a tasty breakfast the next morning, and rode with the couple back to the bus terminal. "You've been wonderful," John told them as he got out of the car. "I'll never forget you." He took down the address Frieda dictated—he would certainly keep in touch—and watched until their car merged into the traffic.

John returned to Canada, and immediately wrote a thank-you note to Hans and Frieda. He was disappointed when they didn't respond, but eventually memories of the trip, and his rescuers, faded.

The following year John vacationed in the same area of Germany. He told some townspeople of his previous encounter, only to be greeted by strange looks. "There's no house in that forest. No one lives there," they told him. Finally John drove to the post office that serviced the area where the couple lived. On the way he recognized the deserted route and the dense forest surrounding it.

But postal workers confirmed what John had already been told. The address Frieda had given him was nonexistent. There was no house in the forest beneath the tall trees. Nor, to anyone's recollection, had there ever been one there. Yet John's thank-you note was never returned. He believes his hosts received it—in one way or another.

⚬⚭⚬

At a church in Chicago a young woman told the congregation how she and a group of friends had been swimming in Lake Michigan off a Chicago pier. Laurie and her friends were the only ones there because swimming was forbidden; the water was too shallow for diving, and there were rocks on the sandy bottom. "But we ignored the signs and swam anyway," Laurie confessed ruefully.

The teenagers had spent at least an hour diving and playing in the waves. Tired, they headed down the pier toward shore. Laurie decided to dive once more. She did, almost brushing the sandy bottom, and then started to swim upward. But something held her back. Horrified, Laurie realized that her foot was caught in a tight rocky crevice. She was trapped!

"I threw up my hand and waved frantically, my fingers just breaking the lake's surface," Laurie said. Were any of her friends still near enough to see her desperate signal? Someone had to. Otherwise she was going to drown!

Suddenly she felt a strong hand grasp her wrist, and pull—hard. Somehow her foot came free, and she burst to the water's surface, her lungs aching. Laurie looked around. There was no one holding her hand or even treading water nearby. Laurie was the only person in the water.

Shakily she climbed onto the pier and walked toward her friends. They were all sunning themselves on the sand, nowhere near the pier.

"You guys," she called, "who pulled me out just now?"

"Out of where?" one of the boys asked.

"My foot was caught and I almost drowned," Laurie told them. She pointed to her right foot. Despite being wedged so tight in the crevice and then pulled out, it didn't have a single scratch on it. Puzzled, she asked, "Which one of you saved me?"

A few years have passed since Laurie's close call, and not one of her friends has ever admitted to pulling her up to safety or even knowing she was in trouble. "It seems unlikely that whoever did it could have completely vanished the moment I surfaced," Laurie explained that day in church. "Perhaps it was a lifeguard of a different kind."

⚬⟨⟩⚬

During a book signing in Lexington, Kentucky, a group of women gathered around my table to tell about their neighbor, Barbara, who had not been able to come and tell me this story herself. Barbara was driving her six-year-old son, Benjamin, to his piano lesson. They were late, and Barbara was beginning to think she should have canceled it. There was always so much to do, and Barbara, a night-duty nurse at the local hospital, had recently worked extra shifts. She was tired. The sleet storm and icy roads added to her tension. Maybe she should turn the car around.

"Mom!" Ben cried. "Look!"

Just ahead a car had lost control on a patch of ice. As Barbara tapped the brakes, the other car spun wildly, rolled over, then crashed sideways into a telephone pole.

Barbara pulled over, skidded to a stop, and threw open her door. Thank goodness she was a nurse—she might be able to help these unfortunate passengers. Then she paused. What about Ben? She couldn't take him with her—little boys shouldn't see scenes like the one she anticipated. But was it safe to leave him alone? What if their car was hit from behind? For a brief moment Barbara considered going on her way. Someone else was sure to come along. *No!* "Ben, honey, promise me you'll stay in the car!"

"I will, Mommy," he said as she ran, slipping and sliding, toward the crash site.

It was worse than she'd feared. Two girls of high school age were in the car. One, the blonde on the passenger side, was dead, killed on impact. The driver, however, was still breathing. She was unconscious and pinned in the wreckage. Barbara quickly applied pressure to the wound in the teenager's head while her practiced eye catalogued the other injuries. A broken leg, maybe two, along with probable internal bleeding. But if help came soon, the girl would live.

A trucker had pulled up and was calling for help on his cellular phone. Soon Barbara heard the ambulance sirens. A few moments later she surrendered her lonely post to rescue workers. "Good job," one said as he examined the driver's wounds. "You probably saved her life, ma'am."

Perhaps. But as Barbara walked back to her car, a feeling of sadness overwhelmed her, especially for the family of the girl who had died. Their lives would never be the same. *Oh, God, why do such things have to happen?*

Slowly Barbara opened her car door. What should she tell Benjamin? He was staring at the crash site, his blue eyes huge. "Mom," he whispered, "did you see it?"

"See what, honey?" she asked.

"The angel, Mom! He came down from the sky while you were running to the car. And he opened the door, and he took that girl out."

Barbara's eyes filled with tears. "Which door, Ben?"

"The passenger side. He took the girl's hand, and they floated up to heaven together."

"What about the driver?"

Ben shrugged. "I didn't see anyone else."

Later Barbara was able to meet the families of both victims. They expressed their gratitude for the help she had provided. Barbara was able to give them something more: Ben's vision. There was no way he could have known—by ordinary means—who was in the car or what had happened to either of the passengers. Nor could the passenger door have been opened; Barbara had seen its tangle of immovable steel herself. Yet Ben's account brought consolation to a grieving family. Their daughter was safe in heaven. And they would see her again.

ANGEL IN THE X-RAY ROOM

Many angel stories occur in hospitals, and that's logical, isn't it? Where better to look for helpers of the spiritual kind?

Mary LaGrange of Greenfield, Wisconsin, would agree. She was concerned when her brother George was admitted to the hospital to have laser surgery on his lower eyelid. He had had a previous surgery on that eyelid because of a bout with cancer, and the laser had removed a small portion of lid and his eyelashes. Now his eye was becoming irritated, and the doctor wanted to do the procedure again.

"George was not comfortable about having a second surgery," says Mary, "so we prayed that someone would help him make the right decision."

On the evening he was admitted, George was still wrestling with the options when a doctor came in. "I'd like to take some pictures of your eye," the man explained. "Just follow me."

More pictures! George inwardly groaned. He'd never seen this physician before, but he followed him down the hospital hallway to a door at the end. The door didn't open easily, and the doctor fiddled with the doorknob, as if he was unsure as to how it worked. But there were the X-ray machines in the room, and the doctor set everything up and took the pictures. "You know," George said, as the session ended, "I'm not really sure I need this treatment."

"Well, it's up to you," the doctor pointed out. "You can do it, but in my opinion, it's really not necessary. The condition could very well clear up on its own."

"Really?" George was surprised. No one else had mentioned this possibility. When the doctor left, George returned to thinking.

By the time the nurse came in that morning, he had made his decision. "We had asked for someone to give us some advice," says Mary, "and that's what we received. George decided not to have the surgery, and he went home feeling very relieved."

About a week later, George stopped in at the hospital accounting department. He wanted to see if that last set of X-rays would be covered by his insurance. But a surprise awaited him. There was no record of any extra pictures taken. "Are you sure?" George asked. "Maybe they're lost."

"What was the doctor's name?" the woman asked.

George hadn't noticed any identification. And there was no record of the doctor's consultation.

The bills never turned up, and George was never bothered by his eye condition again. "The whole experience was amazing," Mary says. She won't forget to ask for help the next time.

An Angelic Rescue

⟨❧⟩

Angie and Andy L. were thrilled about becoming home owners in Kansas City, and they were determined to learn all the skills needed to keep their "palace" in great condition.

A few days after Andy left on a business trip, Angie noticed that the lawn needed cutting. *Wouldn't Andy be pleased if he came home and found the task done?* Angie thought. She'd never operated a lawn mower before, but how hard could it be?

Going out to the garage, she grabbed the gas can and poured gasoline into the mower, just as she had watched Andy do. Unfortunately, she spilled some on the garage floor.

She cleaned it up as best she could, but now . . . where to put the soaked rags? And did she get enough up so it would be safe to start her car, or would it ignite? What if Andy drove into the garage over the spill? This was getting complicated.

Since Angie hadn't met any of her neighbors yet, she felt too foolish to ask them for help, so she phoned her grandmother in Fort Wayne, Indiana, for advice. Her grandmother, Ilean Park, was not a gasoline expert either.

"Call the fire department, and ask them," she suggested.

"Gram, I'd be embarrassed," said Angie. "What if they came with the sirens and the lights . . ."

"What if they didn't, and a fire started?" Ilean countered. Angie agreed.

The firefighters came quietly, reassured Angie that she'd done the right thing, and finished her cleanup. While they were there, one suggested they check the air quality in her new home. Angie nodded her head in agreement.

The firemen were in the basement for what seemed like a long time. When they finally came upstairs, their faces were solemn.

"It's a very good thing we were here," one told Angie. "You have a severe carbon monoxide leak. We've already called your builder and he's on his way."

"Carbon monoxide?" Angie was stunned.

The fireman nodded. "God works in mysterious ways," he told her. "You might have died here alone."

It was a gift from heaven, Angie and Andrew agreed later, when all was calm again. For who would have anticipated anything like this occurring in a brand-new house?

Angie's grandmother knows who to thank. Says Ilean, "I am convinced that Angie's guardian angel was involved."

DID AN ANGEL HELP HER GET TO HER DYING MOM'S SIDE?

⌗⌗⌗

Shirley Miller of Pittsburgh had received a phone call from her brother in Phoenix, which had left her alarmed and upset. "Our ninety-six-year-old mother was in the hospital, and wasn't expected to live much longer," Shirley says. "The family was gathering, and I needed to fly out as soon as possible."

Fortunately she was able to find a seat on a flight later that day. A friend took her to the airport and dropped her in front of her airline checkpoint. So far, so good. But when she arrived at the security line, her heart sank. Passengers were in two lines, each extending the length of the area, and moving slowly. Shirley looked at her watch. There was no way she could get through this line and reach her gate in time. She was going to miss her flight.

Shirley began to pray. *Mom, wait for me*, she said in her heart. A moment later, Shirley saw a woman in a uniform coming toward her. "Hello," she said to Shirley, ignoring the other passengers. "Do you see that line across the room?"

"Yes," Shirley answered. What now? Had she done something wrong?

"If you go over and get into that line, you'll make your flight easily," the woman said to Shirley, and then walked past. Relieved, Shirley wasted no time crossing the room, and got into the much shorter line. It was moving quickly, she noticed. What a relief!

When she looked back at the line she had left, it was still not moving. And she saw no sign of the woman in the uniform. Why had she singled out Shirley from among all those passengers? No one else had been told to move In fact, no one around her seemed to have noticed the woman at all.

"I made my flight and was able to kiss my mother good-bye and hold her hand until she went to be with our Lord," says Shirley. "I'm convinced the woman in the uniform was my guardian angel. How beautiful is that?"

AN ANGEL'S MESSAGE IN STONE

Georgia Lea Horvath and her husband of North Bend, Washington, were grieving the loss of their twenty-six-year-old son, Scott. The three of them had planned a Hawaii trip before he passed. As the departure date approached, neither grieving parent wanted to go. One day, however, Georgia reconsidered. Maybe the trip would distract them. They invited her mother to join them.

The island was beautiful. One morning Georgia and her husband took a walk along the beach where black lava had hardened into the water. All around the Big Island, people would leave names and messages made out of white stones on this lava, so they decided to leave a message: "Aloha, Scott 1/11/72–9/15/98," it read. (*Aloha* means "hello," "good-bye," and "love.") The couple took a picture of it and walked on.

"The next day we took my mom for a walk," says Georgia, "and when we reached that place, she spotted the message right away." Georgia thought it would have been washed away by the waves because it was right next to the ocean. Everyone was thrilled that the writing was still there.

On that day, the Horvaths had planned to take a twelve-hour drive around the entire island. The night before, a neighbor suggested they avoid a certain area. "Don't bother to turn off at the south end of the island to see the most southern tip of the United States," he cautioned them. "It isn't worth the drive on a dirt road, and nothing is there anyway." The couple agreed. This man certainly knew more than they did about tourist attractions.

They had completed the first part of their journey, and Georgia was driving when she saw the sign: TURN HERE to See the Southernmost Tip. "Remember," said her husband, "this is where that man said to go back."

"I remember," Georgia said, and started to turn. Then, at the last minute, she veered back, bouncing down the dirt road. "We're here," she said to her surprised husband. "Let's go as far as we can."

He shrugged. Up ahead he could see more black lava, just like the kind they had seen yesterday. Just then the path ahead separated, and Georgia had to turn left or right. "My hand seemed to turn toward the left," she says.

They drove to the edge of the lava, and stopped. The area was completely deserted, just water splashing along the shore, and once again lots of white stone messages all over from people who had visited. "We got out of the car and started to walk," Georgia says. "Then all three of us stopped. Ahead of us was a message written on a white stone: "Love U 2," it said. "Scott."

All three adults started to weep. "It was a message from Scott," Georgia says. "We know he didn't actually write it, but the fact that we almost didn't go to that area, and when we did stop, there it was . . . well, we were meant to see it." It made their trip, and aided their mourning. Scott was not gone, they knew now, just enjoying a beautiful piece of heaven.

WHAT DO THE LITTLE ONES SEE?

W hen my book *Where Angels Walk* was published in 1992, I was delighted by the positive response from readers. I had expected people to tell me about their own angel experiences, but I was surprised at how many parents wrote about their children's. One morning I settled down with a batch of mail, and opened a typical letter. "You've done a lot of research on angels," a young mother wrote. "Have you ever heard of preschoolers seeing things we adults can't, or being aware of heaven and angels without anyone prompting them?"

Seeing things we can't . . . I recalled Peter, an imaginary companion my four sons had entertained many years ago. Peter hadn't "officially" lived with us, but frequently popped in to visit and to hear nightly prayers or share lunch. As an enlightened parent I had tolerated the boys' fantasy. "Is Peter here today?" I asked innocently. "Does he want a cookie?"

Now, as I read this letter, something occurred to me. No matter how impromptu my questions about Peter, my boys had always answered in unison. "No, Mommy," they said shaking their heads. "Peter didn't come today." Or if Peter was supposedly nearby, four pairs of eyes focused on the same spot in the room. "There he is—can't you see him?" one said, pointing while the others laughed. I had always taken it as a joke. Well, wasn't it?

During the next few weeks I asked my now-grown sons about Peter, and was I rewarded with blank stares. No one recalled our game of pretend. Had it all been make-believe? And if so, why were other parents having the same kind of experiences?

Nita Hannie, of Baton Rouge, Louisiana, wrote me about a difficult time when her son, Patrick, just turned two, was receiving chemotherapy as an outpatient. Patrick developed a low-grade fever, but instead of admitting him to the hospital, the emergency room physician prescribed an over-the-counter medicine. That evening Patrick's temperature rose. "I put him in bed with me, turned out the light, and prayed about what to do," Nita recalls. "After maybe fifteen minutes of silence, Patrick suddenly sat up. Staring at a corner of the room, he said, 'Hi, angel!'"

"Patrick?" Nita whispered in the dark. "What are you seeing?"

Patrick didn't respond. "Hi, angel!" he repeated.

"He spoke with a comfort and familiarity usually reserved for family," Nita says. "He talked for nearly a minute in his own baby jabber, punctuated clearly with the word *angel*, then lay down, smiled at me, and turned over to sleep." A half hour later Nita checked his temperature. Patrick was fever-free.

"Although Patrick has been back in the hospital since then, he continues to be in remission, and is doing well," Nita says. "I believe an angel was in the room with us, bringing healing and comfort, and Patrick saw it."

Patrick knew the word *angel*. Some children did not—yet their experiences were remarkably similar. When three-year-old Danny Agnese of Bethpage, New York, ran across the living room and tripped, his mother, Laura, watched in fear as he fell toward a sharp corner of a table. Suddenly Danny stopped in midair, righted himself, and ran on, uninjured.

Laura was mystified. How could the law of gravity be defied? The next day Danny told her that he had seen "a pretty lady" in his room. "She caught me yesterday so I wouldn't hit my head against the table," he explained. "She said she would take care of me."

Danny had no formal knowledge of spiritual things; he had seemed too young to learn. Then he saw a painting of an angel. "That's her!" he exclaimed. "That's the lady!"

These reports intrigued me. It seemed logical that children were closer to paradise than we adults—hadn't Jesus told us that their innocence and pure hearts were what the kingdom of God is all about? Perhaps little ones, so fresh from heaven, hadn't yet experienced a clear-cut boundary between the two worlds and for a short while could be part of both.

In addition to events happening to children today, I heard from many adults about their childhood experiences. "My parents must have let me out of their sight for a few moments. I remember wandering out to the neighboring highway, close to the center lane, then looking up, and seeing a huge truck coming down the hill toward me," Marsha Wood of Maggie Valley, North Carolina, recounted. "There was something in front of the truck, like the sun's rays, with a shining figure in its center. I was much too young to understand then, but now I realize it was an angel that caused the truck to come to a complete stop, just inches from me."

Reverend Linda Walters, a pastor in Cheyenne, Wyoming, was seven when her younger cousin died of cancer. A few weeks later, she remembers, another little girl mysteriously arrived to play with her.

The child did not attend Linda's school, and didn't seem to live nearby. But Linda was lonely, and accepted her new friend gratefully. The two played happily each day, but when Linda asked her mother for a snack to share, she got a surprise. Neither her mother, nor anyone else, could see the visitor.

"At first my mother was alarmed that I was having hallucinations, and she called the doctor," Linda reports. "He assured her that imaginary friends were normal, so the family played along with me."

The visitor came every day for several weeks, banishing Linda's sorrow. "Then one day she said she had to be moving along, that other people needed her help," Linda recalls. She never saw her friend again, but has never forgotten her.

These letters and others like them put things in a new light for me. Like Linda Walters's mother, I had assumed my sons' playmate was an illusion. After all, children do have rich imaginations, and not every story they tell is true. And yet, could mine have concocted such a perfectly timed practical joke, one that went on for several years before the veil between heaven and earth fully descended? What if Peter was more than just a pretend figure? What if he was a guardian angel?

I guess I'll never know for sure. But recently one of my sons told me about an evening when he was locked out of his truck. "I was in the back of a dark parking lot, miles from home, no stores open, and no way of getting the tool I needed to pop the lock," Bill explained. "Then, all of a sudden, another truck pulled in and drove right to where I was standing. The guy got out—carrying the tool I needed—sprang the lock, smiled at me, got in his truck, and drove away." Bill looked at me. "What do you think of that, Mom?"

I think Peter is still on the job.

Stranded on a Dark Mountain Pass

❧

John White was the general sales manager at a Ford dealership in Kingman, Arizona. Sometimes he drove trade-ins home at night to see if they were fit for resale. The trip to John's home in Bullhead City was a challenge: he had to maneuver through a dangerous mountain pass, but also watch out for unsavory characters known to also travel the road.

One night John had just reached the top of that treacherous mountain pass, when the used car went dead. "No lights, no power brakes or steering," John recalls. Somehow he guided it through the winding curves, pulled it off the highway, and came to a stop in pitch darkness.

Though he was relieved, he soon realized that with no lights it would be difficult to attract help. And what if he attracted a criminal instead? It was hours until sunrise.

An hour or so later, a police car came by, traveling somewhat slowly. John waved with all his might, and the officer spotted him. "I'm heading to a conference in Laughlin, Nevada," the officer told John as he sized up the situation. "I can give you a ride to Bullhead City."

What a relief! John couldn't believe his luck. As the two men talked, John discovered that his rescuer used to be an FBI agent, and now worked for the Flagstaff Police Department. Even better, when they got to Bullhead, the officer volunteered to drive John to his door. "It's not that far out of my way," he said, and a few moments later, John was home, and shaking the kind man's hand in appreciation.

The police car pulled away just as John's wife opened the front door. "I saw the police officer," she said to John. "Is anything wrong?"

"Everything is fine," John assured her, and told her of his luck in being rescued by a police officer. "I hope you said thank you," his wife nudged.

"I did, but I never got his name," said John. "Maybe I should write him a note."

The following morning, John called the Flagstaff Police Department. He was surprised to learn that no one matched the description of his rescuer, and further, none of their officers were former FBI agents. They referred John to the highway patrol, who referred him to the sheriff's department, with the same results. Had he misunderstood? No, he remembered that conversation, almost word for word.

"If it hadn't been for my wife, who saw me getting out of the police car, I might have thought I was losing my mind," John says.

About six months later, it dawned on John that the man could have been a guardian angel. "Maybe I would have been killed on that mountain road, by a car or by criminals, but God had other things for me to do," says John, who has become a Christian.

As for that police officer, he could have very well worked for the police department. Many angels do.

VISION OF GOD'S LOVE

Jim Snyder would consider himself an ordinary man living an ordinary life, surely not one that involves angel sightings. But when his young wife died of pancreatic cancer, Jim was devastated by her loss.

He tried to hold everything together and deal with his grief. But as months passed and Jim's heartache continued, "I began asking God for a sign that everything would be okay, and that I would eventually get through this," Jim says.

One night, about six months after his loss, as he lay in bed trying to fall asleep, he opened his eyes for a moment. There, floating almost casually above his bed, was an angel. "The image was moving, and the face of the angel was surrounded by pillow-white clouds, almost like a wreath," Jim recalls.

Jim could scarcely believe what he was seeing. He blinked several times, but the vision remained. Then slowly it moved across the ceiling. "It had the most peaceful look on its face," Jim says, "and it slowly faded away. I lay there for several minutes, enjoying the calmest and most restful feeling I had ever experienced."

Jim thought about the vision all week. *Was it an angel? If so, why had it been sent to him?*

He was just an ordinary person, wasn't he? Perhaps it had just been a figment of his imagination? And yet there had been that indescribable moment of joy and unshakable faith. . . .

That Wednesday, Jim attended a Bible study meeting and also went to church services. As the groups broke up and people headed home, Jim asked the Bible instructor, a complete stranger, if they could speak privately.

"I told him what had happened," Jim says. "I wanted to know if he thought I was going crazy, or perhaps seeing things that weren't there." The man smiled, as if he was not at all surprised by Jim's words.

He walked to his books lying on the table and picked up his Bible. Turning to a marked page, he handed the Bible to Jim.

"I noted this over twenty years ago," he said, "when I saw an image very much like the one you're describing." Jim could hardly believe it. He looked at the under-lined text. "And an angel appeared to him from heaven, and comforted him" (Luke 22:43).

The brief verse described Jesus's suffering in the garden before His crucifixion. Jim was flooded with understanding. God had not sent an angel to banish His own Son's pain, or even to lift it, for this was not in the heavenly plan. But God had sent an angel—to His Son and to every grieving person—to simply be there, with comfort and understanding. "Life is sometimes difficult," Jim's angel had been telling him, "but you will never go through it alone."

ACKNOWLEDGMENTS

Most books wouldn't be written without the help and encouragement of some wonderful people.

I am grateful for the professional advice and assistance of reference librarians, especially Marilyn Uselmann of the Arlington Heights Memorial Library, Thad Voss of Wheaton College, Theresa Bohm of Wycliffe Bible Translators, Dan Sharon of the Asher Library at Spertus College, and Harriet Leonard of the Duke University Divinity Library. I would also like to acknowledge the helpful research departments at the Christian Broadcasting Network, the Assemblies of God General Council Headquarters, and *Guideposts* magazine. The Reverend John H. Hampsch, CME, Henrietta DePaepe, Pauline Cusack, and authors Charles and Frances Hunter deserve mention for providing me with valuable background material.

I extend special thanks to members of the clergy, including the Reverend George Lane, SJ, of Holy Family Church in Chicago; Dr. Timothy Warner, Trinity Evangelical Divinity School in Deerfield, Illinois; Pastor LaVerne Tucker of Redlands, California; and Rabbi Gedalia Schwartz of the Chicago Rabbinical Council.

Especially helpful were the people at the Loretto Chapel in Santa Fe, New Mexico; the 777th Precinct in Dayton, New Jersey; the Write to Publish Conference at Moody Bible Institute; the Swedenborg Foundation; and the National Centre for Padre Pio, as well as Fran White of the Guardian Angels.

My sister, Susan Fichter, merits special mention for being perhaps the first person to see a book possibility in all those letters.

ACKNOWLEDGMENTS

Grateful notice is due the magazine editors who printed my inquiries, most notably at *Liguorian*, *Our Sunday Visitor*, *Annals of St. Anne*, and *Sonlight/Sun*, as well as those lecture sponsors who allowed me to ask audiences for angel experiences.

A special thank-you to Loyola Press for bringing out this anniversary edition of *Where Angels Walk*.

Finally, I'd like to thank my wonderful husband and family, and my friends, particularly members of the Saint Theresa prayer group, the Hickory Nuts, and the Saint Scholastica Class of '56 . . . Your love through the years has sustained and blessed me.

J.W.A.
Arlington Heights, Illinois

ENDNOTES

1. F. S. Smythe, *Camp Six: An Account of the 1933 Mount Everest Expedition* (London: Hodder and Stoughton, 1937), 262.

2. Charles and Frances Hunter, *Angels on Assignment* (Kingwood, TX: Hunter Books, 1979), 183.

3. Corrie ten Boom, *A Prisoner, and Yet* (Toronto, ON: Evangelical Publishers, 1947), 10.

4. Corrie ten Boom, *The Hiding Place* (New York: Bantam Books, 1981), 202–203.

5. Gordon Lindsay, *Ministry of Angels* (Dallas, TX: Christ for the Nations, 1974), 26.

6. Dawn Adrian Adams, "Rain," *Guideposts*, July 1991, 38.

7. Betty Malz, *Angels Watching Over Me* (Old Tappan, NJ: Chosen Books, 1986). Reprinted with permission.

8. Lee Ballard, "The Flutter of Wings," *Dallas*, May 1986. Condensed and reprinted with permission.

9. W. Doyle Gulligan, ed., *Devotion to the Holy Angels* (Houston, TX: Lumen Christi Press, 1990), 101.

10. Malcolm Muggeridge, *Something Beautiful for God* (New York: Ballantine Books, 1971), 41.

11. Adapted from Raymond Edman, "I Too Saw an Angel," originally published in *Bulletin of Wheaton College*, December 1959. Retold with permission.

12. Hope Price, "He Will Send Angels," *Fate*, May 1961. Reprinted with permission.

13. Billy Graham, *Angels: God's Secret Agents* (New York: Doubleday, 1975), 2–3.

14. W. Doyle Gulligan, ed., *Devotion to the Holy Angels* (Houston, TX: Lumen Christi Press, 1990), 98.

15. Corrie ten Boom, *Marching Orders for the End Battle* (Fort Washington, PA: Christian Literature Crusade, 1969), 89–90.

16. Billy Graham, *Angels: God's Secret Agents* (New York: Doubleday, 1975), 3.

17. W. A. Spicer, *Stories of Providential Deliverance* (Washington, DC: Review & Herald Publishing, 1936), 33.

18. Basilea Schlink, *The Unseen World of Angels and Demons* (Old Tappan, NJ: Chosen Books, 1986), 137.

19. Taken from anecdotes and from Alessio Parente, *Send Me Your Guardian Angel* (Amsterdam, NY: Noteworthy Co., 1983). For more information on Padre Pio, contact the National Center for Padre Pio, R.D. #1 (Old Rt. 100), Barto, PA 19504. Or visit http://www.padrepio.org.

20. Retold with the permission of Pastor LaVerne Tucker, director of Quiet Hour, a worldwide mission outreach headquartered in Redlands, California.

21. At the time I learned this story from him, Sergeant Steven Rogers headed the 777th Precinct in Dayton, New Jersey, an organization for police officers and their families.

22. Reprinted with permission from *Guideposts* magazine. Copyright © 1970 by Guideposts Associates, Inc., Carmel, New York 10512.

About the Author

Joan Wester Anderson has been writing about angels since 1992, penning a total of eight books on the subject (including *An Angel to Watch Over Me* and *In the Arms of Angels*). The original edition of *Where Angels Walk* sold more than one million copies. Throughout the years, Anderson has been a frequent guest on radio and television talk shows. She and her husband live in the Chicago area.

A Note from the Editors

❧

We hope you enjoyed *Where Angels Walk* by Joan Wester Anderson, specially selected by the editors of the Books and Inspirational Media Division of Guideposts, a nonprofit organization that touches millions of lives every day through products and services that inspire, encourage, help you grow in your faith, and celebrate God's love.

Thank you for making a difference with your purchase of this book, which helps fund our many outreach programs to military personnel, prisons, hospitals, nursing homes, and educational institutions.

We also create many useful and uplifting online resources. Visit Guideposts.org to read true stories of hope and inspiration, access OurPrayer network, sign up for free newsletters, download free e-books, join our Facebook community, and follow our stimulating blogs.

To learn about other Guideposts publications, including the best-selling devotional *Daily Guideposts*, go to Guideposts.org/Shop, call (800) 932-2145, or write to Guideposts, PO Box 5815, Harlan, Iowa 51593.

Find more inspiring true stories of how God reaches out to us in
Mysterious Ways

A Bimonthly Magazine from the Editors of Guideposts

Claim Your FREE ISSUE!

Learn more at
Guideposts.org/MysteriousWaysFreeIssue

To receive weekly stories about those inexplicable, chill-down-your-spine experiences that are more than mere coincidences, sign up for your FREE e-mail newsletter at Guideposts.org/newsletters.

Join us on 🅕 **MysteriousWays**